Women as Risk-Takers for God

**Other World Evangelical Fellowship Titles
Published by Baker Books**

Our Time Has Come: African Christian Women Address the Issues of Today—Judy Mbugua

People of the Mandate: The Story of the World Evangelical Fellowship—W. Harold Fuller

Sharing Good News with the Poor: A Reader for Concerned Christians—Bruce J. Nicholls and Beulah Wood, eds.

Teach Us to Pray—D. A. Carson, ed.

The Unique Christ in Our Pluralistic World—Bruce J. Nicholls, ed.

Worship: Adoration and Action—D. A. Carson, ed.

Women as Risk-Takers for God

Lorry Lutz

Foreword by
Evelyn Christenson

Baker Books

A Division of Baker Book House Co.
Grand Rapids, Michigan 49516

© 1997 by Lorry Lutz

Published by Baker Books
a division of Baker Book House Company
P.O. Box 6287, Grand Rapids, MI 49516-6287

New paperback edition published 1998

Previously published in 1997 by WEF in association with Paternoster Publishing, P.O. Box 300, Carlisle, Cumbria CA3 0QS U.K.

Printed in the United States of America

Library of Congress Cataloging-in-Publication Data

Lutz, Lorry.
    Women as risk-takers for God / Lorry Lutz ; foreword by Evelyn Christenson.
       p.   cm.
    Includes bibliographical references.
    ISBN 0-8010-5813-9 (pbk.)
    1. Women in Christianity. 2. Christian women—Religious life. 3. Sex role—Religious aspects—Christianity. I. Title.
    BV639.W7L88 1997
    270'.082—dc21   97-38092

Cover Illustration: Conrad Represents/Rafael Lopez

For current information about all releases from Baker Book House, visit our web site:
                    http://www.bakerbooks.com

Dedicated to
my daughter Sheila Robinson
who has so beautifully used her gifts
to serve lovingly in her home
and faithfully in the church

Contents

Foreword

The battle of the sexes started when Adam and Eve sinned in the Garden of Eden. Although God created man and woman with a perfect relationship with each other and with himself, that harmony was shattered when Eve and then Adam sinned and introduced evil to Planet Earth. For centuries everybody has lived with the results of those broken and imperfect relationships; but God has provided a solution to those, and all ruptured relationships in the person of his son Jesus. To those who receive his son as Saviour and Lord, God restores those original perfect relationships he intended at creation.

In Jesus, the contention, enslaving, competing, striving and abusing of the other sex is replaced by the original Garden of Eden co-operation and completing of each other. When Jesus 'came to set free the captives and those who are downtrodden' (see Luke 4:18), he restored both sexes to a biblically accurate, God-given perspective on their relationship — culturally and spiritually.

Jesus was an example of this task in his whole ministry, culminating with his choosing women to whom he and his angel would announce his resurrection from the dead. Then Jesus, sending these 'second-class witnesses' to break the great news to his disciples, told all the world that he not only had completed that restorative task, but was unalterably committed to it.

Lorry Lutz has powerfully captured this battle and its potential solution in this wonderful book. She rightly sums it up in saying that when we interpret Scripture through the results of the Fall, then we see the effects of sin as having been established by God. However, if our perspective is that of his redemption, the results of sin are seen as unwelcome. Then the need to redeem all from sin's effects becomes our goal — not replacing one dominance with another, but embracing the new order which Christ came to establish.

From the human history of female abuse to the Bible's Old and New Testament accounts of women used by God, Lorry shows us God's intentions all along. Then she skilfully weaves together inspiring life stories of several of today's dedicated Christian women leaders — women who have heard the call of God and, frequently against seemingly insurmountable odds, have sacrificially obeyed that call and are changing this world for Jesus.

My own husband said it so well several years ago to a Japanese secular newspaper reporter in Tokyo. Mirroring his country's then male-dominated society while interviewing me about my seminar tour of their country, the obviously agitated reporter suddenly blurted out, 'How does your husband handle you being the teacher and speaker?' Pointing to Chris, I answered, 'He's sitting right over there. Why don't you ask him for yourself?'

I listened in awe to his bold answer. 'I believe the Christian husband is the spiritual head of his household, God having entrusted him with his wife and children's physical and spiritual care. The Bible says that those to whom something has been entrusted are stewards, responsible for that thing. Thus the husband and father is the steward of the wife and children whom God has entrusted to him. That also makes him the steward of his wife's and children's *gifts and talents* from God. So he is responsible not only to free them to use their talents from God, he also must encourage and assist them to do so. Also, as the steward of these family members, he will give an account to God as to whether he has hindered or helped them in the use of their God-given talents.'

My husband's reply brought tears to my eyes and an answer to my heart for all the people who ask me how Chris and I handle the reversal of roles in our marriage. For the first thirty years he was the successful preacher and pastor while I brought up our children and taught in his church. But now he no longer preaches but works for a Christian college and seminary while I write and travel around the world teaching seminars. When people ask him if he shouldn't be carrying on the out-of-home ministry that I am, his reply is that he was not the one God called and gifted to minister as I do. He didn't decide that, he firmly states — God did.

Years ago, my husband recounts, he humbly released in prayer his wife, children and all that he is to the perfect will of God. I am deeply grateful for a husband who not only makes my obedience to God's call possible, but is so supportive of it.

However, this biblical principle of stewardship of what has been entrusted to us is not just for marriage partners, but also applies to relationships in the body of Christ. In 1 Cor. 4:1–2 Paul says that we are servants of Christ and stewards of the mysteries of God, and thus it is required of all of us to be found trustworthy. We all are responsible and accountable before God for all He has entrusted to us.

The secret of gender harmony is everybody truly wanting and releasing everybody else for God's will, not their own.

The greatest need on Planet Earth, especially among Christians, may not be racial — but gender — reconciliation.

As you read Lorry's book, may you be enlightened, inspired and motivated to let God change you first if necessary, and then the world you influence — so that you can be a desperately needed biblical role model to the generation looking to us for God's perfect will in a terribly askew world.

Evelyn Christenson

Introduction

Before you begin to read this book, let me tell you how it all happened!

I didn't know I was a truck until I moved to South Africa in 1954. At the time it was one of the British Commonwealth countries where they claim 'true English' is spoken. The nickname I'd carried since high school was spelled just like a British truck — a Lorry. But by that time it was too late to change. It didn't bother me, and I hope it doesn't bother you.

It was in those early years as a missionary in South Africa that I learned something else about myself. I had a driving force within me to use the gifts God had given me, though I didn't identify them as spiritual gifts. All I knew was I loved to teach and lead, to plan and organize — and the youth work that God had opened up to my husband and me gave me all the scope I could possibly dream of.

It was quite a juggling act to be wife, mother of five children and missionary. While I knew pretty well what was expected of me as a wife and mother, the tension between responsibilities at home and the ministry was a constant frustration. Whose need was most urgent: the young blacks in Soweto who lived under the bondage of poverty, discrimination and spiritual darkness, or my own five with all the God-given potential waiting to be developed, and whom I loved so dearly?

Fortunately, my husband helped me to keep things in balance, encouraging me, yes depending on me, to give vision and guidance to the youth ministry we had started. At the same time he truly played the role of spiritual leader in our home, making sure we had family devotions and spending quality time counselling and guiding the children in the right direction.

It was during these years that questions about the biblical propriety of my leadership role began to niggle at me. When our mission asked me to teach courses on church history and Christian education at the Bible school, I threw myself into preparation and study with great delight. I loved the interaction in the classroom with sharp young black people, and with older women who were thrilled to have an opportunity to study God's word, and with pastors who needed to strengthen their training.

Now and again I'd ask myself, should I be teaching these African students? Doesn't Paul say in 1 Timothy 2, 'I don't permit a woman to teach or have authority over a man?' At what age do they become men? Or is it all right for me to teach African men but not white men? Is it all right to do this because the mission has asked me to help out because of a shortage of qualified teachers? Or because my husband has encouraged me?

Not only did I teach and lead in Africa, but when we came home for furlough, I spoke in churches and Sunday School classes. Seldom did a pastor refuse my participation, though most of those churches would not have allowed a non-missionary woman to preach on Sunday morning. But then, I wasn't preaching was I? Only giving a missionary report.

Through the years the questions were pushed aside. I felt so comfortable teaching and leading. Others on the staff had gifts of evangelism, wisdom, counselling, discipling, helps and service, leadership-development. I was the idea person; the one who initiated many of the new projects and directions in our ministry. We made up a synergistic whole that God used to develop hundreds of African teenagers into mature Christians at a time when the frustrations of apartheid were becoming more and more intolerable. I believe we left a heritage of leadership-style that is still in use in the body of Christ there today. It didn't seem to hurt our children either. They claim today that our involvement modelled a ministry commitment that has encouraged all five to become workers for the kingdom of God.

After twenty-two years in Africa my husband and I left to begin a new career in the United States. Now I was writing and publishing mission literature — and though I probably had greater influence on more people, this somehow didn't seem to contradict the Scriptures that I should 'keep silent' and not have 'authority' over a man.

The question of the role of women in society had now become a greater issue as secular feminism became more vocal, and the church, in response, seemed to become more resistant. Over the next fifteen years there emerged a good deal of scripturally-based, scholarly literature from a freeing and respectful perspective on the role of women in ministry. I read voraciously anything I could put my hands on — perhaps to find scriptural approval for what I'd been doing on the field for so many years. My heart rejoiced to find nineteenth-century writers like Katherine Bushnell, Jesse Penn-Lewis and Catherine Booth bringing fresh interpretations to Paul's writings. Modern biblical scholars like Gretchen Gaebelein Hull, Catherine Kroeger, Craig Keener and Gilbert Bilezikian, just to name a few, brought new light to the subject.

During these years I was also travelling widely overseas gathering stories and reports for Partners International, an organization that supports indigenous missions in many countries of the world. I began to meet international women and saw the physical and cultural restrictions that bound them. I will never forget staying in a Christian home in Pakistan where the women were virtually prisoners in their own courtyard because men outside the family were not allowed to see their faces and hair. Or talking with the Indian Christian girl whose parents had selected a Hindu husband for her whom she would not meet until her wedding day.

I was troubled that men were given opportunities for training and to attend conferences, while their wives stayed at home — often to carry the full load of ministry while their men were away.

But I also met women of strength and Christian leadership like Dr. Betty Javalera who founded the Philippine Association of Christian Education which before her death was granting a Master's degree in religious education and training Christian teachers for state schools in the Philippines. Or Theeba John who with her husband founded a school and foster-home for Indian tribal children who came directly from the Stone Age. Or Mother George, daughter of American slaves, who served in Liberia for over sixty years, planting churches, starting schools and educating promising young Liberians to take over her work.

God had introduced me to his very special daughters around the world, and when the call came to lead the AD2000 Women's Track as international co-ordinator, I realized he was asking me not only to mobilize them to use their gifts for evangelism and discipleship, but to be their advocate among Christian leaders as God gave me a platform.

Along with the burden to help women be released into ministry was the desire not only to see men and women working together in harmony across denominational and national barriers, but to demonstrate co-operation and unity between global women's organizations. Thus from the inception of the AD2000 Women's Track, the leaders of the WEF Commission on Women's Concerns, the Lausanne Women's network, and the AD2000 Women's Track have been interacting and looking for ways to co-operate. (See the Appendix for the mission statements of these three movements.)

In the South Pacific, Lausanne and AD2000 held a joint consultation for women. In Europe, Hope for Europe, the Evangelical Association of Europe, Lausanne and AD2000 Women's Track co-sponsored a consultation for European women.

From time to time members of the Commission on Women's Concerns, Lausanne and AD2000 Women's Track leaders have met for planning and sharing ideas. As this book goes to press the leaders of all three groups will again meet during the WEF Assembly in Vancouver, Washington. We believe we share the same goals for women, and that we can synergistically work together to make a greater impact on the body of Christ than we would separately.

In 1991 at our first meeting of leaders of these three global women's movements, we drew up a list of ways in which we could work together. In 1992 at the WEF Assembly in Manila the concept of a book on women in ministry was developed at the first full meeting of the Women's Commission. Representatives of Lausanne and the AD2000 Women's Track also attended that consultation.

Not long after that a book committee was set up to include representatives of the three groups. Each organization committed financial resources for research and development of the book, and I was asked to do the writing. I'm grateful for the advice and encouragement of the committee which consisted of Dorothy Dahlman and Ingrid Kern, WEF; Robyn Claydon, Lausanne; and Sharon Mumper, consultant.

Lynn Smith, vice-president of student affairs at Ontario Bible College and Seminary, who is also in the WEF Women's Commission, gave valuable input. Dr. Catherine Kroeger, founder and past president of Christians for Biblical Equality, used her broad knowledge and training to review the historical information in chapter one. I want to thank my dear friend, Ione Larson, who did hours of research at the library and kept my files well stocked with information, and April Hothaus, who spell-checked, formatted and cleaned up after me before the manuscript went to the publisher. Thanks for an invaluable gift of time and talent. And special thanks to my assistant, Betsy Simpson, who kept the Women's Track moving forward while I focused on this project.

This book could not have happened without the co-operation of so many women I interviewed. They opened their hearts, shared their problems, let me into their lives. I wish I could have used all their stories, but length would not permit it. However, the insights I gained from these women added to the book as a whole and I don't believe a single interview was wasted. Thanks to each one of you for allowing me to come into your homes and offices, to invade your privacy and take time out of busy schedules.

And loving thanks to my husband Allen who did everything he could to encourage, motivate and protect my privacy as I wrote. How many times I heard that welcome call, 'Lunch is ready,' as I was in the midst of staring at a blank page. How often he drove me to the airport to send me off for interviews, and was there waiting to pick up my luggage and bring me back to a peaceful house and the laundry done. I'm grateful too for his objective analysis of what I'd written, even when he didn't think it was very good. Thanks, dear friend.

I trust that when you've finished reading, our goals will have become very clear.

- to show the variety of gifts God has given women
- to demonstrate through models of women in ministry how God is calling out and using women to serve him.
- to encourage men and women to work together to build the kingdom
- to encourage respect and acceptance of each other, even though we may hold different biblical interpretations of the role of women in ministry.

Lorry Lutz

Part One

A Look into the Past

One

Unheralded and Unknown

The Lord commanded the word, and great was the company of women[1] who proclaimed it. Ps. 68:11

What women these Christians have!

4th century pagan philosopher Libanius

But you who have the gift of reason were made not for yourselves but for Me, to serve Me with all your heart and all your love.

Catherine of Siena 1347–1380

'Even as a young teenager, Catherine of Siena refused to marry so that she could serve Christ,' I started to tell my young friend Betsy. 'Catherine was so respected in the fourteenth-century church that she was able to instruct Pope Gregory about the problems of the church and charge him to return to Rome to deal with them. When Gregory finally returned to Rome, Catherine almost lost her life when she was attacked by an anti-papal mob.'

The stories I'd been reading about women in church history had gripped my heart and I wanted to share them with someone. Catherine was a woman who had not only risked her life caring for the sick during the Black Death, but had left a deeply moving account of her mystical experiences in her book, *The Dialogue.*

Betsy listened eagerly, her eyes growing big with wonder. 'I didn't know there were women like that in the church,' she said. 'Why have we never heard about them?'

Why indeed? From the time of the early church, women have been actively serving Christ and holding respected positions of leadership, but little has been written about them. Church historians have virtually ignored them.

What do you know about the following women, all of whom have made significant contributions to the life of the church: Paula — Perpetua — Margaret Fox — Julian of Norwich — Junia — Sarah Platt Doremus — Hannah More — Mary Slessor — Pandita Ramabai — Frances Willard?

In this brief overview of godly, committed women who risked family, reputation and even life to serve Christ, we'll touch upon these women's lives, and at the end of this chapter you will find a list of book titles which more fully tell their stories.

There is no question but that women were vitally involved in the work of the early church. Paul refers to no less than ten women in Romans 16, referring to some as 'fellow-workers' a term which he uses to describe male workers in the church as well. He sends greetings to Junia, commenting that she is 'outstanding among the apostles'. John Chrysostom, eloquent fourth-century bishop of Constantinople, wrote of her, 'Oh, how great is the devotion of this woman, that she should even be counted worthy of the appellation of apostle.' Eusebius, one of the earliest of church historians praises the daughters of Philip, who were prophetesses.

The New Testament refers to a number of women house church leaders – Priscilla (with her husband Aquila), Chloe, Lydia, Nymphia and possibly the 'elect lady' of 2 John. There's no clear indication of what these women did, but since most are mentioned without a husband, it seems they were responsible for the gatherings in their homes.

As Paul travelled through Greece he often preached to the educated and powerful, as at the Areopagus in Athens, where people gathered to discuss philosophy endlessly. On several occasions the New Testament reports that 'prominent women' accepted Paul's message.

The New Testament identifies many of these devout and called women such as Suzannah, Jesus' follower and disciple (Luke 8:3); Priscilla, a teacher (Acts 18:26); Phoebe the deacon (Rom. 16:1); and Mary Magdalene, first to announce the resurrection (John 20:18). Though history is generally silent about specific roles of women in the early centuries of the church, there is no doubt that women played a key role in the life of the church.

Structure, hierarchy and canon law were fluid, and the New Testament itself says little about church government, ordination or specific duties of official leaders. Women were able to participate in the private domain, to which culture relegated them, as long as the church met in homes. After the third century, when the church became 'public,' women's roles became more restricted through progressive church councils, as we shall see in the following chapter.

Very early in the church an order of widows developed who were referred to as 'presbyteresses' in a fifth-century *Testament of our Lord Jesus Christ*, a reworking of Hippolytus' *Apostolic Tradition*.

The word deaconess did not come into use until the third century, but deaconesses were honoured in the early church. They visited women in pagan households, ministered to the sick and needy, assisted in the baptism of women and could give communion to women who were sick. A picture in the Priscilla catacomb in Rome dating back to the first century shows a woman serving the Lord's supper to a group of women.

There is clear evidence that early deaconesses were ordained. The ordination prayer quoted in *Constitutions of Holy Fathers*, a fourth-century document, was accompanied by the laying on of hands, and seems to have been worded to counteract those who questioned the practice:

> *Eternal God, Father of our Lord Jesus Christ, Creator of man and woman, who didst fill Miriam and Deborah and Hannah and Huldah with the Spirit and didst not disdain to suffer thine only-begotten Son to be born of a woman; who also in the tabernacle and the temple didst appoint women keepers of thine holy gates: look down now upon this thine handmaid who is designated to the office of deacon, and grant her the Holy Ghost and cleanse her from all filthiness of the flesh and of the spirit, that she may worthily execute the work entrusted to her, to thine honour and to the praise of thine Anointed; to whom with thee and the Holy Ghost be honour and adoration forever. Amen.*[2]

Martyrs

The young church grew rapidly, and so did persecution by the Roman rulers who feared hostility to the state, and failure to honour the emperor as supreme ruler. They accused Christians of witchcraft, magical powers, and rejection of marriage. Christians suffered ten major periods of persecution, beginning with Nero in the first century, and ending with Diocletian in 303 AD. The latter persecution spread throughout the Roman empire from Britain to Arabia, including Christians in Egypt, Palestine and Syria. In his famous *Book of Martyrs* written in the sixteenth century, John Fox wrote, 'It has been said that the lives of the early Christians consisted of "persecution above ground and prayer below ground." Their lives are expressed by the Coliseum and catacombs.'[3] The horrendous stories of persecution are sprinkled with the lives of many women who chose to suffer and die for Christ rather than renounce their faith.

Perpetua

One of the best-documented stories of martyrdom comes from the pen of Perpetua, a young woman of Carthage (in the modern country of Tunisia in North Africa) who recorded the story of her conversion and arrest until the time of her death in March 205 AD. Perpetua was only twenty-two and the mother of a tiny infant. Her father pleaded with her on several occasions to renounce Christianity for the sake of her son and her family.

Perpetua records the last meeting with her father as she appeared before Hilarianus the governor.

> All the others when questioned admitted their guilt. Then, when it came to my turn, my father appeared with my son, dragged me from the step and said, "Perform the sacrifice – have pity on your baby!"
> "I will not," I retorted.
> "Are you a Christian?" said Hilarianus.
> And I said, "Yes I am."
> When my father persisted in trying to dissuade me, Hilarianus ordered him to be thrown to the ground and beaten with a rod. I felt sorry for father, just as if I myself had been beaten. Then Hilarianus passed sentence on all of us; we were condemned to the beasts, and we returned to prison in high spirits.[4]

An observer continues the story describing Perpetua's death. She was stripped naked and thrown into a net. But the crowd was horrified to see this young girl, and her slave Felicitas, in this condition. The women were allowed to put on tunics to cover their bodies, then thrown to a wild heifer which gored them. Perpetua picked herself up and asked that she be allowed to arrange her hair, for she did not believe a martyr should die with her hair in disarray as if in mourning. The two women were then put to the sword by the gladiators.

Blandina

Blandina, described as a homely young servant girl, showed her love for God in great power. During the reign of Marcus Aurelius in the second century, persecution flared, and Blandina was arrested. She was cruelly tortured again and again to the point where even her persecutors became exhausted. But Blandina 'grew in strength as she proclaimed her faith, saying, "I am a Christian; we do nothing to be ashamed of." ' Finally she was hung on a post and left for wild animals to attack her. Church historian Eusebius says 'she was rejoicing and exulting at her departure as if invited to a wedding supper, not thrown to the beasts.'

Wealthy Women

In the early centuries after the spread of Christianity, immorality, frivolity and indecent luxury marked the life of Rome's upper classes. Women spent literally hours painting their faces, and plaiting golden tresses into their own dark hair. Their homes glittered with gold and lavish ornamentation. When they ventured out in public they were carried on litters borne by eunuchs who were their slaves. Even as early as the first century Peter denounced such excesses (1 Pet. 3:3). His warnings were taken to extremes in later years by church leaders who sought to subdue any effort women made to beautify themselves.

While the average woman could not read, and was not encouraged to receive an education, high-born Christian women often studied Latin, Greek and Hebrew and became well-versed in Scripture. There were few copies of Scripture available, and as the majority of people, especially women, were illiterate, canon law had not yet restricted individuals from reading and studying the Scriptures on their own. Wealthy women who had access to Scripture began to denounce and renounce the Roman way of life. One of these was Marcella.

Marcella (325–410 AD)

After her conversion, Marcella of Rome exchanged her luxurious clothing for a coarse brown dress. She turned her palatial home into a Christian retreat, where she held Bible studies and invited famous leaders of the church to teach. In 382 she invited Jerome, renowned father of the church, to teach in her home. Jerome spent three years in Rome while working on the Latin translation of the Scriptures, the Vulgate, which became the official translation of the Roman church for over a thousand years.

While in her home, Jerome frequently discussed the Scriptures with Marcella, and expressed amazement that what had come to him as the fruit of long study and constant meditation, she had learned on her own. Later when Jerome returned to the Holy Land he sent friends to Marcella for copies of the Scripture. Of her understanding of the Scriptures Jerome wrote, 'Her delight in the Scriptures was incredible. She was forever singing, "Thy words have I hid in mine heart that I might not sin against thee" (Ps. 119:11) . . . this meditation on the law Marcella understood not as a mere review of written words, but as something requiring action.'[5] So confident was Jerome of Marcella's understanding that he once asked her to settle a dispute between bishops and presbyters in Rome concerning the meaning of a certain scripture.

The Bible studies in her home were soon called the 'Ecclesia Domestica' or the 'Church of the Household', which became a centre not only for Bible study and prayer but also for ministry to the poor. Marcella became the leader of a large circle of influential women desiring to follow Christ in obedience and devotion. Eventually she established the first convent for women in the West where those who longed to leave the frivolity of Roman society came to devote themselves to prayer, to study of the Scriptures and to good works.

Paula (347–404 AD)

Among Marcella's aristocratic friends was a young woman, Paula, whose family owned the city of Nicopolis, from which Paul reputedly wrote the letter to Titus. When Paula's husband died leaving her with five young children she was inconsolable. Marcella invited her to her home to study the Scripture, and there the wealthy young widow became a Christian.

Under Jerome's teaching, Paula's understanding of Scripture grew, and she longed to serve Christ with all her heart. She began to live more simply, to give away her possessions and to care for the poor and needy. She and Jerome developed a deep platonic relationship. When he returned to his home in the Holy Land, he persuaded Paula to make the journey to see for herself where Christ was born, lived and died. By this time Paula was living a totally ascetic life, wearing coarse clothing, riding an ass and giving so much away that her relatives complained that she would have nothing left to leave her children. Her response was, 'I shall leave them the mercy of God.'

Parting with her youngest two children was heartbreaking. Her youngest son Toxotius stretched out his hands entreatingly as he watched her sail away to the East. Jerome describes how Paula 'overcame her love for her children by her love of God. She knew herself no more as a mother that she might approve herself as a handmaid of Christ. Yet she wrestled with her grief, as though she were being forcibly separated from parts of herself.'[6]

Paula made her home in Bethlehem, living in a mud hut until her convent was built. She founded four religious houses, three for women, and a hospice from which she and her sisters cared for the pilgrims, sick, poor and needy.

She helped Jerome in his translation of the Bible, purchasing ancient books and rare manuscripts to assist in his work. She not only paid Jerome's expenses, but provided women to copy the manuscripts. This was the beginning of careful preservation of the Vulgate and other religious books by nuns and monks for the next one thousand years. She and her daughter, who had come with her to Bethlehem, studied Hebrew and learned to speak it fluently. She gave Jerome wise advice and would question him keenly on the Scriptures which led him to study more deeply when his answers did not satisfy.

Jerome dedicated a number of the books he had translated to Paula and her daughter Eustochium. In defending himself to the critics who felt this was inappropriate he wrote, 'These people do not know that while Barak trembled, Deborah saved Israel; that Esther delivered from supreme peril the children of God. . . . Is it not to women that our Lord appeared after His Resurrection? Yes, and the men could then blush for not having sought what women had found.'[7] Ironically, the lengthy introduction to today's English version of the

Roman Catholic Bible, referred to as St. Jerome's Bible, does not even mention Paula's name.

Mystics of the Middle Ages

Women like Paula found ways to use their gifts and devotion to serve Christ outside the confines of the organized church, which had less and less place for them. Some scholars feel the rise of the mystics of the Middle Ages was a response to the lack of opportunity for women of leadership and ability to use their gifts in the institutionalized church. While women had no official voice in matters of the church, the mystics who received direct revelation from God were honoured.

Julian of Norwich, who lived in the fourteenth century, was an anchoress (a woman who lives a solitary life of silence and prayer, usually in a small room or cell) and spent her life in prayer perpetually enclosed in a room attached to St. Julian's church in Norwich, England. She wrote in her *Showings:* 'God forbid that you should say or assume that I am a teacher . . . for I am a woman, ignorant, weak and frail. But I know very well that what I am saying, I have received by the revelation of him who is the sovereign teacher . . . because I am a woman, ought I therefore to believe that I should not tell you of the goodness of God, when I saw at the same time that it is his will that it be known?'[8]

The establishment of convents offered women an opportunity to devote themselves to God, without the burdens of marriage. Many upper-class marriages were arranged for political or economic reasons without consultation or the consent of the woman. Furthermore, the church taught that even within marriage, sex was only for procreation and distracted from spirituality. Thus the convent came as a release for some women who wanted a more intimate relationship with God or an alternative to marriage, although others were forced to enter the convent. For many women to be 'Brides of Christ' was a route to a more independent and creative life than marriage of that day offered.

The convents provided a place for prayer and devotion, unsullied by the distractions of the world, as well as opportunities for service to the poor, sick and unfortunate. As the convents were established in regions where the church was expanding, the nuns became models of the mercy, love and compassion embodied in the very nature of Christ.

During the Middle Ages the institutionalized church had fallen into avarice, political intrigue and spiritual apathy. Many leaders in the monasteries, both men and women, made an effort to raise the spiritual temperature, to purify the church, and to lift to a higher level the entire population of Christendom.

The discontent which eventually led to the Reformation can be seen in the lives of these early reformers, some of whom were women.

Hildegard (1098–1179)

Hildegard was born in Bingen, Germany, where she became a nun at the age of fourteen. She was familiar with the Scriptures, natural science, philosophy and Latin literature. In later life she ruled a Benedictine convent on the Rhine, and corresponded with emperors and four popes. 'Hildegard was inspired by the Germanic martial ideal,' writes historian Frances Beer. '[She] identifies on this level with her Creator, and sees herself as God's lieutenant. The history of the world is the history of the struggle between the forces of good and evil, and she recognizes her obligation to be militant . . . she seems well suited temperamentally to be a soldier, not one to miss a good fight if there is one to be had. Evidently she does not see the dominant active role as being the exclusive property of the male sex.'[9] Hildegard wrote indignant letters of reproof and defied ecclesiastical authority, in spite of the threat of excommunication. She was the most prominent woman of the church in her day. 'She was taken seriously as a prophet by everyone from Bernard of Clairvaux and the pope, down to the humblest labourers.'[10]

But Hildegard's reforming strength masked a sensitive nature. 'Hildegard several times uses the image of a feather on the breath of God when referring to herself . . . in order to illustrate the way she is used as an instrument of the divine in all her human, bodily weakness,' writes Barbara Lachman. 'She wrote, "I am always filled with a trembling fear, as I do not know for certain of any single capacity in me. Yet I stretch out my hands to God, so that, like a feather which lacks all weight and strength and flies through the wind, I may be borne up by him." '[11]

She wrote at least 77 liturgical songs and produced a lengthy treatise which amounts to a theology of music 'in which all sacred music functions as a bridge for humanity to life before the Fall.'[12]

Hildegard pleaded for reform in the church, despairing over the corruption of the clergy. She admonished her audiences to look to the Scriptures as their authority and to Christ, not the priests, for salvation. She was a woman before her time. It was to be almost four hundred years before the church would be torn apart by another reformer who preached the same message.

Catherine of Siena (1347–1380)

While Martin Luther is credited for the final confrontation in the sixteenth century with a church that had become impure and greedy, and an arrogant papacy lusting for political power, he was not the first to attempt to purify the church. Women like Hildegard and Catherine of Siena had dared to raise their voices against the spiritual decline of the church long before Luther. Catherine, regarded as the most famous of all medieval church women, laboured for peace and reform throughout her short life.

Born in the Italian city of Siena as the twenty-fourth of 25 children, Catherine had a profound religious experience as a young child, seeing a vision of Christ above the steeple of the church. She refused to marry, and repelled the suitor her parents had chosen for her at twelve years of age by cutting her beautiful long hair. For a time her family, exasperated with her zealousness, assigned to her the bulk of household tasks. However her father recognized the unique spiritual qualities of his youngest daughter and granted her permission to live in silence and seclusion in an underground room of their home. Catherine lived in a simple cell with a straw pallet, eventually eating only bread and water, and sleeping no more than two hours a night. Prayer was the staff of her life. At the age of seventeen, after three years of solitude she heard a call from God to purify the church. 'Sweetest daughter, thou seest how she [the church] has soiled her face with impurity and self-love and become swollen with the pride and avarice of those who feed at her bosom.'[13]

In 1363 Catherine chose the life of a religious lay woman, donned a veil of white and a black cape, and served the poor on the streets of Siena. Her overriding burden was the conversion of sinners and she entreated rich and poor, sickly and healthy to repent and be saved. A growing group of devoted followers surrounded her and helped her in her ministry.

The Black Death struck Siena in 1374 and one third of the population of the city died. So virulent was the disease that many went to bed healthy at night and were found dead in the morning. People fled to the country or barred themselves in their houses. But Catherine and her followers stayed in the city and worked indefatigably day and night to care for the sick and dying. She had no fear of death nor concern for her own physical well-being.

After the plague abated, Catherine felt called to work in other cities of Italy to bring people to repentance. However while her fellow-citizens lauded her service at home, many criticized her for contemplating distant mission fields. Once again Catherine sought solace and direction in intimate prayer and received a message from God, 'Does it not depend on my will where I shall pour out my grace? With me there is no longer male and female, lower and upper classes. All are equal in my sight.'[14]

As Catherine's fame and influence grew, she involved herself in what would today be a questionable venture, attempting to persuade church leaders, and especially Pope Gregory, to go on a Crusade to the Holy Land. She believed that this would not only liberate the sacred places, but also help to unify a badly divided church.

She believed the papal move to Avignon under the French monarchy was a tragedy. Indeed the pope lived in lavish luxury and political intrigue. Catherine exorted the pope to return to Rome which had been the centre of church leadership for centuries. She attempted to be the mediator in a quarrel between Pope Gregory and the city of Florence, which he had excommunicated.

History does not agree on whether or not Catherine's influence affected Gregory's move back to Rome. He died shortly after his return, and Catherine moved to Rome to assist the new pope, Urban VI, still hoping to bring about reform in the church. After some years of failing health, Catherine died at the age of thirty-three in Rome.

'It is with Catherine of Siena that I think we see most clearly just how far-reaching can be the force of a mystic's personality, or "charisma" to fall back upon a woefully misused term that simply means "Holy Spirit" ' writes Carol Lee Flinders. 'She is so passionate in her convictions and in her affections, so fully engaged in life as to belie conventional assumptions about sainthood and what it means to renounce the world.'[15]

Church historian, Philip Schaff, writes, 'She was excelled by none in her own age in passionate effort to save her people and help spread righteousness. Hers was the voice of the prophet, crying in the wilderness "Prepare ye the way of the Lord". '[16]

Women of the Reformation

When Martin Luther finally brought the growing Reformation sentiments to a head by nailing the Ninety-five Theses to the church door at Wittenberg in 1517, life for men and women of the church in Europe changed for ever. Reformation zeal spread like wildfire, and penetrated even the monasteries and convents.

Katherina von Bora was a nun in the Cistercian convent in Nimbschen, Germany. There she learned farming and to write German and understand Latin. But strict silence was enforced and friendship between nuns discouraged. Even speaking to a visitor took place through a latticed window.

Yet, somehow, the teachings of the Reformation slipped into the convent and stirred up new passions and convictions. One can only imagine how the silenced nuns slipped notes to each other and whispered surreptitiously when the abbess was out of hearing. Katherina approached her parents and friends for help to leave the convent but they refused. Then a daring plot evolved. History is not clear about the exact role Luther played in helping eleven nuns to escape. But one dark night a vendor appeared at the convent delivering barrels of herring. Eleven nuns rode out inside the barrels to an uncertain future.

Martin Luther was faced with the problem of what to do with these nuns. Eventually all but Katherina were married. The man he recommended was not acceptable to Katherina and she refused. She did, however, send word to Luther that she would be willing to consider either a Dr. Nicholas von Amsdorf, one of Luther's staff, or Luther himself.

Luther had not thought of marriage for himself, expecting to be burned at the stake as a heretic at any time. Certainly Katherina faced the same possibility as a runaway nun who had accepted the teaching of the Reformation. Only under the protection of certain sympathetic rulers were they safe.

But Luther wrote to his friends, 'While I was thinking of other things, God has suddenly brought me to marriage . . . God likes to work miracles.' They were married in June of 1525, and enjoyed more than twenty years of a tumultuous but happy union.

Katherina Bora Luther became the revered matriarch of the Protestant parsonage. A mother of six, she fulfilled all the expectations of the woman of Proverbs 31. She looked after orchards and gardens and served hundreds of people who came through the Luther home during the hectic Reformation days. She turned part of her home into a hospital, and her eldest son, who became a physician, testified that she treated the sick as well as any doctor.

The Reformers improved attitudes towards sex and gave dignity and spirituality to marriage. But at no time in history had ministry for women been so limited as in the Reformation. Women were now devoid of service even in monasteries and religious orders, and found little avenue for ministry outside their homes and children.

Jeanne of Navarre

During the post-Reformation period, Jeanne, mother of the future King Henry IV of France, protected the Huguenots (French Protestants) and worked to spread the gospel and foster the study of theology. She recalled what Calvin had written to her when she became a Protestant, 'Unless we betake ourselves daily to the Holy Scriptures the truth that we once knew oozes away little by little till it is all gone, except that God shall come to our aid. In His infinite wisdom He has seen fit to prevent you from descending to such a pass.'[17]

Her husband opposed her conversion, and for a time locked her up as a prisoner in her own home. They fought bitterly over their son Henry – one determined that he would not attend mass, the other forcing him to study under Catholic tutors. After her husband died she issued strict orders renouncing Catholic practices in Navarre.

Though her son returned to the Catholic church after his marriage and ascent to the French throne, he signed the Edict of Nantes which gave religious toleration to the Huguenots for many years.

Outside the Catholic, Lutheran and Reformed churches, smaller offshoots of the Reformation gave women greater scope for ministry. Linda Mercandante writes, 'The Anabaptists of the Radical Reformation opened new possibilities in Christian life to women, and as early as the 1520's in Germany and the Low countries, women were preaching. . . . Although this trend did not last, a precedent had been set. Pietists, too, with their emphasis on a lively personal appropriation of faith . . . stressed a "spiritual priesthood of all believers" and encouraged women to exercise their gifts for the edification of all – though not usually in the public assemblies of worship.'[18]

New Opportunities for Women

The humanistic awakenings of the Renaissance (fourteenth to sixteenth centuries) had opened some doors for upper class women to gain an education and follow less conforming roles. But during the next three centuries tremendous changes in society as a whole were to bring new opportunities for women to gain education and to become involved in social reforms. As we have seen, however, these changes did not generally affect women's opportunities in the church.

The Industrial Revolution brought people together in urban conditions, at the mercy of landlords and mill-owners. Many women were forced to work in factories and shops instead of fields and farms. Social evils not only became more pressing but more visible, and women began to take more public roles in trying to rectify them.

To try to summarize the impact of women of God in the great social movements of abolition, prohibition and suffrage, and especially on world missions, is an impossible task in this brief chapter. Here are just a few glimpses of these unheralded heroines of the last three centuries.

Margaret Fell Fox (1614–1702)

The wife of George Fox, founder of the Quaker movement, spent her long life bringing encouragement and comfort to the persecuted Friends, as they were also known. Born in Lancashire, Margaret was a member of the English nobility, and married Judge Fell with whom she produced nine children. George Fox often visited Swarthmoor, the Fell estate. Margaret caught his vision of the Inner Light on his first visit. 'He opened for us a book that we had never read in, nor indeed had ever heard that it was our duty to read in . . . And he turned our minds toward the light of Christ as they had never been turned before.'

To become a Quaker in the seventeenth century was no easy decision. Margaret risked loss of comfort, the esteem of her neighbours, and even her freedom, but enthusiastically threw herself into the Quaker cause, opening her home to the persecuted, raising funds for travelling preachers and relieving their sufferings in prison. After the death of Judge Fell, she continued to hold regular though illegal meetings in her home. For this reason she was arrested and imprisoned for four years, surviving under the most dire circumstances. She accepted her imprisonment nobly, assuring the judge, 'What I suffer is for the Lord's sake, and I am freely given up to His will, and pleasure, what He permits and suffers to be done unto me, in which doing I shall rest content whether it be mercy or cruelty.'

As soon as she was released she continued visiting Quakers in jail, and on remote farms and villages to preach about the Inner Light. She was imprisoned twice more in her lifetime for her Quaker activities.

In 1669 George Fox wrote in his journal: 'I have seen from the Lord a considerable time before, that I should take Margaret Fell to be my wife.' Both George and Margaret regarded their marriage as a spiritual union. Though they loved each other deeply and were completely at one in their purpose and calling, they were seldom together. Their ministries called them to serve in different parts of England, and they were both imprisoned at different times. During their twenty-eight year marriage the longest interval they were together was two years.

In her long ministry of spreading the Inner Light of Christ, Margaret had the blessing and encouragement of her husband, who believed in the work of women in the Church. Quakers were in agreement with Paul's words, 'There is . . . neither male nor female, for you all are one in Christ Jesus' (Gal. 3:28).

One of the contributions Margaret made was to organize women's meetings so that women might be used for the service of God. They not only studied Scripture but were trained in midwifery, social welfare and other helpful ministries. Ruth Tucker explains, 'Attending women's meetings . . . was almost as controversial as preaching. Despite the fact that these women were involved in the traditional female activities, involving deeds of charity, the very fact that they were meeting without the supervision of a man drew heavy criticism.'[19]

Margaret Fox courageously defended the Quakers, taking advantage of her noble heritage to visit Charles II several times to bring petitions on their behalf. When James II became king she made another appeal which influenced him to set forth his Declaration of Indulgence for all Nonconformists, bringing some relief to the Friends.

Margaret wrote sixteen books and many pamphlets as her enduring legacy to the Quakers. One of her best known is a 20-page pamphlet entitled *Women's Speaking Justified by the Scriptures*, published in 1666 while she was in prison. She emphasized the theme that the 'Spirit is poured upon all flesh, both Sons and Daughters.'

When Margaret was seventy-six she made another lengthy horseback ride to London to see her husband George, who was by then too ill to travel. Though ten years her junior, he was weakened by his many imprisonments and arduous journeys around the world to take the message of the Inner Light. He died nine months after her visit. Margaret lived another twelve years and died aged eighty-eight, still mentally vigorous and full of wisdom and spiritual understanding.

Hannah More (1745–1833)

Vivacious and intellectual, Hannah More spent the first thirty-five years of her life moving in the social circles of London. (The Encyclopedia Britannica cross-references her as a 'Bluestocking.') She was a gifted playwright and became friends with such renowned writers as Dr. Samuel Johnson, who encouraged her to publish her writing.

At the age of thirty-five she came into contact with a group of influential Anglicans who believed that Christians must make a social impact and work for change in society. Many believe that this small group of Christian activists, known as the Clapham Sect, had much to do with abolishing the slave-trade in the British empire, ending child labour, and even helping to protect England from the French Revolution.

It was at a meeting of the Clapham Sect that Hannah met John Newton, a former slave-trader and author of the beloved hymn, 'Amazing Grace.' Another important leader of the Clapham Sect, William Wilberforce, a member of parliament, used his influence to bring down the slave-trade. In 1789 Wilberforce took Hannah to visit the Mendips, a mining area in the West of England. The poverty and ignorance she saw appalled her. With her sisters she began teaching the children in this region to read and taught them the Scriptures. Out of this grew one of the first Sunday Schools in England. Incredibly, she and her sisters were condemned and persecuted by the curates of the church for this action because of the prevailing belief that education of the poor would destroy their interest in farming and other menial tasks.

Hannah also wrote many of the tracts for the Clapham Sect to counteract the demoralizing tendencies of the French Revolution which were flooding England. With the help of her sisters and friends, she produced three tracts a month for three years, advising the poor to cultivate sobriety and hard work, and to trust in God and the kindness of the gentry. Over two million of these tracts were sold at a penny each. When she died she left her estate of about thirty thousand pounds, income from her writing, to seventy Christian organizations.

Women in Missions

While some Roman Catholic missions had been pushing into China and India as early as the seventh century, there is little historical evidence that women pioneered these ministries. Perhaps studies will reveal pioneering women in China, India and other places where the gospel was planted in these early attempts who were as valiant and determined to serve God as the women we've met in the early European church.

As information about conditions in places like India and China became available, men responded to the call to serve in faraway lands. In 1793 William Carey sailed to India from England to become the 'Father of Modern Missions'. But little is said about his long-suffering wife, Dorothy, who felt no call and did not want to take her four small children to India. In the end, after much persuasion by her husband and his partner, Dorothy agreed to go. But she never acclimatized to the strange language and customs of her adopted land. The Careys lived in destitute circumstances, often without money even to buy bread. Within a year, five-year-old Peter died, and Dorothy was never the same. Over the years she retreated into her own confused mind, and was later described as wholly deranged. Ruth Tucker writes, 'While other women willingly died for the cause, she suffered years of mental torture for a cause to which she was not committed. She was deprived of the simple joys of home and family and was later remembered only for her "reproachful tongue" and her "insanity." '[20]

British mission agencies, such as the London Missionary Society, pioneered in many parts of the world – India, the South Seas and West Africa. Contrary to Carey's experience, their reaction indicated that wives were indispensable to the work. Nevertheless many agencies simply listed the man's name followed by a small m. to indicate he was married.

Catholic nuns had pioneered mission work almost two centuries before Protestant single missionaries. Doors opened slowly and only the most courageous and visionary of women would venture into the uncharted heathen regions.

Mary Slessor

Perhaps the best known of these early pioneers is Mary Slessor, who responded to God's call after the death of her brother who had long felt he should be a missionary. Born in Scotland, Mary went to Nigeria (then known as Calabar) under the auspices of the United Presbyterian Church. She was disappointed to find the missionary community emulating the British lifestyle with high teas, fancy hats and gloves and social occasions which were as foreign to this lower class mill worker as village life in Africa.

Because she wanted to live with and like the Africans, Mary moved inland. 'She discarded the Victorian missionary's hat, gloves, boots, bustle, long curls, and sometimes even her outer dress. She spent time in African houses, sleeping beside big sweating bodies, eating native food, going barefoot, suffering local diseases – but awake, aware, curious, asking questions, categorizing information, applying it,' writes Miriam Adeney.[21]

Mary Slessor spent forty years in Africa, moving ever farther into the interior among warring people immersed in witchcraft. She rescued twins who would have been killed by the community, and raised seven adopted children. She opened up the interior of Nigeria to the gospel and served as an intermediary between tribal factions.

*   *   *   *   *   *   *

As American missions began to develop in the nineteenth century, they looked to British missionaries as models. This was especially true for wives of missionaries, whose roles had been primarily limited to child-bearing and caring for husbands and children. They were neither recognized as missionaries, nor expected to have a ministry, though many, of course, did. Both European and American agencies were slow to send out unmarried women as missionaries, and those who were sent were forced to be part of a missionary family, and under the rule of the male head of the house.

From the beginning of the nineteenth century American women were deeply involved in praying and supporting home and foreign missions. Cent-societies raised thousands of dollars for missions. By 1818 the number of such societies rose to ninety-eight in spite of the constant criticism they received. The secretary of a Female Cent-Society wrote to the editor of a mission publication asking advice. 'Some members had become uncertain as to whether it be right for females to meet together for prayer, on account of some apostolical prohibition.'[22]

A mission leader of that day who held a relatively liberated view of women in missions preached on the subject, warning women not to take advantage of their freedoms. As far as their financial contributions were concerned he warned, 'Women may also promote the Saviour's cause by measures of a private nature, especially by devising, suggesting, and recommending schemes of benevolence the execution of which naturally must be left to the men.'[23]

Sarah Platt Doremus (1802–1877)

By the middle of the nineteenth century the women of the church could no longer wait for the existing boards to send single missionaries and to focus on the needs of women and children. The plight of women in Asia particularly caused concern and fervent prayer. By 1900 more than 48 women's missionary societies were recruiting, funding, sending women to, and supervising them in mission fields around the world.

What finally broke the dam, to allow such an outpouring of women missionaries, recruited, sent, financed and prayed for by women's societies? R. Pierce Beaver gives three major reasons:

(1) Higher education for women gave women new opportunities and vision. The teaching profession emerged as a respected outlet for women.

(2) The American Civil War brought the gifts of women to the fore as they organized, volunteered, and focused on a target around which they could mobilize their efforts. 'The War was the most effective school for women in initiative and public affairs in the course of the nineteenth century,' writes Beaver.[24]

(3) In 1834 British women founded the 'Society for Promoting Female Education in the East', and sent women teachers to Malaysia, Java and Siam. When the reports of this ministry spread in North America, women prepared to organize as well, though the initial effort was dampened at the request of the leader of the American Board of Missions.

However in 1861 the first women's missionary society was formed in North America, the Woman's Union Missionary Society of America. Sarah Doremus became the first president and served until her death in 1877. Her home became the centre for departing and returning missionaries, and she became known as the 'Mother of Missions.'

Beaver describes her as 'one of the most remarkable laywomen in the whole history of American Protestantism.' She organized a society for the relief of Greek women then suffering under the Turks; started services in the New York prison and encouraged the organization of the Women's Prison Association. She served on the board of the New York Bible Society, founded the House and School of Industry and helped found a children's and women's hospital. She was also one of the founders of the Presbyterian Home for Aged Women.

With such obvious gifts and commitment, it is no wonder that the Woman's Union became an effective ministry, supporting more than a hundred women missionaries in Burma, India, China, Syria, Greece and Japan in its first twenty years. Fifty-eight of these were native-born women workers from their own countries, a cutting edge strategy that few other missions followed for decades. Mrs. Doremus's leadership became an inspiration to women around the country, and denominational women's missions emerged in ensuing years.

The role of women in missions cannot be overestimated. Missionary wives faithfully followed their husbands to foreign lands, many never to return home again. Many died on the mission field, often buried beside two or three children who had preceded them. As single missionaries joined them, they established schools and hospitals, planted churches and translated the Scripture.

On the home front the mighty power of prayer grew out of women's gatherings in homes and churches as they lifted their concerns for women and children in foreign lands before the Father. They inspired their children by their involvement, prayer and sacrifice. They brought their daughters to mission society meetings; they enrolled their babies in 'mission cradle rolls.' They invited missionary families home for Sunday dinner and into their homes for rest and renewal — ever exposing their children to the joys and challenges of overseas ministries. Ralph Winter declares that it was the prayers and involvement of women in missions in the nineteenth century which brought about the Student Missionary Movement of the early twentieth century. By 1929, sixty-seven percent of all North American missionaries were women.

Even as God was raising up missionary women from the western world, He called out women in 'heathen lands' to risk all to serve him too. Records are skimpy at best, but here and there one reads of a woman like Mrs. Chang, a Buddhist in China who became a Bible-woman. Because of her Christian witness, she was captured during the Boxer Rebellion in 1899–1900 and hung by her thumbs to die until neighbours intervened. Or Fatima Hanum a Turkish Bible-woman who was forced to flee Constantinople because of persecution in 1902. One of the most famous of Christian women leaders in India was Pandita Ramabai.

Pandita Ramabai (1858–1922)

Pandita Ramabai had memorized 18,000 Sanskrit verses by the time she was twelve years of age. Her father, a Brahmin priest and wandering guru, believed that women should be educated, contrary to Hindu practices of her day. When Pandita's parents died of starvation, she and her brother continued to wander on a religious pilgrimage for four thousand miles throughout India, seeking truth. While living in Calcutta Pandita was exposed to Christianity, and thereafter continued to compare the Christian and Hindu scriptures.

Even while studying the Bible she was asked by Hindu scholars to lecture to high-caste Indian women about their duties because they recognized her brilliance. As she read the Hindu scriptures, she discovered that all had a very low view of women – 'that women of high- and low-caste, as a class were bad, very bad, worse than demons, as unholy as untruth and that they could not get Moksha as men. The only hope of their getting this much-desired liberation from Karma and its results . . . was the worship of their husbands. The husband is said to be the woman's god; there is no other god for her.'[25]

Pandita decided to help raise the standards of women and children in India. She was concerned about the plight of widows. In 1880 there were twenty-three million widows in India, fifty-one thousand below the age of ten, ten thousand below the age of four. They were blamed for the deaths of their husbands and were made to shave their heads and wear white mourning for the rest of their lives. When she herself became a widow after only nineteen months of marriage, she became even more aware of the social rejection and degraded position widows suffered in India.

In 1883 Pandita visited England and came under the influence of the Anglican church where she saw the tremendous difference between Christianity and Hinduism in the treatment of women. She wrote, 'I realized, after reading the fourth chapter of St. John's gospel, that Christ was truly the Divine Saviour He claimed to be, and no one but He could transform and uplift the downtrodden womanhood of India and of every land.'[26] She began to take her first steps to faith in Christ, though she still considered herself a Hindu.

From England Ramabai went to study in the United States. She returned to India to open a school and home for illegitimate children, widows and orphans and to crusade for the rights and improved treatment of women. In 1891 Ramabai came to full conversion and experienced the personal presence of the Holy Spirit. She named her mission 'Mukti,' which means salvation.

Over the years her mission expanded to include care of unwanted babies, training for the blind, and solace for the crippled. She established the House of Mercy, a home for unmarried mothers. She organized bazaars so that her women could sell their crafts and set up skills-training programmes. She bought a printing press and taught her girls to set type and operate the press. The orchards and gardens surrounding the mission provided food for hundreds.

During the famine of 1896 Pandita travelled around India to collect six hundred starving widows and children and brought them back to the mission. A great revival broke out at the mission during the overcrowded days of the famine and hundreds of girls were converted. They were baptized in the nearby Bheema River.

During the last fifteen years of her life Pandita translated the entire Bible into Mahrathi – the only complete translation in the world done by a woman. As she lay on her deathbed, she asked God to spare her long enough to do the final proofreading of the translation. God answered her prayer, and on the tenth day, when she had proofed the last page, she peacefully 'fell asleep.'

Francis Willard (1839–1898)

Back in the United States women were fighting a different battle as they saw the widespread use of alcohol destroying their families. While the women's temperance movement was not primarily an evangelism or missions movement, it opened up doors for women to preach and evangelize. The strategy was 'gospel temperance' – the belief that conversion would bring sobriety to drinkers and conviction to those who made and sold liquor.

The early prohibition movements were led by men, but drew great interest from women. However when Antoinette Brown, a delegate to the Temperance Convention in New York in 1853, attempted to speak she was booed off the platform for three hours. With such rejection, women realized they must form their own organizations. Frances Willard helped found the Women's Christian Temperance Union and served as president from 1879–1898. The WCTU became the largest women's organization in the world, with several million members by 1890. Its missionary branch, the White Ribbon Missionaries, organized chapters in Asia, Africa and Latin America.

The WCTU emphasized evangelism. Women spoke in prisons, police stations, to railway employees – wherever they could get a hearing. Women also demonstrated outside saloons, calling upon men to turn to God and away from drunkenness. Willard described the women's activities as functioning outside the church not because they wanted to but because the church 'is afraid of her own gentle, earnest-hearted daughters.'

Francis Willard was born in an abolitionist home. The family cellars became a refuge for runaway slaves on the Underground Railway.[*] Her family became Christians during the Finney revivals in 1829 and she was converted during a bout of typhoid in 1859. Willard attended Oberlin, the first co-ed college in the

---

[*] The Underground Railway was a secret organization set up to help slaves escaping from the Southern states to reach safety in the Northern states and in Canada.

United States, and became president of Evanston College for Ladies. She was the first woman to serve as president of a college which granted a degree.

In 1876 Willard had a special call from God. She writes, 'While alone on my knees one Sabbath in the capital of the Crusade State [Columbus Ohio] . . . there was borne in upon my mind, as I believe, from loftier regions, the declaration, "You are to speak for woman's ballot as a weapon of protection to her home and tempted loved ones from the tyranny of drink," and then for the first and only time in my life, there flashed through my brain a complete line of argument and illustration.'[27]

However when Francis presented her vision to promote suffrage in order for women to protect their homes, the WCTU rejected her. They did not want to sully their skirts with politics. Francis dropped out of the WCTU for a year and joined Dwight L. Moody who had asked her to come and serve as an evangelist with him in Boston. He encouraged her to speak of temperance and suffrage as well as the gospel. Once again she faced opposition, and left the campaign after a short time. However she wrote, 'I deem it one of the choicest seals of my calling that Dwight L. Moody should have invited me to cast in my little lot with his great one as an evangelist.'[28]

In 1879 Willard was elected president of the WCTU and served until her death in 1898. Her skills as an organizer, administrator, politician, orator, and visionary developed the WCTU into the largest and most efficient women's organization in the nineteenth century. The movement eventually lead to the passing of the Nineteenth Amendment in 1920, giving women the right to vote.

Willard's goal was 'the Christianizing of society.' She worked with labour groups, black organizations and other alliances as well as the church. She called it 'gospel politics.' Politics at best is a difficult game, bringing criticism, rejection and public scrutiny upon those involved. But in the late nineteenth century it was particularly difficult for a Christian woman to follow the call of God and the urgency of her heart in the public arena; to maintain her dignity and demonstrate the fruits of the spirit under the chastisement not only of society as a whole, but especially of the brothers and sisters within the body of Christ who denounced her participation on the basis of her gender.

Francis Willard is but another example of women of God through the ages who responded in obedience to God's plan for their lives, and were willing to pay the price.

Why has it been such a difficult struggle for a woman through the ages to respond to God's call? What obstacles became insurmountable? What attitudes and cultural mores kept her in her place? We'll find some of the answers in the next chapter.

Notes

1. The word for *company* is feminine in Hebrew.

2. Philip Schaff, *History of the Christian Church,* vol. 3, *Nicene and Post-Nicene Christianity, AD 311–500* (Grand Rapids: Eerdmans, 1979), 260–61.

3. William Byron Forbush, ed., *Foxe's Book of Martyrs* (Philadelphia: Universal Book and Bible House, 1926), 11.

4. Quoted in *Christian History* (Worcester, Pa.) 8, no. 1 (1988): 32.

5. Edith Deen, *Great Women of the Christian Faith* (Uhrichsville, Ohio: Barbour, 1959), 20.

6. Ibid., 31.

7. Nancy Hardesty, "Paula: A Portrait of Fourth-Century Piety," *Christian History* (Worcester, Pa.) 7, no. 1 (1988): 17.

8. Elizabeth Alvida Petroff, "The Mystics," *Christian History* (Carol Stream, Il.) 2 (1991): 32.

9. Frances Beers, *Women in Mystical Experience in the Middle Ages* (Woodbridge, Suffolk: Boydell Press), 1992.

10. Petroff, "Mystics," 33.

11. Barbara Lachman, *The Journal of Hildegard of Bingen* (New York: Bell Tower, 1993), 168.

12. Ibid., 32.

13. Deen, *Great Women,* 55.

14. Caroline T. Marshall, "Catherine of Siena," *Christian History* (Carol Stream, Il.) 10 (1991): 9.

15. Carol Lee Flinder, *Enduring Grace: Living Portraits of Seven Women Mystics* (San Francisco: Harper, 1993), 126.

16. Philip Schaff, *History of the Christian Church,* vol. 5, *The Middle Ages, AD 1049–1294* (Grand Rapids: Eerdmans, 1979), 204.

17. Deen, *Great Women,* 87.

18. Linda Mercadante, "From Hierarchy to Equality" (master's thesis, Regent College, 1978), 23.

19. Ruth Tucker and Walter Liefield, *Daughters of the Church* (Grand Rapids: Zondervan/Academie Books, 1987), 230.

20. Ruth Tucker, *Guardians of the Great Commission: The Story of Women in Modern Missions* (Grand Rapids: Zondervan/Academie Books, 1988), 17.

21. Miriam Adeney, "Esther across Cultures: Indigenous Leadership Roles for Women," *Missiology* 15 (July 1987): 324.

22. R. Pierce Beaver, *All Loves Excelling* (Grand Rapids: Eerdmans, 1968), 33.

23. Ibid., 34.

24. Ibid., 86.

25. Tucker and Liefield, *Daughters of the Church,* 344.

26. John Woodbridge, ed., *Ambassadors for Christ* (Chicago: Moody Press, 1994), 170.

27. Nancy Hardesty, *Women Called to Witness* (Nashville: Abingdon Press, 1984), 18.

28. Tucker and Liefield, *Daughters of the Church,* 273.

For further reading on the lives of the women in this chapter see:

Beck, James R. *Dorothy Carey: The Tragic and Untold Story of Mrs. William Carey.* Grand Rapids: Baker, 1992.

Beers, Frances. *Women in Mystical Experience in the Middle Ages.* Woodbridge, Suffolk: Boydell Press, 1992.

Bordin, Ruth. *Frances Willard: A Biography.* Chapel Hill: University of North Carolina Press, 1986.

Buchanan, James. *The Expendable Mary Slessor.* New York: Seabury Press, 1981.

Catherine of Siena. *The Dialogue.* Edited by Richard J. Payne. New York: Paulist Press, 1980.

Clark, Elizabeth. *Women in the Early Church: Message of the Fathers of the Church.* Wilmington, Del.: Michael Glazier, 1983.

Flanagan, Sabina. *Hildegard of Bingen: A Visionary Life.* New York: Routledge, 1989.

Foster, Richard, and James Bryant Smith, eds. *Devotional Classics: Selected Readings for Individuals and Groups.* San Francisco: Harper, 1989.

Gies, Francis and Joseph. *Women in the Middle Ages.* New York: Harper & Row, 1980.

Haile, H. G. *Luther.* Garden City, N.Y.: Doubleday, 1980.

Hardesty, Nancy A. *Great Women of Faith: The Strength and Influence of Christian Women.* Grand Rapids: Baker, 1980.

Hopkins, Mary Allen. *Hannah More and Her Circle.* New York, 1947.

Jantzen, Grace. *Julian of Norwich: Mystic and Theologian.* New York: Paulist Press, 1987.

Jones, Mary Gladys. *Hannah More.* Cambridge, Mass.: Cambridge University Press, 1952.

Kunze, Bonnelyn Young. *Margaret Fell and the Rise of Quakerism.* Stanford, Calif.: Stanford University Press, 1994.

Labarge, Margaret Wade. *A Small Sound of the Trumpet: Women in Medieval Life.* Boston: Beacon Press, 1986.

Ramabai, Pandita. *A Testimony.* 9th ed. Kedgaon Poona Dist., India: Ramabai Mukti Mission, 1968.

Roberts, William. *Memoirs of Hannah More.* 2 vols. London: Seily & Burnside, 1834.

Sheils, W. J., and Diana Wood, eds. *Women in the Church.* Oxford: Basil Blackwell, 1990.

Steer, Douglas V. *Quaker Spirituality, Selected Writings.* New York: Paulist Press, 1984.

Two

The Historical Obstacle Course Women Faced

'Woman . . . why are you crying?' . . . Jesus said to her, 'Mary.'

John 20:15,16

God gave women healing release through tears. Perhaps women can best appreciate the clean feeling and the alleviation of pain that tears can bring. Mary demonstrated the deep pain she felt over the loss of her beloved Lord, spilling out in tears of sorrow. And Jesus understood and accepted those tears. In spite of Jesus' model of respect, concern and compassion for the women he met in his lifetime, his revolutionary relationships and attitudes did not change society's general view towards women. While Christianity has given women greater freedom and respect than any other religion, in many ways the view of women as inferior, unequal and of little value has been perpetuated even by leaders of the church through the ages.

Our purpose in this book is to encourage Christians to recognize the way God is using women today – not to denigrate the church or male leadership. But in order to be honest and fair we will take a look at the way society and cultures have cruelly mistreated women, just as we have re-examined history when we have sought reconciliation with other ethnic and national groups of people.

Sin has built barriers between men and women through the centuries. Many of these roadblocks to self-esteem and freedom exist around the world today even in the church. Whatever your theological position on women may be, it is time to recognize each other's 'respected interpretations' among true believers. We need to begin practising the Golden Rule more earnestly in relation to women who feel called to serve, without gender hang-ups. We need to recognize that there is much more at stake here than Paul's teaching on the role of women.

The Curse

It all began in the garden. Adam and Eve lived an ideal life in a perfect environment. But one day as they walked through the garden, Eve saw the beautiful tree of the knowledge of good and evil. The fruit looked delicious, and the thought of knowing even more, of being more like God intrigued her. Suddenly the great Beguiler stuck his head around the tree, inviting her to help herself. When she pulled back reminding him that God had told them they would die if they ate it, Satan used all his charms on her. He's a wily fellow even today, and he deceived her by telling her that she wouldn't die. She would just become wiser.

Meanwhile Adam stood there silently. He knew better, for he had heard God's command not to eat of the tree even before Eve's creation. Why didn't he speak up? Why didn't he pull Eve away? Could it be he wanted that knowledge even more than Eve? There was no resistance when she offered him a bite.

Adam and Eve both disobeyed, and both suffered the consequences of their sin. But Scripture places the responsibility on Adam. 'For if by the trespass of the one man, death reigned through that one man, how much more will those who receive God's abundant provision of grace and of the gift of righteousness reign in life through the one man, Jesus Christ' (Rom 5:17).

But Eve has borne the major brunt of the consequence of sin which entered the world at the Fall. Besides the predicted results of pain in many childbirths, and her over-dependence on her husband, she also ended up tilling the hostile earth with him. And of course, all will die!

From the beginning of time woman has suffered abuse, has been used, overworked and undervalued by almost all societies. She has been considered weak, lacking in intelligence, sexually seductive, emotionally unstable. Jesus honoured women, taught them, healed them, treated them with equality, assigned them to proclaim his message, while most cultures (even those who knew nothing of the story of the Fall) continued to consider women of lower status.

The Old Testament never again mentions Eve or her culpability, and she is referred to only twice in the New Testament, where Paul points out that Satan thoroughly deceived her. 'This provided more than enough biblical warrant for Jewish males of Jesus' day to justify their debasing treatment of, and oppressive discrimination against women,' writes C.C. Cowles in *A Woman's Place*.[1] Two centuries before Christ, Jesus ben Sirach wrote, 'From a woman sin had its beginning, and because of her we all die.'[2]

The Old Testament honours women, and nowhere does it teach their inferiority or culpability. But the patriarchal society of the day in which the Old Testament was written reflects the sin permeating people's hearts. Abraham lied about Sarah and put her in jeopardy to save his own skin; Lot offered his virgin daughters to the men who demanded his male guests for homosexual acts. David's lust for a woman's body led to his ordering that her husband be put in a dangerous position and killed in battle. Absalom performed public sex with his father's ten concubines to flaunt his victory – never mind how the women felt.

Cultures Everywhere Reflect the Effect of the Fall.

Gretchen Gaebelein Hull reflects on the impact that patriarchalism in any society makes on both men and women. 'Women cease to be partners in a "one flesh" union and become possessions, treated as objects to be picked up or discarded at the will of the men who control their destinies. Perpetuating the family or the clan or even the institution of patriarchy itself becomes the overriding consideration, not justice – and certainly not the human rights of women.'[3]

Whether you believe that the control and rule of men over women is a prophetic outgrowth of the Fall, or a command of God for all human relationships, no one can deny that the results have gone way beyond what God intended. They have dehumanized both men and women. To some degree almost every culture in the world reflects a negative attitude towards women.

Greek and Roman women were considered generally inferior, and in many places were secluded within their homes, discouraged from associating even with other women. Their legal status was that of a perpetual minor. The belief was held that a dream about a male child was a good omen, while dreaming about a female was bad.

The story of Pandora's Box (circa 800 BC) is one of the earliest secular stories of woman as the source of sin. It was said that Jupiter ordered a beautiful woman to be created, but Vulcan gave her a deceitful mind. When she came into the presence of men, she opened her casket and allowed all the evils of mankind to escape. Katherine Bushnell, author of God's Word to Women, believes that early Jewish writers who were influenced by Greek philosophy reconciled the story of Eve with the story of Pandora.

While Greek philosophers did not necessarily reflect the day by day life of the people, their writings were influential and taught what they thought was the highest good. Generation after generation of Greeks expounded and expanded the teachings of the great philosophers, so that even in the time of the New Testament Greeks were known for their philosophical debates. 'All the Athenians and the foreigners who lived there spent their time doing nothing but talking about and listening to the latest ideas' (Acts 17:21) writes Luke about Paul's opportunity to debate with the philosophers at the Aeropagus. We read that a Greek woman Damaris risked her reputation to listen to Paul on this occasion, and believed (Acts. 17:34).

The following are some of the 'words of wisdom' that have come down to us through the ages from these philosophers.

Pythagoras (580 BC) taught that had there been no Eve, Adam would have remained happy and immortal [and alone I might add!].

Socrates (470 BC) taught that woman was halfway between a man and an animal. He asked, 'Do you know anything at all practised among mankind, in which in all these respects the male sex is not far better than the female?'[4]

Plato (428 BC) an ardent follower of Socrates, passed his low view of women on to his most influential disciple, Aristotle (384 BC), who taught that males were to be the dominators, while females and slaves were meant to be dominated, and that all females were inferior to males. Aristotle wrote, 'We should look upon the female state of being as though it were a deformity, though one which occurs in the ordinary course of nature.'[5]

Philo, a contemporary of Paul, was a prolific Jewish writer. He believed that the rational part of a person is masculine and should rule the feminine. His concept was that woman is 'endowed by nature with little sense.'

Women in Jewish Society

Jewish women in Palestine had greater freedom to go out of the house, go to the marketplace or to work in local shops than Greek women had. The New Testament tells of women who followed Jesus, drew water at the public well, were healed on the street, sat at his feet to learn, and in general were visible. The Babylonian Talmud calls on a husband to love his wife as he loves himself.

Yet on the whole the Talmud, commentaries on the Law, and other Rabbinical writers indicate that any public life for a woman was frowned upon by the religious leaders of the day.

A Jewish woman had no say in the choice of her marriage partner. In a contractual arrangement of ownership she passed from father to husband, without inheritance or any legal rights to land or personal finances. She was instructed to keep her head covered in respect to her husband. Some rabbis commended women who veiled their faces even in their own homes, so that their children never saw them. A woman was to obey her husband in all matters and to show him deference such as standing behind him while he ate. Jewish literature is full of joy over the birth of a son, and sorrow over that of a daughter.

In case of danger the husband must be saved first, then the sons, followed by the wife and daughters.

Josephus, the famous Jewish historian writes, 'The woman, says the Law, is in all things inferior to the man. Let her accordingly be submissive, not for her humiliation, but that she may be directed; for the authority has been given to the man.'[6]

In the Temple and synagogue worship women were to be absolutely silent; they could not participate in the worship in deference to the 'dignity of the congregation.' One rabbi wrote that 'it would be better that the Torah be burnt than spoken from the lips of a woman.'[7] Women were allowed only in the outer courts of the Temple, and forbidden to enter any Temple area while menstruating or within forty days of giving birth (eighty days for a female child).

Jewish men in Paul's day were warned not to sit among women because 'evil comes from them like a moth emerging from clothes.' If a man was seen talking with a woman in public it implied they had an inappropriate relationship. 'The end result of indulging in chatter with a woman, the Sages thus warned, was hell . . . Indeed so important was this matter, later rabbis reasoned that "God himself avoided speaking with a woman." '[8]

The Church Fathers

But the incarnate Son of God spoke freely, lovingly and publicly to women, modelling a new attitude and relationship. The Church Fathers did not seem to understand what Jesus was saying by his revolutionary actions. Instead, they continued to perpetuate the results of the Fall which infiltrated all societies, pagan and Christian, often pushing them to the extreme. There was no doubt a broad gap between the policies of the Church as reflected in the early writings, and the practices in society. Thankfully, we have already looked at the qualities and contributions of women throughout the ages, evidence that in spite of scorn and denigration, many women were able to rise above these negative pronouncements and were encouraged by loving husbands or sympathetic leaders.

A quick overview, however, of statements made by godly and respected theologians will give some idea of the courage and spiritual energy needed by any woman stepping out of the prescribed role.

Tertullian, an early church father, seems to have been considerate of his own wife, when he wrote her a letter charging her not to marry a pagan if he should die. Some reasons given were, 'Who would be willing to let his wife go through one street after another to other men's houses, and indeed to the poor cottages, in order to visit the brethren? . . . Who will let her creep into jail to kiss the martyr's chains? Or bring water for the saints feet?'[9]

Tertullian vigorously opposed heretical sects of his day. Perhaps the strength of his comments about women are due largely to his revulsion against sexual excesses in these pagan religions. His most frequently quoted statement about women is heartbreaking to women who love the Lord.

> You are the devil's gateway; you are the unsealer of that [forbidden] tree; you are the first deserter of the divine law; you are she who persuaded him who the devil was not valiant enough to attack. You destroyed so easily God's image. On account of your desert, that is, death – even the Son of God had to die.[10]

Jerome, whose friendship with Paula was discussed in chapter one, reflected the growing aversion among church leaders to sexuality. Though he experienced long and respected friendship with women once they adopted a celibate lifestyle, he equated woman with 'body' and thus with sexuality and evil. He warned Paula not to take her daughter to public baths because she might see the totally revolting sight of a pregnant women. He is quoted as saying 'nothing is more vile than to love a wife like a mistress.'

Origen, a third-century North African scholar, also had problems with women. 'Certainly women should teach what is good, but men should not sit and listen to a women . . . even if she says admirable things, or even saintly things; that is of little consequence since they come from the mouth of a woman.'[11]

Theological discussions of the wife's place being solely in the home rather than in the public domain date back to the third century, as church polity about formal and hierarchical leadership developed. It seems that as long as the church met primarily in homes, women were involved in every area of ministry without restriction. But as the church moved out of homes into the public sphere, restrictions on deacons and the order of widows appeared.

John Chrysostom, a third-century theologian whose *Summa Theologia* became the Roman Catholic theological textbook for centuries, wrote that God appointed different domains for men and women. The 'more necessary and beneficial aspects to the man and the less important, inferior matters to the woman.'[12] The fact that he testifies that Junia, mentioned in Romans 16, is a female apostle makes his observation even more striking.

It is painful to read how through the centuries writer after writer imbibed this lie of Satan. The great North African Bishop of Hippo, Augustine, is recognized as one of the most influential thinkers in Christendom. His *Confessions* are recommended reading for a moving account of the struggles of a carnal man as he plumbs the depths of the reality of God.

Yet even Augustine was not immune from the taint of discrimination against women. He taught that Eve was created to be man's helper specifically for the production of children. He equates all sexual desire with lust. He encouraged a man to love what is human in her but to hate what pertains to a wife, which led to the conclusion that only man possesses the full image of God.[13]

A few observations from church councils reveal how the status of women was gradually lowered over the years. In 533 the Synod of Orleans abolished the office of deaconess 'on account of the weakness of her sex.' In 538 the Council of Orleans forbade married clergy to sleep with their wives. The Council of Tours (567) blamed women for luring men into sin, comparing them to serpents who shed their skins to become more alluring. The Synod of Tours a few years later declared that women were impure by nature. The Council of Vienne in 1312 restricted women from partaking of communion while pregnant or menstruating. This practice continued throughout the Middle Ages.[14] Remember that these decisions were not made by pagan councils or anti-Christian bodies, but by men of the church who believed they were following the counsel of the Holy Scriptures.

The Reformation

Did matters change after the Reformation? Not much. In some ways it was more difficult for women who wanted to follow a life of ministry and devotion to God, for Protestant women no longer had the convents as an outlet. Martin Luther believed in marriage, in educating children (including girls), and in the inherent value of women, even conceding that if no man were available it might 'be necessary for a woman to preach'.

But Luther had also imbibed the philosophy and moral values of his day. He wrote, 'Take women from their housewifery and they are good for nothing.' More cutting was his remark, 'If women get tired and die of bearing, there is no harm in that; let them die as long as they bear; they are made for that.'[15]

John Knox wrote of women in 1558, 'Nature doth paint them . . . to be weak, frail, impatient, feeble and foolish; and experience hath declared them to be inconstant, variable, cruel and lacking the spirit of counsel.'[16]

No wonder men did not consider women's conversation enlightening or interesting. In her book *The Weaker Vessel* Antonia Fraser argues it was the 'learned woman' that terrified men. For a man, education was a prized experience. For a woman, it was frowned upon as the drug called learning.

'How could a woman be "modest" if she knew too much? Above all, education increased a woman's vocabulary, and one thing a seventeenth-century man could not abide was a talking woman.'[17] Even in the 1990s, 43 percent of women in less developed countries are illiterate (as compared with 24 percent of men).[18]

Attitudes Around the World

As noted earlier, attitudes towards women in almost every culture of the world have been harmful. For example, Aboriginal tribal elders of Australia selected a marriage partner for a girl at birth, promising her to an older man. Naturally, she had nothing to say about the matter and if she rebelled, was abused.

Violence again women is an age-old problem, but one that is gaining international attention. At least 75 percent of refugees in the world are women and girls, fleeing war and violence. Approximately one quarter of the world's women are violently abused in their own homes. Some of the worst offenders are: Papua New Guinea: 60 percent abused; Thailand: 50 percent; Korea: 60 percent; Pakistan: 80 percent. In the United States, domestic violence is the biggest cause of injury to women – more than rape, road accidents and muggings combined.[19]

In 1996 almost two million girls around the world underwent female genital circumcision. In Somalia up to 90 percent undergo the most extreme form in which all external genital parts are cut off. The highest numbers of mutilations occur in Nigeria, Ethiopia, Egypt, Sudan and Kenya. Considered a rite of passage from girlhood to womanhood, circumcision is said to make girls desirable for marriage, ensure virginity, and keep them from sexual wrongdoing. It is practiced mostly by Muslims, though Muslim leaders would deny that they encourage or condone it.

Even without this invidious practice, Islam has accepted the same negative attitudes about the inferiority of women as the rest of the world. In Pakistan the sharia law requires two female witnesses to equal one male witness in a legal case. (And two Christian men or four Christian women!) 'This takes into consideration the more emotional nature of women,' writes Said Abdullah Seif Al-Hatim.[20] The Koran says that women are created inferior to men, and that it is permissible to flog a wife under certain circumstances.

As in many other cultures, Muslim women are held responsible for seducing men. Al-Hatim describes the need for women to cover all but their hands and feet in public so as not to tempt men, since man's sexual drive is 'like a disease'. Al-Hatim defends polygamy partly because of the shortage of men in society, but also because a woman must respond to her husband's sexual demands as often as he needs her, and pregnancy and menstruation may interfere with his fulfilment.

While Islam had access to the story of Adam and Eve, Hindus developed their own explanation for the inferior status of women. The sins she had committed in a former life caused her to be born a women, valued less than a cow. Her husband is her god, and serving him is the only way to gain merit. Before the law intervened, an Indian widow committed 'sati', throwing herself on her husband's funeral pyre. Today more than five thousand young Indian brides die a different fiery death each year, as their husbands and in-laws set fire to them, seemingly in an accident in the kitchen. The 'dowry death' releases the family to seek another bride, and another dowry. More of these cases are being prosecuted today, but very often the local authorities turn a blind eye.

The killing of thousands of female foetuses in India has become a national scandal. A report states that out of one thousand abortions committed in a Bombay hospital following ultrasound to determine the sex of the child, 999 were female. Many mothers simply walk out of the hospital leaving behind infant daughters. A picture in a magazine shows cribs lined up outside the hospital, with three or four baby girls in each one, free for the taking. The Indian government's Department of Women and Child Development states, 'In a culture that idolizes sons and dreads the birth of a daughter, to be born female comes perilously close to being born less than human.'[21]

A proverb in Buddhist Sri Lanka states, 'She is born a woman because she committed a thousand sins in the previous world.'

In one tribe in Ghana a widow is forced to marry one of her husband's relatives to bear children for her dead husband, but is then often left to fend for herself and her children. In other parts of Africa there are taboos against women eating nutritious food like eggs, milk and chicken which are reserved only for men.

And what does the famous Latin 'machismo' stand for? Scott Bartchy defines it as a term which 'signifies a kind of animal strength by which one creature controls another and thus establishes his self-identity and place in the pecking order.'

Increased sensitivity to and awareness of sexual harassment in North America would jeopardize the future of any person making insulting statements publicly about women today. But only a few years ago a Texas senator quipped, 'Do you know why God created women? Because sheep can't type.'[22]

The 20th Century Church's Problem?

To be fair, many positive changes have occurred in the status of women in spite of the prevailing attitudes we have discussed. Changing attitudes is a slow process, whether those attitudes be towards slavery, race or women. Wherever Christianity has gone, a women's place has vastly improved. But sometimes the church is slower than society, as in the case of the abolition of slavery, which Christians defended with vehemence from Scriptures. Sometimes people outside the church take a lead in the process of justice and change, and though their motives and methods may be wrong, the change they are calling for may be right.

Probably one of the saddest accounts of how the attitude of church leaders limited and affected women's roles in ministry is the story of twentieth-century missions in North America. As noted earlier, by 1929, 67 percent of all foreign missionaries from the United States were women and over forty women's mission boards had been formed. Women recruited single missionaries, sent them out to work primarily with women and children, financed them and organized national prayer movements. The World Day of Prayer was founded by the Federation of Woman's Boards and the Council of Women for Home Missions in 1919.

But leaders of the mainline churches resisted this movement, opposing the appearance of women in public meetings, and their assumption of leadership roles in churches on the mission fields. In his landmark book on the history of women's mission societies, R. Pierce Beaver writes, 'The church has always been the bastion of male arrogance and power, and the men were most reluctant to share control and ministry with the women.'[23]

The mainline mission boards began increasing pressure on the women's organizations to merge. The chief spokesperson for the women's missionary boards, Mrs. Helen Montgomery asked, 'Are men ready for it – are they emancipated from the caste of sex so that they can work easily with women, unless they be the head and women clearly subordinate?'[24]

Evidently not. For example, in 1884 the Methodist Church drew up a new constitution which brought the women's organization under its rules. 'It took all the initiative and power from the women, deprived them of effective administration and ended their appointment and assignment of women missionaries.'[25]

Many men felt these organizations were part of the emerging women's rights and suffrage movements. 'The spectacle of lady missionaries, officers and executives of the Boards addressing mixed audiences, speaking before the assemblies . . . and presiding over their own meetings filled conservative males with horror.'[26] However, the leaders recognized the ability of the women to organize and to raise funds even beyond what the denominational boards were doing. They pleadged that the women would not lose their influence or control if they became part of the mainline mission boards.

By 1920 all but a handful of the women's mission boards had disappeared. Seldom did the mainline missions replace the leadership with another woman when the female leader retired or died. While the missions promised to bring the 'best-qualified person into leadership, regardless of sex.' Beaver comments, 'It is amazing that so seldom is this best-qualified person a woman. It is most rare for a man to be succeeded by a woman. A woman's peculiar gifts are lost in the direction of world mission in consequence of her progressive exclusion – the power of heart as well as intellect, the important feminine intuition, her impatience with bureaucratic procrastination and endless discussion before action, and her readiness in faith and hope to take a risk.'[27]

Beaver believes that the 'greatest loss consequent to the end of the distinctive, organized women's world mission movement has been the decline of missionary dynamism and zeal in the churches.'

We ask again, where did these attitudes arise? Why has it been so difficult for women to use their gifts in ministry? Up to this point we have looked at the effects of the curse and its resultant impact on cultures. Sin has built a barrier between men and women which has degraded women and men – a barrier which Jesus broke down. 'For he himself is our peace who has made the two one, and destroyed the barrier, the dividing wall of hostility' (Eph. 2:14). Though referring here primarily to Jew and Gentile, it is not out of context to include the rest of the social package – man and woman, slave and free as in Galatians 3:28. Socially the world is recognizing that the barriers should come down. What is still standing in the way of many Christian women to step out and use their gifts in obedience to God's call?

The Theological Tension

For Christians the most powerful influence on women's ministry has been the Scripture passages which deal with this issue. There are in fact, only three major passages which seem to deny women equality and opportunity in ministry – 1 Cor. 11:3–10; 14:33–35 and 1 Tim. 2:12. Throughout history, church leaders have generally inferred their position on women, changing as it frequently did, from models or lack of them in Scripture, from decisions made by all-male church councils, from cultural practices revealed in Scripture, or by focusing on individual verses rather than the Scripture as a whole.

Very few councils, assemblies or church boards have approached the question from a neutral or purely objective position. Yet throughout the centuries a lone voice here and there challenged the accepted traditions, asking insightful questions, and suggesting alternative interpretations.

In 1923 Katherine Bushnell wrote *God's Word to Women*, taking a fresh look at hundreds of passages of Scripture which she believed gave women greater freedom and opportunities in ministry.[28]

In recent decades a rash of books on both sides of the issue has been published. While liberal theologians and radical feminists simply pooh-pooh the writings of Paul as a woman-hater, or as spurious, other scholars are biblically-based evangelicals and hold to the inerrancy of the Scriptures. Perhaps the major difference is that the non-traditionalists attempt to start from a new perspective, taking the whole Scripture into account, rather than focusing on isolated passages.

While we will leave it to these scholars to delve into the theological issues more thoroughly, it is interesting to consider some of the various points of difference, based on interpretations of Scripture.

The following attitudes come from the same Scripture but are interpreted differently from traditional and non-traditional viewpoints.

Traditional interpretations	*Non-traditional interpretations*
Women have spiritual equality before God, but limited freedom in the church and family. *Gal. 3:28*	Women have spiritual equality before God and social equality as people. *Gal. 3:28*
God commanded woman to allow her husband to rule over her. *Gn. 3:16*	God declared that as a result of sin, man would rule over woman. *Gn. 3:16*
Men and women are created equal before God but the woman is secondary to man as a 'helper'. *Gn. 2:18*	Men and women are created equal and woman is an equal 'helper.' The Hebrew word for helper is also used to describe God as our helper. *Gn. 2:18*
Man as 'head' is ruler and authority over woman. *1 Cor. 11:3*	Man as 'head' is source, nurturer and servant-leader. *1 Cor. 11:3*
Woman must have man's authority on her head. *1 Cor. 11:10*	Woman has her own authority on her head. *1 Cor. 11:10*
The New Covenant does not relate to women's role in the church. *Acts 2:17, 18*	The New Covenant changes women's role in the church. *Acts 2:17, 18*

Traditional interpretations	*Non-traditional interpretations*
Women may pray and prophesy in private. *1 Cor. 11:5*	Women may pray and prophesy in public. *1 Cor. 11:5*
Phoebe is described as a servant. *Rom. 16:1*	Phoebe is described as a minister (the same word is translated minister elsewhere for men). *Rom. 16:1*
All apostles in the New Testament were male.	The woman Junias is called an apostle. *Rom. 16:7*
Gifts of pastor, teacher, leader limited to men. *1 Cor. 14:33, 34 (1 Tim. 2:12)*	No gender limitations on gifts. *Rom. 12:3–8 (1 Cor. 12:7–11; Eph 4:11–13)*
Disciples would not accept testimony of a woman. *Luke 24:11*	Jesus instructed Mary to go and bear witness of the resurrection to his disciples. *John. 20:17*
Women must not teach men. *1 Tim. 2:12*	Women listed as 'fellow-workers' – same word Paul used for male colleagues – *Rom 16:3,6*. Priscilla honored for teaching Apollos. *Acts 18:26*
Elder to be husband of one wife, therefore must be male. *1 Tim. 3:2*	Elder requirements must be broader than listed in Timothy. For example, if he must be a husband, then Paul is disqualified
Wives must be in submission to their husbands. *Eph. 5:22*	Mutual submission encouraged in *Eph. 5:21* (the word submission does not appear in 5:22).
Women are to obey their husbands as Sarah obeyed Abraham. *1 Pet. 3:6*	At times Abraham was told to listen to Sarah's instructions – picture of mutual submission *Gen. 21:12*
Women leaders in Old Testament [e.g. Deborah, Miriam] are to be considered exceptions because there were no men available or spiritually up to the task.	God says he called those women to leadership along with the men. *Mi. 6:4*

As you've read through these columns, you've probably identified yourself with the right or the left. But perhaps you have done as so many do today, and picked a smorgasbord of choices from both sides. Perhaps you believe it's all right for a woman to sing hymns of praise and testimony in the church, but not to preach or teach. Some churches permit women to teach adult Sunday school classes, but not to preach. For years it's been acceptable for women to evangelize and plant churches on the mission field, but not at home. (Does this smack of racism?)

In some churches women are permitted to pray, but not to prophesy. Others may insist that elders are male – but not require them to be good teachers, to be hospitable, or even to manage their own families well, as is so clearly stated in Timothy.

Like Calvinism and Arminianism, both positions can be defended from Scripture. Some applications have changed as culture has changed. While we no longer 'give each other a holy kiss' – or at least most of us don't (2 Cor. 13:12); enrol widows under the care of the church (1 Tim. 5:9); or insist that everyone lift up 'holy hands in prayer' (1 Tim. 2:8), we recognize these were proper and expected in the culture of the early church. And most of us have no problem today with those who lift their hands in prayer, choose to care for widows, or greet each other with a 'holy kiss'. We would hope that we are not condemned for *not* following those practices either.

Most women leaders I have interviewed for this book are not optimistic that the church will soon change its attitude towards women's roles. In fact, the two sides seem to be becoming increasingly polarized. We seem to be learning to love and work together across other divides such as Calvinism and Arminianism, pre- and post-millenialism, and charismatic and non-charismatic. But church leaders seem to be digging in their heels on this tug-of-war, and saying 'not another inch' or we'll slide down the slippery slope of radical feminism, or back into the Dark Ages. The women who have taken risks to follow God's call simply ask for love and acceptance, and the recognition that they stand before their Master, responsible for their decisions and obedience.

While this has been a difficult chapter to read, it is necessary for Christians, both men and women, to recognize the extent of these sinful attitudes and resultant demeaning of women through the ages. We need to realize that in many parts of the world these injustices continue. The reinforcement of negative attitudes by the church has affected how women look at ministry. Even today many women feel guilty exercising gifts of leadership. They have a 'gut feeling' that they are stepping out of place. There is a strong sense in some churches today that woman belongs primarily back in the home. And while this may indeed be true for the majority of women, at least while their children are small, it has hurt many women who have an additional call of God on their lives.

Knowing the historical barriers women have faced, we can better understand the courage and sense of divine call necessary for women to step out into ministry. It is with great joy and satisfaction that I tell the following stories of women who, in the face of great obstacles, are risk-takers for God.

Notes

1. C. S. Cowles, *A Woman's Place* (Kansas City, Mo.: Beacon Hill Press, 1993), 66.

2. Sirach 25:24, as cited by Aída Besançon Spencer, *Beyond the Curse* (Nashville: Thomas Nelson, 1985), 18.

3. Gretchen Gaebelein Hull, *Equal to Serve* (Old Tappan, N.J.: Revell, 1987), 87.

4. Cowles, *Woman's Place,* 43.

5. Cited in Patricia Gundry, *Woman Be Free* (Grand Rapids: Zondervan, 1979), 18.

6. Craig S. Keener, *Paul, Women and Wives* (Peabody, Mass.: Hendrickson, 1992), 165.

7. Ibid., 49.

8. Ibid., 162.

9. Catherine Kroeger, "The Neglected History of Women in the Early Church," *Christian History* (Carol Stream, Il.) 7 (1988): 17.

10. Ruth Tucker and Walter Liefield, *Daughters of the Church* (Grand Rapids: Zondervan/Academie Books, 1987), 103.

11. Ibid., 106.

12. "The Wife's Domain," *Christian History* (Worcester, Pa.) 7, no. 1 (1988): 34.

13. Tucker and Liefield, *Daughters of the Church,* 124.

14. Ibid., 131, 133, 161.

15. Ibid., 173.

16. Naim Attallah, *Woman* (New York: Quartet Books, 1987), 12.

17. *Time,* 17 September 1984.

18. *PRB Media Guide to Women's Issues* (Washington, D.C.: Population Reference Bureau, 1995), 26.

19. UNICEF, *The State of the World's Children,* 1995.

20. Abdullah Seif Al-Hatim, *Woman in Islam* (Pakistan: Islamic Publications, 1979), 33.

21. Quoted in the *Washington Post,* 14 February 1993.

22. Cowles, *Woman's Place,* 44.

23. R. Pierce Beaver, *All Loves Excelling* (Grand Rapids: Eerdmans, 1968), 102.

24. Ibid., 181.

25. Ibid., 104.

26. Ibid., 105.

27. Ibid., 201.

28. Katherine C. Bushnell, *God's Word to Women* (Oakland, Calif.: Katherine C. Bushnell, 1923).

Part Two

Women Who are Taking Risks for God

Introduction to Part II

I pray that your love may abound still more and more in real knowledge and all discernment, so that you may approve the things that are excellent, in order to be sincere and blameless until the day of Christ; having been filled with the fruit of righteousness which comes through Jesus Christ, to the glory and praise of God.

Phil. 1:9–11 (NASB)

We are now going to meet twelve women who have obeyed God's call to follow his leading in ministry. Before we begin looking at their fascinating stories we should realize two things:

First, these women have followed the dictates of their own hearts. We may not agree with the decisions they have made as they have interpreted God's will for their lives. They are human and have made mistakes; they have sinned and disappointed their Maker and those they work with.

But they are women of courage, of spiritual insight, and above all of obedience to the heavenly vision God has revealed to them. We should not judge them for their weakness; nor put them on a pedestal. We can simply learn from them that it is God who gifts, calls, and enables. They will not stand before us in judgment, but before the one who has asked them to respond courageously to his call.

Secondly, as I write this book, all twelve women are still alive and active in ministry. Thus it is with much prayer that I write about them, knowing that the enemy would dearly love to cause them to fall or to discredit their ministries. Before you begin reading these stories, will you take time to pray for God's protection and his continued anointing upon their work?

Three

Her Maker is Her Husband – Elena Bogdan, Romania

Sing, O barren woman, you who never bore a child;
burst into song, shout for joy, you were never in labour;
because more are the children of the desolate woman that of her who has a husband,
says the Lord.
enlarge the place of your tent, curtains wide, do not hold back;
lengthen our cords, strengthen your stakes.
Do not be afraid; you will not be humiliated.
You will forget the shame of your youth and remember no more the reproach of your
widohood.
For your Maker is your husband- the Lord Almighty is his name.

Isaiah 54; 1,2,4,5

An urgent knock on the door startled Elena Bogdan. Who could be coming to visit her in the middle of the morning? She looked through the peephole to see two men dressed in business suits.

'Who's there?' she called out. But even before they answered she knew these were Ceaușescu's secret police, known throughout Romania for their brutality.

Her heart pounding, Elena responded, 'My husband is not at home. Can you come back later?' She glanced around the room, frantically wondering what to do. There in plain view sat the suitcases of documents and the boxes of Bibles and Christian literature she and Traian had brought home just a few days before in preparation for their next round of underground deliveries. Traian worked with Christian Solidarity International which kept the plight of persecuted Romanian Christians before the West. The pounding on the door grew more insistent as the police shouted, 'We have a search warrant; open up.'

Defiantly Elena shouted, 'I won't open the door. Come back when my husband is home.' Only twenty-six years old, Elena with her sparkling brown eyes and rich chestnut hair would be temptation enough if she were caught alone by the police. But the thought never entered her head. She raced to the window in the futile hope that she could at least get rid of the names and addresses of Christian families who had been undergoing persecution by the Communists. She and Traian had been taking food and money to many of these families, impoverished because the head of the house was in prison. But a quick glance told her the house was surrounded. There was no time to burn the evidence for she could already hear the police breaking down the door with a heavy object.

Terrified, she tried the telephone. Thank God they had not cut the wires. Even as the door finally gave way, Elena gasped a plea to her friend that Traian should be warned.

For eight hours the police interrogated Elena at the local police station. Where was her husband? Who provided the money for their work? What were the names of others in Timişoara with whom they were working? They demanded that she write out an explanation of what she and Traian were doing.

But even as they shoved paper and pencil in front of Elena, she refused to put anything in writing. Traian had warned her from his previous prison experience that the police would use against her anything she wrote down.

Instead she turned every question into an opportunity to tell these angry men, 'Jesus loves you and we love you too and want you to be saved.'

In her heart the verse kept ringing, 'On my account you will be brought before governors and kings as witnesses to them and the Gentiles. But when they arrest you, do not worry about what to say or how to say it . . . For it will not be you speaking but . . . the spirit of your Father speaking through you' (Mt. 10:18,19–20). And the Holy Spirit kept reminding her that the only way these men could hear the gospel was if Christians were arrested.

As the day wore on it became obvious that the police had a watertight case against Elena and Traian. They wanted her to bring him back to the police station for questioning the next morning. They spoke about a six-year prison term – and worse if Traian did not turn himself in. And then they released her, no doubt believing Elena would lead them to her husband.

When Elena returned to her darkened home and saw the damaged door, she realized she could not stay there safely overnight. It seemed that Traian had received the warning, but where was he? It was dangerous for her to wander the streets at night looking for him, so she stayed with Christian neighbours. The next morning she slipped out of the house very early to the home of Traian's parents, relieved to find him there.

After their joyous reunion, Elena told him about the six-year imprisonment hanging over their heads. Traian's immediate reaction was, 'I'm not going to spend the best years of my life in a communist prison. Let's escape.'

But escape was easier said than done. The borders were relentlessly patrolled by secret police; documents were checked on public transport. The Danube which separated Romania and Yugoslavia was guarded not only by foot soldiers, and observation towers, but also by soldiers who travelled in patrol boats back and forth every half hour. Elena had heard stories from people who tried to escape. 'Those guys with military boots, twenty-year-old young men full of energy and brainwashed, start beating you up, kicking you in the stomach, in the kidneys, in the mouth. They knock out your teeth. If you lose consciousness they revive you and start all over again. If a woman is caught she is raped and then beaten just as badly as a man. And after that, they give you over to the police who put you in prison for several years,' she had been warned. 'And if the patrol boat catches you in the water, they just push their harpoon in you and leave you dead on the water, or simply run the boat over you and the engine chops you up.'

However, Elena's greatest fear was not capture or death, but leaving Romania and the people to whom God had called her. Couldn't they be witnesses in prison, as she had been to the police who interrogated her?

Elena and Traian stayed with his parents for a night or two as they debated the pros and cons of escaping from Romania or facing the prison sentence. She concedes that this was one time when she found it difficult to be submissive to her husband. But they finally agreed that they should escape.

Elena admits it was hard to leave behind everything she had worked for so long. 'I had worked so hard training to be an electrical engineer, and to get a good job. It was not easy to buy your own apartment under the Communists. But I saved and furnished my house. And then I had to leave my house, my job, my friends, my church. And worst of all – to leave Oltenia [the poorest and most neglected province of Romania] where God had called me.'

Knowing it was too dangerous to stay with Traian's parents, they moved to the home of Christian friends in Timişoara. But after a few nights, their friends were shaking with fear that the police would come, and they would also be in trouble. They pleaded, 'Please, we don't want you to feel that you are not welcome in our home, but we are afraid.'

So Elena and Traian knew they had to flee into the mountains until they could decide how to escape the country. They made several surreptitious forays back to their home in the middle of the night to get some of their things. While at their friends' home, Elena was able to put together a tent. They carried only immediate necessities – a blanket, a lamp, some changes of clothing, and as much Christian literature as they could carry to distribute as they travelled.

'We knew we couldn't buy food. There was no food without ration coupons. Sometimes we went to the homes of Christians and they gave us their food.

But we also knew that the ration is so small that when they gave us food, they were taking it from the mouths of their own children.' Elena recalls. 'We ate edible weeds a lot of the time.'

May, 1982 – springtime in Romania. Under other circumstances a hiking trip into the beautiful Carpathian Mountains would have been a dream come true. Elena and Traian had only been married five months. They had met when a small group of Christian young people formed a mission group focused on Oltenia in southern Romania.

Elena had grown up in a Christian home, but after she moved to the city of Timişoara to study electrical engineering, she had gradually lost her faith and taken on the philosophy of her friends around her. 'At school I heard that there is no God, that you cannot believe in somebody that you cannot see and touch. My only goal in life was to be independent.'

Elena even attempted to join the Communist party, but was rejected. 'Probably because my father had been a Christian and when he became mayor of our town, he walked into his office with a Bible,' she surmises.

But once she gained her independence, home and job she began thinking, 'What happens when I die?' She understood there was a part of her that is spiritual, that cannot be seen and touched. She could not deny the existence of her soul.

It took many months for Elena to reflect on her spiritual need. She found herself praying, 'God you know that I don't believe in you, and maybe I'm talking to myself right now. But God, if you are there, I need you. If you are there, help me to believe in you, because my life doesn't make any sense.'

Nine months later, an American missionary passing through Romania shared John 3:16 ('For God so loved the world that He gave His only begotten Son that whoever believes in Him should . . . have eternal life.' NASB) in a meeting 26-year-old Elena was attending, and she accepted Christ. She seemed to hear the Lord say to her, 'Count the cost, because I cannot be second or third in your life. I can be either first or not at all.' Elena testifies, 'I counted the cost and I chose Jesus as my Saviour, and I've never been disappointed.'

From the start Elena was filled with fervour to tell people about her new-found love. Every day she prayed that God would give her the opportunity to witness to someone. 'And every day,' she recalls, 'God brought by at least one person with whom I could share his love.'

Elena found the best opportunities to witness came on the trains by which she travelled frequently as part of her job. One day she sat in a compartment with several country women from the southern province of Oltenia. Elena began to talk with them about the Lord and found them responsive. They mentioned their daughters attending boarding school in a village where Elena would be disembarking and she asked their names and for permission to visit them.

As soon as Elena had time she went to the dormitory and asked the matron if she could see the girls. Since Elena was not a relative, the matron was very suspicious. But Elena told her she'd met their mothers on the train and they had encouraged her to visit their daughters. She wanted to take them out for an ice-cream.

The matron relented and Elena spent a delightful time with the girls, as she told them about Jesus. As she got to know them, she was overwhelmed with the spiritual darkness in Oltenia, and God seemed to burn the people of that region on her heart.

On one of her first holidays after her conversion Elena travelled to Oltenia, witnessing in homes, coffee-shops and restaurants. Somehow she was oblivious to the danger, and found people ready to listen and open to accept Christ. It was during this time that a group of young people in Timişoara heard about her burden for Oltenia and offered to form a mission group to work in the southern province. Whenever they had a free weekend, two or three of them would travel by train to towns in Oltenia to witness in public places.

Once Elena sat at a table in a restaurant with several young men, and when the meal was served, she asked if it would be all right for her to thank the Lord for her food. This opened up a lively conversation, and an invitation for her to join them to visit a seriously injured friend in the hospital. Elena still remembers how she walked into the hospital room, crowded with relatives and friends. It seemed as though the Lord opened a pathway right to the young man's bed, and she was able to share the gospel with him. When his relatives realized what she was doing they shouted, 'Lady, leave him alone.' But the young man in the bed asked her to pray for him, and she learned later that he told his friends, 'You don't know how much good she did me today.'

On another visit to Oltenia, village people reported her to the police for spreading 'religious propaganda.' A police truck picked her up and brought her in for questioning. As she shared her faith with the interrogator, she could see his attitude changing. He finally told her to get on the next bus out of town before his supervisors came back.

One of the members of the mission group was Traian Bogdan who had been risking his freedom and life for several years as part of Christian Solidarity International. He often visited families to pray with them after the father or son had been imprisoned, and brought them food and other assistance. Traian was tall and thin, with gentle brown eyes and a fair complexion, and Elena could only describe him as 'beautiful.' Within a few short months they were engaged and married in December, 1981.

And now what should have been a belated honeymoon was a journey of desperation. Instead of enjoying the glorious mountain scenery, far from the environmental desecration that the communists had inflicted upon this oil-rich country, they spent their energies trying to work out how to cross the border. The northeastern borders into Hungary and the Ukraine were heavily patrolled. The Danube, snaking between Yugoslavia and Romania for hundreds of miles, was carefully guarded by the Romanians, since Yugoslavia had a relatively open policy towards fugitives from Ceauşescu's tyranny.

They never spent more than a week or two in the same place. Traian seemed to have a nose for the secret police, and when he said, 'Let's go,' Elena packed up and moved. Now and again they stayed with Christian friends whom they had visited in the past. How good to have a bath and 'real food.' How wonderful to catch up on news of family and friends. But always there was the constant preoccupation with, 'How are we going to get out of the country?'

Many times Elena said, 'Let's just go back home and face the risk of going to prison.' She had an overwhelming sense of deserting the people to whom God had called her. She pleaded with Traian, 'All of us are fleeing when it gets tough. Who's going to stay here and tell these people about Jesus? The ones who are afraid to talk about him anyway? Let's just go to prison.'

But deep in her heart she was also afraid, not of prison itself, but what the secret police would do to brainwash and break her. 'They were demonically evil,' she states flatly. 'They would turn you into an informer – into one of their instruments, and control you by fear. That was something that at the time I did not feel I had enough emotional strength to overcome. And that was the only reason I still considered escaping the country.'

The beautiful spring moved into the summer. And Elena and Traian kept moving too. Sometimes he would leave her behind and find his way back to Bucharest, a city of over two million, where he could slip into the homes of friends unnoticed, trying to make plans or get the latest information on border conditions.

Late in the summer they spent ten days at the beach, relaxing in the sun, trying to forget what lay ahead. But for Elena this became a spiritual drought. After ten days she realized that she had not shared the love of Christ with any of the people they had been mingling with.

She began weeping, saying to Traian, 'I don't know what's wrong. Is there sin in my life, or maybe I'm not doing very well during my quiet time? I've not been able to share the gospel with anyone during these days.' She began to pray fervently, 'Lord if you don't need me, take me home, because the only reason I want to live is for you.'

Traian's prayer that day still rings in her ears, 'Lord, please help me to be worthy of my wife's call.' And she realized then how strong the call of God was upon her life, even stronger than self-preservation.

For a day Traian took over the cares of daily living, cooking and washing clothes, so that Elena could spend the time alone in prayer and Bible study. The next day was to be their last day on the beach. With joy and freedom in the spirit, she went around telling each person they had met about the Lord Jesus, and leaving Christian literature with them. She wasn't at all surprised that they responded with hunger and appreciation, promising to read the literature. God had prepared their hearts.

As the autumn and cold weather drew closer, Traian and Elena had to make a decision about their escape route. They could not live in a tent eating berries and weeds much longer. Every avenue of escape had its drawbacks. They could not agree. Finally they came to the conclusion that each should work out a way of escape and they would leave separately. It seemed sensible for Elena to leave first, so that if she were captured Traian could notify people in the west as well as exerting pressure from the Romanian side.

At first Elena shared her ideas with him, but he vetoed each one. 'I think I was a bit more of a risk-taker than Traian,' Elena explains. 'He was trying to find a method that would guarantee him a hundred percent success in his attempt to escape. There was no one hundred percent guarantee. You had to take risks. I told him, "Let's give God the chance to show his glory. Let's give him the chance to protect us and not try to do it all." ' Traian agreed but added, 'Yes, but God gave us wisdom.'

By this time he had decided that one of the wisest ways to escape was by home-made submarine under the Danube. Elena refused to consider such an attempt, but Traian proceeded with his plans. He went to Bucharest where his friends helped him build a simple tube-like construction with an air pipe to the surface to take him across the Danube underwater. He and his friends drove a car back to the Danube with the contraption on top of the car. Only God knows why they were not stopped.

Elena can still point out the spot in a tributary of the Danube just north of Severin, where she lives today, where they slipped the 'submarine' into the water to test it. It sprang a leak and sank to the bottom!

By early October Elena had made up her mind to cross the Danube on an air-mattress. The thought was terrifying to her for she could not swim, and still remembered when she was almost drowned in the river at fourteen years of age. She and Traian were staying with friends in the town of Craiova. They decided to part there before Elena made her escape attempt. Traian was to return to Bucharest alone to continue researching ways to escape.

Did Elena have a sense of foreboding as they kissed each other the morning he left? They did not say goodbye to each other, but in her heart was the thought that they might not see each other again. However, she brushed it aside and sent him on his way. The sense of danger, apprehension and constant risk overcame the possibility of loss. They were both beyond awareness of their personal reactions. The situation had become so tense, it had to be brought to a close.

Now Elena's plans for escape were crystallizing. She asked her friends to give her an air-mattress to escape, but they refused. They feared that if she were caught the police would force her to tell them who gave her the air-mattress. And beyond that, they did not want to have the responsibility upon their shoulders if the attempt failed and Elena drowned.

The day before she planned to leave was spent in prayer and fasting. She felt as though her mind switched into neutral. She prayed, 'Lord, if you say no, no problem. I will stay here with my husband. And this is how I will know, if you give me the air-mattress by ten o'clock tomorrow morning. I believe you are going to express your will through these people. If they are afraid, fine, but I am going to give that to you.'

By nine o'clock the next morning, Elena had the air-mattress and was on her way. She had decided to cross the Danube from the back garden of her mother's home in Pescari. Though the river was more than a mile and a half wide at this point, she knew the banks well and was familiar with where the soldiers were positioned. A submerged island halfway across would give her a resting spot among exposed branches of trees. Also just across the river in Yugoslavia was a quarry. Often as a child she had been able to discern the movements of the workers on the other side, and she felt that if she headed there she had a better chance of being rescued once she landed.

But the journey from Craiova to Pescari was fraught with danger. She travelled by train from Craiova to the river. Then she took a commercial passenger boat to within seven kilometres of her home town. How would she explain the air-mattress in her suitcase if she were searched? What if the soldiers asked for her identification papers and recognized her?

As she neared home, a greater fear crossed her mind. She could not let her mother or brother know what she was doing. They would stop her escape, convinced that she was safer with them than if she fled the country. And if anyone in town recognized her, and told her family, that would put them in danger if the police questioned them. So as she neared the town she asked the Lord to allow her to get to her mother's house without being seen.

Suddenly a heavy storm broke, driving everyone off the streets, and she was able to slip into her mother's back garden, and the hayloft above the house without being seen. She slept fitfully that night, imagining what it would be like to be downstairs in her mother's home, talking with the family, eating a hot meal. The next day she spent in prayer. At one time she heard a voice saying, 'May it be done according to your faith.' She remembers saying, 'O

Lord, please don't do it according to my faith, because I really don't have any. I believe in your grace and I am really depending on your grace.'

Another time Isaiah 41:10 came to her: 'Do not fear for I am with you . . . I will uphold you with MY righteous right hand.' (NASB) But the enemy told her that perhaps these were just coincidences – the air-mattress, the rain storm. 'And then the Lord gave me a vision of a white hand from heaven . . . reminding me that he would protect me with his righteous right hand.'

During that day she decided she had better be ready to hide under the hay, should anyone come up to the loft for anything. When she heard footsteps climbing the ladder, she covered herself, and her brother noticed nothing amiss. In fact when he finished his work, he jabbed the pitchfork into the hay, just missing her head.

As the darkness of the night settled around the village Elena crept down the hayloft stairs and through the back-garden to the river's edge. She had decided to use the back-garden gate to make a stronger raft, and to lift her air-mattress out of the water. She had come prepared with a few tools – a rope, a knife, a raincoat.

Standing on the edge of the dark waters, moving so swiftly past her, Elena could see the lights of the village, and the stars above. It was a brisk October evening and she shivered even before she pushed herself off from the shore. As soon as she hit the water the air-mattress submerged under her weight, drenching her. Surprisingly, the water was warm. It was difficult to steer the heavy gate towards the trees sticking out of the submerged island halfway across the river – her point of reference. Instead the fast-moving current began taking her east toward the curve in the river, and closer to the soldiers' lookout. The water had carried her beyond any hope of getting to those trees.

'Lord,' Elena cried out, 'you told me, "Fear not for I am with you; I will protect you and help you." ' And suddenly she found herself transported to the other bank, a short distance from the quarry. To this day she does not know how she got there. 'I believe that to be physically transferred to another place was a miracle . . . I was a Baptist and I did not expect miracles.'

As she pulled herself onto the steep shore of freedom, her body felt like lead. Exhausted, she could only lie on the bank thanking God that she had made it safely. Now she gathered her few belongings together and, shivering in the sharp night air, made her way to the quarry, hoping that some of the workers would hide her until she could make her way out of Yugoslavia.

But instead, they turned her over to the police. Yet how differently these police treated her. They gave her a uniform to wear while her clothes were drying, and a hot drink. The authorities held her for two weeks for illegal entry into the country, but she learned later that this was for her own safety. Ceauşescu was paying a state visit to Yugoslavia at that time, and if she had been caught wandering around the country, she would have been returned to Romania post-haste.

Elena spent more than six months in refugee camps, most of the time in Italy, before her application to be admitted to the USA was granted. During that time she was able, through friends in Romania, to inform Traian of her safe arrival. They had previously agreed on contact points and even to use a false name, Victor, for her correspondence. In the ensuing months she received letters post-marked India, Sweden, and other countries, letters which Traian had given to 'underground' visitors in Romania to post for him.

In May, 1983 Elena entered the USA with refugee status. For some months she stayed with other Romanians who had fled their homeland, but she found an extreme paranoia among them. It was obvious to her that they suspected her of being an informer. The Communists used this tactic to divide and weaken the Christians, spreading rumours until it seemed everyone was suspicious of everyone else. It was especially hard for Elena because she could not speak English and was totally dependent on Traian's friends.

Eventually she was able to move to Chicago where she learned English rapidly. It was there in December that she received the fateful phone call from Romania, 'Traian is dead.'

Recent letters from him had told of several failed escape attempts. Once he had tried escaping on a train and the police had questioned him for 24 hours before letting him go. They had not realized that he was a hunted man, but from that point he sensed that his life was in danger. He moved to another safe house, but now the authorities knew he was in Bucharest. He wrote to Elena, 'If something happens to me and I die, please continue my ministry.'

Now the worst had happened. Traian had been missing for two months. He'd been hiding out with friends and had gone out to use a public phone to finalize arrangements for escape by ship on the Black Sea. He'd never returned. After two months without any word of his whereabouts, his body was found hanging in the attic of the very house of his friends where he'd been hiding. Those who found him said there were no signs of decay or that he had died by hanging. They felt it was made to look like suicide but they were not allowed to have an autopsy done.

The taint of suicide still hangs over his death, though Elena does not believe it. She recalls Traian's words when another underground worker's body was found hanging in an outhouse. 'A Christian doesn't do that because this is a sin you can't repent from.'

Yet the news of his death was devastating. 'I felt so many times like throwing myself on the floor and crying and screaming. But God enabled me every time to fall on my knees instead.'

Elena had memorized much Scripture since she'd become a Christian just three short years earlier. Now Scripture flooded her mind – 'Thank God in all things, for this is his will concerning you.' But she cried out to God, 'Lord do you want me to give thanks for my husband's death?'

God seemed to say, 'Yes, if you believe that I love you so much that I gave my Son to die for you. Not only that, when you were wandering through the door of sin, I stretched my holy arm and I brought you out of sin and to the cross and cleansed you with the precious blood and blessed you with the Holy Spirit. Now that you are my child, do you believe that I love you less? If you believe that I am sovereign, and not one sparrow falls to the ground without my knowing it, would you be willing to trust me and thank me?'

During the hours of wrestling with God and dealing with the pain of her loss Elena decided not to remarry. 'I wanted to use all the time that God had invested in me to put back in his service. And I needed an answer. That was the time the Lord spoke to me through Isaiah 54: 4,5 "Do not be afraid; you will not suffer shame. Do not fear disgrace; you will not be humiliated. You will forget the shame of your youth and remember no more the reproach of your widowhood, for your Maker is your husband – the Lord Almighty is his name." '

What was she to do with her life? She had no desire to work as an electrical engineer, but she had no income or permanent home. However a kind Romanian pastor's family had taken her in for a few months and at his suggestion she applied to Denver Seminary. Graciously the Lord provided a scholarship and a local church in Denver took her under its wing. Seeing no possibility of ever returning to Romania, Elena became an American citizen. After her graduation from seminary she took a job as associate pastor in a Denver church.

But the winds of revolution were stirring in eastern Europe. Elena felt God calling her back to work 'underground' from Austria and went through the process of applying to an American-based mission and raising support. By the time Elena returned to Europe the communist government had fallen and she was back in her beloved Romania.

In Bucharest, friends helped her find Traian's grave. She learned that several pastors had refused to conduct his funeral because it would place them under suspicion. And the one who did take the service was followed and questioned many times by the police.

As soon as possible, Elena headed back to Oltenia where she made contact with a pastor in the town of Severin, not far from the banks of the Danube. The spiritual darkness was as heavy as ever. Most Orthodox churches were cold and empty, except for holidays and weddings. The priests warned people against Protestant heretics. The sense of the occult and latent communist oppression permeated the community.

But Elena had come with a message of light and love, and her young adult group in the church mushroomed to more than a hundred. As she taught the word of God, these young people who had grown up under atheistic teaching, soaked in the truths of Scripture. However, as the work grew the pastor became more authoritarian, demanding that Elena wear a babushka on her head. 'It seemed he suddenly remembered that I was a woman and that I had to wear my scarf to cover my head and that I had to be quiet in the assembly . . . and that was not why I had came to Romania. If I had to be quiet I would have stayed in America because that was the best place in the world I have ever lived, and the years that I spent in Denver were the best years of my life. And that is when I realized that the issue of women in ministry was beginning to come up.'

In 1993 Patrick Johnstone was to write about Romania in *Operation World*.

> *The 1989 revolution removed the Ceauşescu 'dynasty' but not Marxist controls or attitudes. There remains a heaviness and pessimism because of unrelieved poverty and the deep wounds caused by the excesses and cruelty of the Ceauşescu regime . . . Some leaders in the Orthodox Church oppose Protestant and foreign evangelistic outreach. One Orthodox leader has called Protestantism 'the biggest heresy in Europe.' . . . The transition from severe persecution and restrictions to freedom to worship and witness has been difficult. Pray for flexibility and vision for the leadership and also wisdom in handling those of their number who openly or secretly served the atheist authorities in the past . . . Few pastors have had formal training. The Pentecostal churches are in a theological crisis: 80 percent of their number have had no formal training. The result is often petty legalism . . . Ethnic divisions infect Christians too . . . the shameful treatment of Gypsies needs an application of the Cross of Christ.*[1]

A prominent Christian leader returned from ministering in Romanian churches and warned, 'Unless the Romanian church changes its attitude towards women in the church, women's influence by the year 2000 will be exactly zero.'

Elena was to experience the tensions of these observations in her ministry as she began to find her own way to serve God in Oltenia. Her mission gave her permission to start her own ministry – as long as it was not on the doorstep of the church, and as long as she did not take converts with her.

She rented a hall which seats one hundred and put an advertisement in the paper. The first week 45 people attended. After three months 13 were ready for baptism; three months later another 17, and so on until a hundred believers were meeting each week. It became clear to Elena that this was no longer simply a Bible study or discipling class, but was indeed a church.

Though people of all ages attended the meetings, most were young people who enjoyed the contemporary worship style she introduced and the practical applications of God's word. Her style of leadership attracted more educated young people – young people who dressed in slacks and jeans and girls with smart hairstyles and make-up. Elena observed that to many Christianity had become a subculture that seemed to declare 'godliness means ugliness.' But as Elena offered an alternative, God raised up some of the brightest young students to follow him.

Within six months Elena organized the Emmanuel Bible School so that young believers could be trained and discipled close to home. She formed the Emmanuel Christian Mission and registered it with the government and was able to purchase two adjoining houses in the centre of the city for classrooms. Professors from Denver Seminary and Columbia Biblical Seminary came to teach short-term courses. Very soon twenty students were enrolled in the programme. Several showed such great potential that Elena planned to send them overseas for further training. This could only be a miracle of God in the poverty-stricken darkness of Oltenia.

Elena keeps short accounts with her students. High standards of godliness and confession of sin are part of the daily experiences at Emmanuel. Her home is open to all and she spends hours counselling students and members of her congregation. Sessions of prayer and repentance are common, for Elena constantly has to deal with her own sharp tongue and quick judgments. Yet she will be the first to confess when they are brought to her attention and expects the same of her disciples. 'I would rather have a sold-out team of very committed Christians than have a lot of them that do not understand and do not have a high regard for Christian values,' Elena explains.

Even as God was blessing and building the work in Severin, the enemy was seeking to destroy it. Elena began receiving criticism and rebuke from Christian leaders in other parts of the country because she was now pastoring her own church. She struggled with bitterness.

'I remember one instance when I felt so hurt in my heart by one of the leaders. It was so painful that I felt I couldn't pray for or love him. If I did pray for him, I would tell on him to the Lord. "Look, Lord at what my brother is doing!" But that was the moment that I realized a root of bitterness came into my heart and I had to say, "This is the time I have to stop praying for him and start praying for myself because I have a problem," ' Elena confesses.

But matters were to get even worse. For as the work in Severin grew, her mission realized that not only had a church grown out of Elena's work, but that she was pastoring that church. At a missions conference in Europe the matter came to a head with one of the mission leaders. 'When the issue of women in the ministry came up he became very emotional about it, and I have to admit that I had become emotional too,' Elena recalls. She did not want to leave the mission and grieved over the decision she had to make, for the mission insisted that a male missionary be sent to take her place.

So reluctantly she turned to her home church in Denver, which recognizes women in leadership, and came under the umbrella of its denominational mission. For some time Elena had found that her lack of ordination caused problems. Every time the church held a baptism, wedding or communion, she had to call in a pastor from another church. This caused confusion in the minds of her congregation. Is Elena our pastor or not? Sometimes she had to depend on leaders who were against her leadership. Before one baptism there was great discussion in the performing pastor's church about whether or not they should allow Elena's converts to 'desecrate their baptismal waters.'

Therefore when the mission of her home church agreed to become her umbrella organization, Elena decided to request ordination. She wrote:

'I believe that the ministry to which God has called me requires ordination. Some functions involved in this work, such as the observance of sacraments, cannot be lawfully performed without ordination. Likewise, the pastoral and teaching role in which I have been for the last two years is ordinarily filled by an ordained minister. Even though God, in his grace, has used me in the planting and developing of Emmanuel Evangelical Church of Severin, in order to continue with the vision God has given me, I would feel much more confident and thus more efficient, if I had the official recognition, blessing and authority of our presbytery.'

But while the local presbytery agreed to ordination, the denomination did not. Instead, a male missionary was sent to Severin with the full intention of becoming the senior pastor. For Elena this was a heartbreaking time, as the dissension affected congregation and students alike, causing some to leave. 'I asked the Lord to take me home because I saw the ministry being destroyed and I would rather die than see my baby die. And I had to learn my own lessons here, that it's not my work, it's God's work, and it's God's baby. And I had to learn to let go and to trust the Lord more.'

Elena's understanding of the biblical role of women in ministry is very basic.

1. God created male and female in his own image.

2. Though the woman was cursed, Deborah is an illustration of a woman leader. 'Why didn't God ask Lapidoth, her husband, to be the prophet and judge?' Elena asks. Instead God chose to speak through a woman.

3. In Christ we are equally saved, equally developed, equally gifted by the Holy Spirit, because the Lord has given gifts as he wills and not according to sex. 'One day the Lord will come and ask me, "What have you done with

the talent that I have entrusted to you?" ' she states. 'And on that day of judgment I cannot make excuses, "Lord, the men that you have given me did not allow me to use it." I am responsible before the Lord to invest those talents . . . and reproduce myself to the maximum into the kingdom of God.'

From her personal intuitive nature she understands God as an equally loving Father. 'I have a picture of my heavenly father, our Daddy, holding a boy and a girl on his lap. They are both his children on his knees and we both hug him and love him, and he holds us both. And I can't see him pushing the girl off his knee and saying, "You girl, get away, because I need to talk to my son a little bit." I am his child, and he paid the same price for me as he did for my brother in Christ.'

In spite of the disappointments Elena continued to reach out for new opportunities to share the gospel with her countrymen. Though not in her original plans, a contact with a Christian Gypsy woman opened up a whole new area of ministry. Gypsies have long been the despised and hated people of Europe. Hitler destroyed more than 500,000 Gypsies in the gas chambers during World War II. All the Gypsies of Lithuania, Estonia, Poland and Luxembourg were eradicated.

Romanian Gypsies number more than two million. But after the fall of Communism, Gypsies suffered violent persecution. Mobs burned their homes and beat their occupants sometimes to death. More than 150,000 Romanian Gypsies fled to Western Germany in 1991 and 1992 – but most were deported and sent back.

Nomadic because of constant persecution, Gypsies today are settling into communities. They usually live in separate sections of town, with few amenities and jobs available to them. In recent years revival has broken out among Bulgarian and Romanian Gypsies and large congregations have grown. However, in Oltenia, Gypsies, remained unloved and unreached.

In December 1994, a Christian Gypsy woman died. Before her death she had requested that she have an evangelical funeral. Her family members came to Elena to ask if she would perform the funeral. Seeing this as a potential evangelism opportunity, Elena took a team of students with their musical instruments to the village of Garla-Mare, about two hours drive from Severin. Though the Gypsies speak their own Romany language, most adults also understand Romanian, so they were able to take in the message of God's love that Elena preached that day.

Elena and the team stood around the body in the home of the deceased, and Elena declared to them, 'I want you to know that the kingdom of God has entered your village and God has something very important to tell each one of you today.' The team sang, read the Scriptures and preached, and many eyes glistened with tears as the Spirit of God touched their lives.

When the funeral was over crowds formed around the team asking questions, 'How can we get rid of swearing? How can we get rid of alcohol?' The conviction of sin was upon them, and when Elena asked if they would like to meet regularly, they quickly assented. More than two hundred people came to the first meeting. The head man of the village had requested the use of the town hall since it was winter and miserably cold standing outside on the muddy ground. But before the first week's meeting, the Orthodox priest had gone from house to house telling people not to go to the meeting, and persuading the town council not to open the hall for a church. Instead the people crowded into the small Gypsy homes, filling three and four rooms with eager listeners week after week.

Elena found discipling the Gypsies difficult. Many made their living by stealing, so much so that the local Romanians ceased giving them jobs. Those who had gone to Germany to 'work' came back with stolen goods. Some of the men actually asked, 'Sister Elena, we have a problem now. How are we going to live? Now that we are Christians we can't steal any more and none of us has a job.'

When Elena asked from whom they stole they admitted they stole from each other, but most of the big stealing was from the government's collective farms. Elena believes this is a demonic stronghold for these people and she leads them through prayer and repentance and rejection of the powers of darkness.

When the first group of seventeen candidates was ready for baptism, the Bible school students spent a whole afternoon interviewing them. They reported that four of the candidates felt they did not pass the requirements. One man said he was going to Germany to 'work' and he didn't feel he should be baptized until he had that trip behind him because he was going to have to lie to cross the border.

Since the church in Garla-Mare started, a second Gypsy church in Punghina has started. This congregation is trying to build its own meeting hall. Elena appointed two teams of Bible school students to work with them every weekend. The Bible School closed for the '95/'96 school year so that students could do a year of church-planting under Elena's supervision.

The students live in Gypsy homes at weekends, suffering the attacks of fleas which seem to infest them, getting along without sanitation facilities and eating food provided by their hosts. But the rugged conditions don't seem to faze them. They teach adults to read, hold Bible classes for children, and continually lift biblical standards of honesty, integrity, forgiveness and a respectable work ethic before the people. Most Gypsy children in this region attend only a year or two of school, and the students try to convince their parents of the importance of education.

Elena has developed a heart of love she never knew she had for the Gypsies. But she is realistic enough to realize that only God can change a culture that has been passed from generation to generation for hundreds of years. 'I believe that the only thing that can change these people is the Gospel of Jesus Christ. They need to develop a new value system and experience inner healing. You need to develop a whole new generation of people to undo, to deprogramme them from a lot of the dysfunctional patterns of life and thinking.'

In March, 1995, Dr. Norman Hoyt, head of the missions department at Columbia Bible Seminary, and his wife, Ginnie, returned for a second stint of teaching at Emmanuel. The Hoyts served not only as well-loved teachers, but as wise counsellors for Elena. They recognized that it would be difficult for her to find an evangelical mission that would allow her to pastor a church and to appoint her female students as pastors in the church-planting ministry. They agreed to help her find an alternative so that she would not have to go through another painful change.

After spending five weeks teaching at Emmanuel, the Hoyts planned to leave for the United States on the 31st March. Elena had originally planned to return with them for deputation meetings, but because of her schedule decided to leave the day before. The shocking news reached her in Denver that the aircraft on which the Hoyts flew had crashed nine minutes after take-off from Bucharest airport. There were no survivors.

Elena returned to Romania a few weeks later to hold the Hoyts' funeral on the plaza outside the theatre where the Severin church meets. They were buried in the tiny Severin cemetery where a beautiful white marble tombstone reminds visitors that these American missionaries died serving Christ and loving Romanians. And Dr. Hoyt's promise was kept. Friends at Columbia formed an umbrella organization under which Elena can freely follow the call of God upon her heart.

Today Elena continues the dream she had first captured when she studied in Denver. 'I envision that this church in Severin will become the mother of many churches, and that the more this church grows, the more students it will equip. And the more students it equips the more churches we will plant. In that way we will fill the land of Oltenia with the gospel of Jesus Christ by means of saturation church-planting.' She adds, 'I don't have the concept of saturation church-planting down, but I sure understand the philosophy of it.'

Within a year of establishing the church in Garla-Mare, her dream seemed to be becoming a reality. The church began praying and making plans to plant five more Gypsy churches in other towns. Students began two more Gypsy churches in the villages of Recea and Danceu. Some of the Gypsy adults are already showing leadership qualities, and one young man is a student in the Bible school.

Elena knows that the tension over women in ministry will probably be a lifelong struggle – one that she has to learn to handle more graciously. 'I trust the Lord. I started this ministry from scratch. It's his work done through a woman. And I believe that what he started he will carry to completion.

'I did not go into anybody's ministry to divide it or to be divisive because of my sexual identity. And I have no intention of doing that. I will carry on the ministry the Lord has started to the degree that he will bless it and to the degree that he will strengthen me.

'My purpose is not to promote the kingdom of women, and not to promote my own programme, but the kingdom of God. But I want all the men and women the Lord raises up within Emmanuel Christian Mission to be able to serve the Lord to their fullest potential and not be hindered by human opinions.'

Remembering the times when she has been deeply hurt by the cutting remarks and rejection of Christian leaders, Elena knows she must cast herself more fully on the Lord. She often prays, 'Lord, don't you feel how it hurts? Lord, give me joy. Help me to love them. Help me to pray for them.' Elena realizes that God is purifying her through the pain she suffers. 'It's not how badly they hurt me, but how I respond to that hurt that is important to the Lord.'

Notes

1. Patrick Johnstone, *Operation World* (Carlisle, U.K.: OM Publishing, 1995), 464.

Four

Using the Media to Spread the Message – Elizabeth Mittelstaedt, Germany

'Now write it on a tablet before them and inscribe it on a scroll, that it may serve in the time to come as a witness forever.'

Isaiah 30:8 (NASB)

'Record the vision and inscribe it on tablets that one may read it fluently.'

Hab 2:2 (margin)

'Dear *Lydia* . . .

'The doctors who examined me recommended I abort the baby because of my illness. I was very confused; I looked for a church and found one. I went in and fell on my knees.

'No one was around yet I felt a presence . . . I didn't know how to pray, but I said, "Please God, help me." As I set out for the hospital sadness lingered in my heart. Yet I knew that this presence remained with me.

'After examining me, the doctors declared the baby too big to abort. I felt relieved . . . Today I am happy to have a baby. Thank you, *Lydia* for all the help and direction for my life.'

Niculita, Romania

When Elizabeth Mittelstaedt, editor of the Christian women's magazine *Lydia* read these words, memories flooded her mind. During the communist regime her mother had contracted a serious case of diphtheria. Medicines were difficult to find and the doctor did 'the best he could'. He gave her kerosene-lamp oil but warned, 'Don't bring the child you're carrying into the world with this [infected] blood. You're dying anyhow.'

Elizabeth could still see her mother's grief-stricken face as she recounted travelling by tram to hospital to have an abortion. Abortion was routine in communist Eastern Europe. Women helped each other with crude instruments and many died. At least she had a legitimate excuse to go to hospital for the procedure.

As she stared out the window into the bleak winter landscape, she kept asking herself, 'Should I have this abortion?' A sense of foreboding gripped her heart and a voice seemed to say, 'Don't kill this baby!' Maria was not a Christian at the time and didn't connect the inner warning with God. But even though the pregnancy was endangering her life, she heeded the silent voice and turned round to go home. A few months later she delivered a sickly little girl, and though no one expected her to live, the family named her Elizabeth.

Maria, now a Christian, does not like to speak of this incident, but she recently told Elizabeth, 'Remember, God watched over you even before you were born. God really loves you.' Then she added, 'And I'm so glad to have you. You've brought a lot of joy into my life.'

It's not surprising that one of Elizabeth's early interviews for *Lydia* was with Susan Howard who played Donna on the TV series *Dallas*. Everyone in Germany knew who shot JR. But what they didn't know was that Susan had become a Christian during the series. At one point in the story she was supposed to abort her baby, but she refused to play that role. Eventually the scriptwriters changed the script, and Donna delivered a Down's syndrome baby. Thousands of letters poured into the station lauding Donna for her decision, just as Niculita commended *Lydia* for its encouragement in difficult decisions women have to make. In-depth interviews, such as the one with Susan Howard, which reveal the heart issues women face have made *Lydia* the most widely read women's magazine in Europe. It is published in German, Romanian and Hungarian with a total circulation of almost two hundred thousand subscriptions and an estimated one million readers. Doctors in Germany have ordered dozens of copies – they can't keep them in their waiting rooms!

An article in *Today's Christian Women* asserts that Elizabeth holds a critical role in shaping the future of Germany and is influencing thousands of European women. Author Julie Talerico writes, 'Since the crumbling of the Berlin Wall, pornography and cult magazines have flooded the new territory. But *Lydia* is filling a moral vacuum, teaching former communists and atheists Christian values . . . With a very low percentage of Germans born-again, many *Lydia* readers aren't Christians but are finding answers in the message of Jesus Christ.'[1]

Wherever Elizabeth goes, men and women recognize her. Her heart-shaped face with strong cheekbones and broad smile has a cover-girl quality. She's known from her many speaking appearances all over Europe, and from her picture on the editorial page of the magazine. When someone driving the Mittelstaedt's family car was involved in an accident, the police came to a meeting Elizabeth and her husband, Ditmar were attending to verify its ownership. Looking at her driver's licence, the officer smiled at her, 'Oh, you're Elizabeth Mittelstaedt, the editor of *Lydia*!'

Fame has never been her goal, but writing to impact others has. Even in her youth Elizabeth dreamt of writing poetry. Her favourite poet was a young Communist, Petofi Sandor, who wrote that it was a privilege to die for one's homeland. Her teacher was a faithful Communist who played martial music over a loudspeaker on the main street of the town, and taught her to read Marx and Lenin. When the national anthem was played her heart burned within her, and she wanted to march to the beat of the drums. She dreamed of becoming a writer who would influence others and change her world.

Again and again her teachers taught there was no God. But when she was nine years old, Elizabeth and her whole family accepted Christ when a missionary passed through their town. She went to church with her mother hoping that none of her school friends would see her and taunt her for the rest of the week.

The time came when she had to pay the price for her faith. As a top student, she was offered the opportunity to study at the university to be a teacher. But in order to take up the scholarship she had to become a member of the Communist party. After long discussions with her parents, she refused the scholarship. Elizabeth was broken-hearted.

Seeing her daughter's hopelessness, Maria urged her to develop a practical skill. She bought her a sewing machine and sent her to study with the local seamstress. By the time Elizabeth was seventeen, she was designing clothes for a clothing factory in town, not realizing that God would use her innate gift for design and form in a special way in the future.

One day Elizabeth heard that a missionary would be speaking at the church. She expected a brawny man who could tackle lions and crocodiles. Instead she saw a tall Swedish woman who was travelling through Eastern Europe speaking about Jesus Christ. Elizabeth was so impressed she promised God, 'If ever you need a woman again, I would love to work for you.'

Elizabeth's response touched the missionary's heart. Olga Olson recognized potential in the frail-looking young woman who had come to hear her. She saw anguish and longing in the wide-set blue eyes, and when she spoke with her, she knew that Elizabeth was deeply depressed about her future. Though the Communists would not allow young people to study in the West, Olga was able to find a way to get Elizabeth out of the country and to a place where she could attend Bible school.

The night Elizabeth got on the train for the West no one at her factory knew that she was leaving. Tearfully, she parted with her family, believing that she would never see them again. It was only after she left that she learned that church leaders were very upset that a woman was going off for Bible training. In fact, she was the first woman from her country to do so. In the general council some pastors fought to bring her back, but the school would not agree to their demands. Several years later when Elizabeth reported on the revival in the children's camps she'd led and how God had worked through her ministry, one of the pastors came to her after the service pleading, 'Forgive me. I have despised women all my life. But I will not do it after this because God used you.'

During her three years in Bible school, Elizabeth often cried – not out of homesickness, but because she had no sense of calling on her life. Other students knew exactly what they were going to do, but she feared that if she returned to live in Eastern Europe she would never get out again. Yet during college vacations she was able with the help of the Swedish missionaries to slip into Romania, Hungary and Yugoslavia to take Christian materials and hold children's camps. 'I was very young looking,' she explains, 'very skinny and most of the time they overlooked me at the borders.'

She experienced one frightening incident when she was traveling by train from Timişoara to Cluj in Romania. In her excitement about the coming children's camp, she foolishly began telling her fellow passengers what she was doing. Suddenly the train stopped and she was told to get off. Grabbing her suitcase, she hid behind the station, wondering what had prompted this unscheduled stop. Horrified, she saw police entering the train and searching the compartments. God had protected her from arrest and given her a warning about being too open with strangers. A subdued Elizabeth got on the next train to Cluj, resolved not to risk her being arrested again.

These experiences helped prepare her for *Lydia's* ministry, for she has an insider's understanding of life under the Communists. Women often express their amazement that she is so intuitive about the Eastern European mind, even though she lives and writes from Germany.

In her last years at Bible school a new complication arose, for a German student from Canada began to show an interest in her. Ditmar Mittelstaedt had come to study in western Europe. His parents had emigrated to Canada from Germany some years before. They had no desire to return to Europe, but Ditmar felt God's call on his life for Europe and decided to study there for a year. By the time he was ready to return to Canada, he pleaded with Elizabeth to marry him.

'I said no to the marriage three times, because I felt that God would not take me out of this country,' Elizabeth confesses. But true love won the day. She agreed to an engagement if she could stay on one more year in Eastern Europe to finish her commitments under the Swedish mission. It was a difficult parting, knowing that the next time they would see each other would be in Canada nine months later. And even more difficult for Elizabeth who spoke rather broken German, and no English at all.

She made her wedding dress and put it on so that her family could see her in it. Everyone cried as they took her to the plane, once again believing this was the last time they would see each other. On the plane Elizabeth prayed, 'God, if this is not your will, let the plane crash. I don't want to marry the wrong man.' Three weeks after her arrival in Vancouver, Elizabeth and Ditmar were married. Even as she stood in front of the altar, repeating her vows, she was thinking of the irrevocable step she was taking. 'I gave up my country, my call and my family to follow one man.'

After their marriage Ditmar moved from college to college to complete his education. He served as an associate pastor of two churches. Elizabeth did her best to fit the role of pastor's wife. But her dreams seemed to have been shattered. When she had seen Olga Olson on the platform of her church it had been a shock and an exciting revelation. She had never seen a woman on a church platform before. Then God had called her to serve him, and she had started children's camps, youth groups and women's ministries in many parts of Eastern Europe during her Bible school days.

Yet here in North America she could barely speak the language, and she felt unqualified and inept. 'I believed when I married, those ministries were closed,' she relates. 'Now the call was for me to be a helpmate. I ironed his shirts, I cooked his meals and I wanted to make him the best pastor ever. I tried my best . . . but I was so empty.'

Finally an older woman in the church counselled her, 'Elizabeth, why do you try to hide your gifts? Don't you think that you could complement your husband? You are not competing with him; you could be a team.'

Responding to this wise advice Elizabeth's directions changed. 'I no longer feared that I had no place in God's vineyard. I can do something too. I do not need to be the wife who rules over him, and doesn't iron his shirts or cook his meals. I can do all these things, but I do not need to stand before God empty-handed – except for ironed shirts. When I stand before God he is not going to ask me what did your husband do? He's going to ask me what I did with what he gave me. From that point on I changed my whole vision.'

Over the next three years Ditmar completed his studies at Fuller and then at Northern Baptist Seminary in Chicago while he served area churches. During that time Elizabeth says, 'I learned English quite well.'

One day Ditmar came home with the astounding news, 'Honey, I'm called to missions and we are going to the mission field.' They had no specific place in mind though they had received an invitation to go to India. But Ditmar secretly felt called to Germany, and God providentially opened the door for them to go.

However when they arrived in Germany, Elizabeth realized how poor her

German really was. When a salesman came to the door and heard her broken German he shouted at her, 'Auslander, raus' (Foreigner, get out)! Elizabeth was crushed and told Ditmar, 'Honey, we'll never make it in this country.'

It seemed to Elizabeth she was back where she had started. Ditmar began an international correspondence school and she tried to help him any way she could. 'I kept my house neat; I tried to be a friend to my neighbours. Even though my language still wasn't very good, I supported the women in the church wherever I could. But in my heart I ached for more.'

One of the aches in Elizabeth's heart was for a baby, but as the years passed it became evident that God would not give her this desire. They decided to adopt a child. The first little boy died before the adoption could be completed. They tried a second time, but this time just four months before delivery, the birth mother changed her mind and kept her baby. Ditmar consoled the grieving Elizabeth, 'I don't know how many times we need to break our hearts. Let's just see what God has for us. Maybe he has a better plan.' But Elizabeth was to go through deep tragedy before God's plan became clear.

One morning, about a year after the adoption had failed, Elizabeth had an early morning dental appointment to have three crowns made. The elderly dentist worked on her back teeth, forcing her jaw wide open. After two hours Elizabeth lost all sensation in her jaw and couldn't control the muscles, so the dentist's wife held her jaw open for another three hours.

That night Elizabeth experienced excruciating pain. When she returned to the dentist, he began extracting teeth, thinking that was causing the pain. But nothing helped. Night after night she would wake Ditmar to pray for her in her agony. For six months she was in constant pain, collapsing many times. Finally they flew to the Mayo Clinic in Rochester, Minnesota where she underwent six days of tests.

The news was devastating. There was nothing they could do about the nerve damage. 'The damage is permanent. You can go to the ends of the earth and you will find no help. We are sorry, but we can offer no relief from the pain,' the doctors told her.

Returning from the Mayo Clinic, Elizabeth wondered how she could face the constant pain, and whether life was even worth living. One day as she was walking across a bridge over a small river, she looked down into the water and a voice seemed to say, 'JUMP'. Even though the water wasn't deep enough to drown her, the sharp rocks below would certainly have killed her. Yet the temptation lasted only a second.

As she looked across the bridge to the pretty little German village beyond with its geranium window-boxes and white picket fences God seemed to say to her, 'Inside those nice homes there is a lot of pain and brokenness for women.' She knew that the two world wars had left many wounds. Women hid behind their facades and covered up their pain.

'I could feel how God loves this continent and how he loves the women,' Elizabeth recalls. 'In that moment my heart was broken about what broke his heart. I can't explain how God breaks your heart; it just happens. So I said, "God I would love to help, but what can I do?" ' And that was the day God put the idea of the magazine in her heart.

Elizabeth had never written an article or taken a journalism class. The very idea of publishing a magazine was frightening. But when she finally shared the vision with Ditmar he was excited. 'Honey, I know just how we can do this.' Right from the beginning Ditmar was her encourager, promoter and business manager.

Others weren't so sure the magazine would fly. One publisher told her they had done a survey and discovered that German women weren't readers, and would not be able to support a magazine of more than ten thousand copies, the minimum required to be financially viable. The largest Christian magazines in the country were generally subsidized by a denomination.

After hearing these discouraging reports, Elizabeth returned to her little room under the roof where they were living at the time and cried out to God, 'You see, God, nobody wants this magazine.' And she said she heard God saying, 'But I want it!'

There seemed to be a wonderful presence of God in the room that day and she felt as though she could ask him for anything. For a moment she thought of asking for a baby – she was thirty-nine and her time clock was running down. But then she thought, 'What would it be like to be without pain for just one hour? Could I ask for that?' And then out of the blue the Scripture came to her mind, 'Ask of me and I will make the nations your inheritance' (Ps 2:8.).

Elizabeth broke down and cried, 'God you know I want to have ten thousand women more than a child or an hour without pain. Give me ten thousand women.' She kept this prayer a secret as the magazine came off the press.

For the first issue Elizabeth and Ditmar used household money and litera-ture funds from their mission. They sent complimentary copies to three hundred churches and subscriptions began rolling in. For the third issue they printed seven thousand copies, and then had to reprint an additional three thousand – making a total of ten thousand. Elizabeth couldn't believe that God had answered her prayer so quickly. But she wasn't satisfied to stop there and she prayed again, 'God, it would be so nice if you put one more zero at the back.' By the end of its tenth year *Lydia* had a circulation of more than ninety thousand in Germany alone and was well on the way to reaching Elizabeth's second goal.

From the beginning *Lydia* has aimed at top quality – four-colour pictures, coated paper, well illustrated and professionally designed. It can compete with women's magazines anywhere in the world. But the most important feature is its focus – helping women know Christ, know how to manage their lives as Christian women and how to build Christian marriages and train their children. In the very first issue Elizabeth encouraged her readers to send in their personal experiences, and dozens of stories of ordinary women who have found victory over problems in their lives have found their way into the pages of the magazine.

Elizabeth has learned that criticism comes with the territory. Though she seldom writes about beauty care and dress ('other magazines can do that much better') when she does she's sure to receive letters of criticism from certain branches of the church. Eastern European churches are still very conservative about make-up, so Elizabeth is sensitive to this audience.

She has been successful in skirting the charismatic issue which has divided Europe's churches. She does not permit discussion of divisive theological issues or the denigration of different beliefs. She feels one sign of success is that readers differ in their perception of the magazine. Some say, 'It's a Baptist magazine,' and others say, 'It's a Pentecostal magazine.' forty-nine percent of readers are from the State (Lutheran) Church.

One topic that is sure to bring a lot of response is the role of women. 'God called me to encourage women to find their gifts and use them – it doesn't matter where, in the home, in their neighbourhood, in their society.' She has dealt with the questions of women keeping silent in the church, the woman as 'helper' and as submissive to her husband. One article told the stories of Susannah Wesley, Joni Earickson and Mother Theresa as women whom God has used. Even though she knew she would receive criticism, especially from pastors, she felt the time had come to speak about this question 'God so impressed on my heart that this is one way to encourage women. I felt he said, 'Elizabeth, so much gets lost because seventy percent of the church is women and they just sit and do nothing. It would be so much faster to reach the lost and I could accomplish so much else if the women would work, but no one is there to encourage them to do what they can.'

Whenever Elizabeth deals with the issue of women in leadership she knows she will face opposition. But she is confident that God has led her and she's not afraid. 'When I don't know I have his blessing,' she states, 'I go shaking in the night. But I wrote in the editorial [regarding the article about women] that God wants to use women "We don't send soldiers into battle with just one arm. . . . not that we want to rule; we want to help. And God has created us for that." '
And because of this transparent spirit, the magazine has not suffered because of criticism, even though as Elizabeth says, 'Sometimes it's hot.'

Elizabeth is the first to admit that she couldn't do this without a marvellous staff. Though her German has improved, she still depends on skilled editorial help to see that every mistake is caught. But her greatest source of encouragement and strength is Ditmar. Though he continues as director of the International Correspondence School and field moderator of their mission, much of his time is spent as business and personnel manager of the *Lydia* office.

The vision of the wise woman who counselled Elizabeth back in Chicago has been fulfilled – Elizabeth and Ditmar are indeed a team. Sometimes Elizabeth is concerned that she is the one who is recognized and given the public affirmation, but Ditmar seems to flourish as her visibility increases. 'I try very hard to acknowledge him. But through the years I think he has accepted who he is and . . . he is happy about it. At the office, he's the boss and I'm the editor . . . he doesn't interfere with discussions of artwork or layout, and I don't enter into personnel and financial matters.' Elizabeth explains. 'But he knows this is God's call on my life, and he would be afraid to touch that.'

At home, it's a different story. In the small town of Asslar, an hour's drive from Frankfurt, they live in a small but graciously appointed cottage just five minutes from the office, where they can escape the pressures of deadlines and bottom lines. A wall of books lines Ditmar's study, evidence of his studious nature. But there is a love of beauty in both of them that can be seen in the simple floral decorations on the dining-room table, or the open vista from their living room into a small manicured garden with a tinkling fountain. Their dog, Annie, greets them enthusiastically at the door. Their home is an oasis, not only physically, but emotionally.

Because of Elizabeth's continuing poor health, Ditmar willingly takes over many of the chores at home. His favourite is to run down to the local 'Bäckerei' for wonderful German pastries. 'But I'm careful not to make him a cleaning lady – no-way – and I'm not going to boss him about like a little boy, either,' Elizabeth comments. 'It is giving and taking – and it's not perfect.'

Elizabeth believes in mutual submission 'I believe that God asked me to submit to my husband, but God asked him to love me. Only I can decide if I will submit to him, and only he can decide if he loves me. It wouldn't be a pure, clean relationship if we didn't talk over what we think. We talk about how I feel, how I see it. He doesn't need to agree a hundred percent, but that is my side of it. Then he tells me his side, and we try to resolve it somewhere in the middle.'

Elizabeth and Ditmar help each other to keep short accounts with God. They have developed times of prayer and blessing during the day both privately and together. They have their devotions in the morning and always close the day together in prayer. If either one fails to have personal devotions, the other one checks up to find out what happened.

'But I don't want to present an unrealistic picture, suggesting that we don't have struggles,' Elizabeth explains. 'At home, I'm not a big editor; I'm his wife. Sometimes he comes after me and says, "You didn't do your job." And sometimes we have tears and he'll say "You have to find another manager." But when we come home we clean it up and go on. I can't stand going to sleep [with something like that on my mind]'.

Ditmar marvels at Elizabeth's dogged perseverance and fortitude in spite of frequent illness. A bout of Lyme's disease contracted in Romania on a photography assignment for the magazine nearly cost her her life. Ditmar does his best to nurture and protect her, but he does not hold her back from following the vision God has given her. He was right behind her as the idea of a Romanian *Lydia* emerged.

Elizabeth longed to help women in Romania who had suffered so much during the communist control and Ceauşescu's rule. She knew of the suffering of women forced to have many children; of those who abandoned children on the streets because they could not care for them; of the physical deprivation and lack of trust in the society. She began to dream how she could use some of the same stories translated, and the same pictures and layout. This will be our little baby, she thought.

But the little baby would cost a lot of money and Elizabeth didn't think she could start without at least a two-year commitment. Where would the money come from?

She spent a day in her room praying. But for hours there was no answer. Finally towards evening she seemed to hear God saying, 'What was the first promise I gave you for the German *Lydia*?' She remembered the verse, 'Ask me for the nations' and God reminded her there was an 's' at the end of nations. There was her answer to take the risk of another edition of *Lydia*.

This time she did something she'd never done before – she asked her readers to make it possible for Romanian women to receive the same blessing that they were receiving. She reminded the German women that they have had many 'firsts' – the first Bible in the vernacular, the Reformation, the Moravians as first missionaries. She challenged them that perhaps now God wanted women to do something. The response was overwhelming. Money began pouring in, mostly from East German women who had themselves suffered under Communism. They gave sacrificially; one woman sent her whole monthly disability check. Elizabeth felt so bad she sent half of it back.

Another woman sent all her savings. But she wrote to Elizabeth, 'Don't say thank you. You have to understand why I give it.' She had been abused by her parents, grandparents and husband. When she was 38 years old somebody brought *Lydia* across the Berlin Wall and gave it to her. After reading the magazine she gave her heart to Jesus. She wrote, 'The situation didn't change, but healing came in my soul. Why didn't somebody tell me earlier? Why did I have to wait for 38 years? I don't want Romanian women to wait so long.'

The Romanian edition has been underwritten since its inception. Whenever Elizabeth travels to Romania and meets the women whose lives have been changed through *Lydia* she thanks God that her pain has been turned into such joy for others.

Throughout her pain-filled life, Elizabeth has seen her burden for those without Christ grow. 'My heart breaks about the lost world – some who have never heard about Jesus and others who have heard but don't understand; they're blind. Everything I put together in the magazine I ask myself, how will I reach them?

'Years ago I read about someone who prayed every day. "God please make me creative today or give me one idea." That has become my favourite habit too. With so many responsibilities and such a busy life, I ask God to make me creative and give me good ideas. I'm putting a magazine together, and I always need to have new ideas. I am so amazed at how creative my God is and how he never runs out of ideas. Even if I live in just a narrow little world, I do not need to worry that I cannot find a new angle to reach women.'

Elizabeth challenges herself as she challenges her readers: 'Lassen Sie sich inspirieren, und sagen Sie mit Maria: Ich bin bereit. Herr, was hast Du für mich zu tun?' (Be inspired and say with Mary: I am ready. Lord, what do you have for me to do?)

Note:

1. *Today's Christian Woman,* January–February 1992, 27.

Five

The Gift of Giving – Dr. Lee Hyung-Ja, Korea

After this, Jesus travelled about from one town and village to another proclaiming the good news of the kingdom of God. The twelve were with him and also some women who had been cured of evil spirits and diseases; Mary (called Magdalene) from whom seven demons had come out; Joanna the wife of Cuza, the manager of Herod's household; Suzanna; and many others. These women were helping to support them out of their own means.

Luke 8:1–3

Bankruptcy! Lee Hyung-Ja couldn't get the disgraceful thought out of her mind. Day after day she mulled over solutions in her head. Before her father-in-law died and left his businesses to her husband, his oldest son, life had been very comfortable. Their three children were lovingly cared for by their nanny and Lee Hyung-Ja had even dreamt of getting back into studying oriental art again.

But now their world was crashing around their shoulders. Instead of prosperity, her husband, Choi Soon-Young (Korean women don't take their husband's name at marriage), revealed that the baking business he had inherited was over a million dollars in debt, and another family company was in serious financial crisis. They could not even pay the interest on the loans.

Lee Hyung-Ja even thought of running away to America to avoid facing disgrace before her friends and family. Seeing her husband's despair and depression, she worried about his health. In desperation she prepared to visit the home of the president of the bank that held their loan.

As she entered his study, bowing graciously before him, the bank president must have wondered at the courage of this petite woman dressed in traditional white mourning clothes. Her silken black hair was set in the latest fashion, framing her alabaster complexion. Her round face showed little expression until she smiled, and then her serene brown eyes twinkled with inner joy. In a soft and gracious voice, belying her strength and perception, she explained her husband's business situation. But the president refused her request. In spite of her embarrassment, Lee Hyung-Ja was driven by the crisis in her family to return to face the bank official again. And he eventually responded mercifully to her plight, and extended the loan.

In the midst of these pressures, Lee Hyung-Ja came under deep conviction from God. 'Why haven't I been trusting the Lord in these matters?' she asked herself. Convicted of her lack of faith, she began getting up to pray at four in the morning. The early morning times of prayer filled her heart with the consoling presence of God and the confidence that he had the answers to their perplexing problems.

In her prayer times, Lee Hyung-Ja began receiving specific answers about her husband's business – ideas they had not thought of before. As she shared these with Choi Soon-Young, he could see the wisdom of her suggestions and began implementing them. He couldn't understand her ability to comprehend the complex intricacies of the business, but he realized that God had revealed them to her in prayer.

The two began praying together at four in the morning every day. And more and more Choi Soon-Young turned to Lee Hyung-Ja for answers to their business problems. He even called her from the office to pray about urgent decisions and listened to the answers God gave her.

Lee Hyung-Ja recalls these experiences. 'Our gracious Lord started to reveal his will through voices, visions, prophesies, dreams and most of all through the word of God. He answered most of my prayers faithfully, but sometimes I failed to interpret them correctly. Through those detailed instructions, my husband's business revived again. Please do not think that I still pray in that kind of format. When most of the problems were solved, most of those intense, momentary gifts were taken away. Nowadays I pray based on the word of God, which is very good.'

Incredibly, the business turned round during a time of financial and political crisis in South Korea. The couple now faced the challenge of what to do with their growing wealth. 'I had tithed my husband's monthly salary, but when his businesses turned round, we prayed that we would give the tithe of our business as long as we live,' Hyung-Ja explains.

As they began to analyze their profits they realized even the tithe would be too large a sum to give to one church. Lee Hyung-Ja admitted the enormous profits flowing out of their new construction company became a test – would they really tithe such a huge amount? With their first tithe from the business they gave an interest-free loan to build a church which is now the largest Methodist church in the world.

Lee Hyung-Ja grew up in tormented times in Korea. Born in 1944, during the thirty-five year Japanese occupation, she remembers nothing of the suffering her people endured. The Japanese promoted the fiction that the Koreans were incompetent and uncultured. The Japanese language was taught in schools, but few Koreans were permitted to receive higher education. Hyung-Ja's father was one of the exceptions. He was trained in Japan and became a professor of law.

Lee Hyung-Ja's family had been Christians for several generations. Missionaries had come to Korea in the mid-nineteenth century when her great-grandmother became a Christian. In 1941, just before the outbreak of the Second World War the Japanese ousted all western missionaries, but a strong church remained. Confucianism which was integrated into Buddhism, however, provided the philosophical backbone of the country. Over half of the Korean population still identifies itself as Buddhist.

With the defeat of the Japanese in the Pacific, Korea finally gained its independence and formed a constitutional government in 1948. Almost seven hundred thousand Japanese were evacuated from Korea, but the country was left in shambles, with little trained leadership. The Japanese had taken everything out and put nothing into the beleaguered peninsula during its long occupation.

Hyung-Ja's first vivid memories of turbulent times were of the austerity during the Korean War. As North Korean soldiers under the leadership of Russia, and later China, invaded the south in 1950 the city of Seoul was totally destroyed. Refugees from the north, including thousands of Christians escaping the Communists, fled south ahead of the army, carrying their few possessions. Bridges across the Han River were blown up and many lost their lives trying to cross.

Though she was only eight years old, Hyung-Ja remembers how her grandfather built a safe shelter for the family in a farmhouse in the country outside Seoul. But she also can visualize dead bodies strewn on the streets. 'Sometimes we had to walk over them,' she reminisces sadly. Providentially she didn't know of the headless bodies found in the jails, and the trenches filled with dead Koreans. As food shortages mounted, her mother sold her precious possessions one by one to purchase rice. 'Sometimes she cooked rice porridge to make the rice last longer,' she recalls. Eventually the family, too, fled further south. Ewha Women's University where her father taught established a temporary campus in Pusan, where it remained until the cease-fire was signed in 1953.

Confucianism taught women to be subordinate and to practise endurance. Their main role was to manage the large extended family and to produce male heirs. Women were originally denied the opportunity to participate in life outside the home. But gradually attitudes towards women changed, and Ewha Women's University was but one evidence of the growing opportunities given women in Korean society. Dr. Helen Kim, president of the university, also taught a weekly Bible study at the Christian high school which Hyung-Ja attended. 'She was an authentic role model whom everybody looked up to and respected as a Christian liberator in a good sense. Korean women were in the darkness of Confucianism and social oppression,' Lee Hyung-Ja explains, 'but when Christianity settled in Korea, the darkness was slowly removed and the liberation of women began. Dr. Helen Kim was used by God to place the status of women in its proper perspective.'

When the Republic was established in 1948, women were given constitutional rights to equal education. Lee Hyung-Ja herself became a beneficiary of this law, and studied oriental art in a Korean college. As a child her teachers scolded her for drawing in class, but as she grew older they recognized her artistic gifts. Even today one of her greatest joys is collecting original works of famous Chinese calligraphers, some dating as far back as the eleventh century. She has her own personal collection. One of her dreams is to build a museum to house the works of famous Korean artists. Hyung loves to encourage Christian artists for she believes art is a special communication from God.

After a near-fatal bus accident while in college, Lee Hyung-Ja's health deteriorated. She'd had plans to go to France after college to study art. But her family was concerned about the pressures of study and travel in her weakened physical condition. Instead, her father decided that it would be better for her to marry and began making surreptitious inquiries.

Choi Soon-Young, a thirty-two-year-old bachelor was looking for a suitable wife. His sister began asking her friends at the university if they knew of someone for her brother. When Hyung-Ja's name was proposed, family members on both sides looked the possible match over. Both sets of parents were well-impressed with the choice.

How did Hyung-Ja feel? 'I would have to say that on the first day I met him, I was not really very impressed,' she admits. 'But as time went by I came to love and respect him.' Following their marriage in 1968, the couple had three children, a daughter and two sons.

Lee Hyung-Ja has had an intimate relationship with God from childhood. She remembers seeing a stream of sunlight pouring into her kindergarten classroom and being overwhelmed by its beauty. 'I was momentarily so enraptured by the shining light that I felt I was in a world of fancy,' she remembers. But as an adult she believes she had experienced the presence of God in the bright light.

Now as she and her husband experienced the power of early morning prayer, and the answers that had changed their lives, she longed for even more of his presence and direction in her life. One morning shortly after the business began turning round, Lee Hyung-Ja was on her knees before dawn, pouring out her heart to God. Suddenly an indescribable force overpowered her, and she fell to the ground. She heard a voice commanding, 'Light every dry branch, and pass the torches from mountain peak to mountain peak, Raise the torch of the Holy Spirit high above and pass it unto the end of the world.' God had called her to a new ministry which would encircle the world and out of this vision the Korean Centre for World Mission was officially organized in 1977.

God had begun working in Hyung-Ja's life in a special way since she and four women started meeting for prayer in Hyung-Ja's living room a year earlier. As they prayed for God's leading, for his mercy upon their politically unstable nation, for the economy in crisis, for their families and churches, for revival in their own nation, God began to send others to join them.

A network of Bible studies and prayer groups grew across the city. Called 'Torches' these groups focused on people in different walks of life – military personnel, artists, doctors, lawyers, hairdressers. Much of this growing ministry was supported by Hyung-Ja's tithes. She purchased a building to accommodate three hundred people, and soon saw the Torches outgrow their facilities.

One day as Lee Hyung-Ja was visiting the home of a friend, she received a call from her husband's office. He had desperately been tracing her for he wanted her advice. He had the opportunity to buy a large plot of land on Yeouido Island in the centre of Seoul. They had been praying together about purchasing property to expand the facilities of his fast-growing life insurance company. But this offer, right on the Han River in the most desirable part of the city, was beyond even their imagination.

Choi Soon-Young told her there were two sites available. Would she pray for the more valuable riverside property? Hyung-Ja laughed at the impossible request, but promised she would pray. Later when the purchase was settled she asked him which property he had been able to purchase. 'Why, the riverside portion of course,' he responded. 'Didn't we ask God for that?'

The months of intense prayer took their toll on Hyung-Ja. 'We prayed for the most minute things,' she explains. 'We engaged ourselves in prayer to the extent I almost got sick.' Her husband expected to have all his prayers answered, almost as though she were a direct link with heaven for his business enterprises. But Hyung-Ja knew that God did not always answer in that way. Sometime he said no; sometimes his answers were slow; at other times immediate. Sometimes it was hard to tell what God was saying. And sometimes she misread his direction.

Some have even accused her of neglecting Bible study because of her focus on guidance through prayer. But Lee Hyung-Ja learned through this special time of intense prayer that she could not neglect reading God's word, and it became an integral part of each day. She often prayed conversationally, interspersing her words with a line of Scripture or a verse of a hymn.

But now she was entering what was to be the most disturbing period of prayer for guidance. As she began praying about the building to be erected on Youido Island, her heart was restless and uncomfortable. It seemed God was saying this should be a skyscraper – a building taller than any in Seoul.

She prayed asking whether 40 stories was the right number, but had no peace. 'Lord is it 45–50–55?' Still no assurance that God had directed her.

Finally she sensed the Spirit of God saying the building should be 60 stories high. Agonizing before the Lord, she pleaded that only the Spirit of God would be heard. And for the third time the response came clearly, 'Sixty stories.'

One has to understand Korea's serious security problems with communist guns aimed at Seoul only 30 miles from the border. Once they had totally destroyed the city. In order to maintain better security, the government had outlawed any building higher than fourteen stories.

No wonder Hyung-Ja hesitated to tell her husband about the direction she had received. She admits that though her husband is pleasant most of the time, he can be very sharp in certain aspects. 'I act cautiously towards him,' she explains. And her fears were justified, for Choi Soon-Young became very angry when she told him about her ridiculous conclusion. 'That's impossible,' he retorted, and wouldn't speak to her for several days. In his own heart he was troubled that Hyung-Ja had received direction, and he had not.

Yet when he returned from his next trip to Philadelphia, he brought with him pictures and designs of skyscrapers. Baffled, Hyung-Ja asked him why he had brought them back. His response was, 'Didn't you tell me God wants us to build a 60-story building?'

Soon-Young proceeded to draft the blueprints. Hyung-Ja added her suggestions like the ground floor restaurant with its fountains and coloured lights dancing to classical music. Everything in the building was to be of the latest design and luxury, from the expansive marble entrance halls to the exquisite 60th floor private dining-room with windows on three sides overlooking the city. And the shape of the gleaming building would represent praying hands. It was a fabulous dream. 'But,' Choi Soon-Young reminded her, 'if it fails it will be not only a financial loss, but a disgrace.'

Now the struggle began in earnest. Choi Soon-Young visited the Blue House, the official residence of the president, to appeal to Park Chung Hee for special permission, but was refused in no uncertain terms. No one seemed to understand that God had ordered this building. Lee Hyung-Ja visited the wife of the mayor of Seoul, asking her to influence her husband to grant the rights. But she became angry and accused Hyung-Ja of asking her to take advantage of her husband's position to gain her ends.

So confident were the couple of God's leading, that they decided to go ahead with foundations. Choi Soon-Young dug foundations three stories below ground, deep enough to sustain a 60-story structure. Three levels down, they struck water which to this day provides the source of water for the entire building.

Then in 1979 the political turmoil that had been writhing for years came to a head with the assassination of President Park. Somehow in the confusion and restructuring that followed, the 'fourteen-story' law was rescinded for a short time, long enough to grant permission to Dr. Choi to proceed with the project. Six years later the gleaming '63 building' stood as a witness to God's leading and faithfulness. Within two years every office and shop space was leased with a waiting list as vacancies occur. 'God just committed the care of the building into our custody,' says Lee Hyung-Ja. 'I take pride in being a caretaker of the building, a symbol of Korean economic development.'

During the construction of the building, business profits continued to increase so that every financial obligation was met. An astute business man, Choi Soon-Young continued to expand his companies under the umbrella of the Shing Dong Ah Group. The original life and fire insurance companies, with thousands of agents, were based in the '63 building.' He added construction, shipping and international trade. And with every new business, the profits grew – and the tithe poured into the Korean Christian World Mission Trust which they had organized in 1977.

According to Korean custom, 'it is generally the wife's responsibility to handle all the finances, whether a large sum, or as small as a mouse's tail,' Lee Hyung-Ja explains. 'The wife is to thank her husband as the financial provider and must be a wise manager of the funds.' In Lee Hyung-Ja's case the tithe of all the companies is placed into the trust, and she and an executive committee makes decisions as to how the funds are to be used.

In the early years she used the money to develop the 'Torches' and concentrated on domestic issues. One of her favourite projects was the 'Hallelujah Soccer Team.' This professional team plays all over Asia against national teams, winning two or three championships a year. The Torch Centre Christians love to tell of how thousands of Asians cheer enthusiastically for the team, shouting over and over again 'Hallelujah! Hallelujah!' when a goal is scored. These strong, well-built young men not only glorify Christ as they witness between halves at the soccer matches, but deeply admire their benefactor. It's an impressive sight to see them stand in unison, bowing in respect when Lee Hyung-Ja walks into the room.

Other domestic programmes continued to expand. One Torch organization provides encouragement and funds for Korean artists – traditional dancers, dramatists, musicians, champion Taekwondo performers. Leading Christian artists perform in the finest facilities with Hyung-Ja's backing.

But with the vision God had given her of the torch of the Holy Spirit passing to the ends of the world, Hyung-Ja began to broaden her focus. She has made large grants to the Far Eastern Broadcasting Company and the Torch Trinity Graduate School of Theology, which trains Korean missionaries.

A growing concern, however, was the inadequate facilities at the Mission Center. Yet land prices had rocketed in Seoul, now a city of over ten million people. Where could she build a large enough facility to house all the visions and dreams swimming in her head?

One Saturday as she was praying with some of the pastors at the small Mission Center, God gave her three conditions for answering her prayer about a new Mission Center.

1. She would have to ask her husband to provide the funds to build the new Mission Center.

2. God convicted her of criticism of another Christian organization to which her husband had given funds for a new building, when she needed the funds to build a larger Mission Center. She would have to stop criticizing and mend the relationships.

3. God challenged her to go to the wife of one of her husband's contractors to ask for a favor in building the new Center. She admits 'It hurt my pride to pay a visit to my husband's subordinate.'

Not long after she had made this agreement with the Lord, her husband received a call from the Blue House. Years before he had sold to the government a large piece of property on a hillside which was now a part of southern Seoul. He was asked if he would be willing to purchase it back.

Choi Soon-Young came home with the news and asked his wife, 'Do you really want it?'

Hyung-Ja stood silent for a moment, marvelling at God's dealings, but wondering how to answer.

'Do you have any funds [in your trust account]?' he asked.

Hyung-Ja told him the amount of donations the Torches had been collecting for the new building, and the amount of the loan available on the old property. It was only enough for three hundred of the available four thousand p'iangs (1 p'iang = 2 square meters). Disappointed, Hyung-Ja didn't answer him immediately. Reconsidering, Soon-Young offered one thousand p'iangs (the amount she'd been considering) and in the end gave her all four thousand p'iangs.

Today the Korean Center for World Mission, also called the Torch Center, backs onto a rugged hillside in the Yang Jae district of southern Seoul. Heavily forested, with pathways meandering through the lush gardens, it provides a sense of peaceful seclusion in the midst of a teeming city. A magnificent mosaic sixty-three feet high, made from six million pieces of glass covers the outside front wall of the Torch Center. It depicts the Good Shepherd, welcoming all to his loving care.

Since its completion in 1991, the Torch Center has become the centre of mission training and vision for Koreans of all denominations. Love Hall, which seats 3500, houses the finest pipe organ in all Asia. Hyung-Ja travelled to Austria personally to place the order for the organ to be built. Joy Hall, on the lower level, seats another thousand. In 1995 four thousand delegates from 186 nations met at the Torch Center for the Global Congress on World Evangelization. Sponsored by the AD2000 & Beyond Movement, this mid-decade evaluation of progress in fulfilling the Great Commission, met here in 1995, was the guest of Dr. Lee. (Hyung-Ja was granted an honorary doctorate conferred by Trinity Evangelical Divinity School.)

Sixty students receive their doctorate of missions each year under scholarships granted by the executive committee of the Torch Center. The largest theological library in Korea is housed here.

The second floor of the administration building is given over to Hyung-Ja Lee's offices and her and her husband's boardrooms. (He serves as the chairman of the Torch Center board.) One can see something of this remarkable woman's personality in these private quarters. Orchids and floral arrangements grace the sun-filled rooms. Valuable pieces of oriental art interspersed with brilliantly coloured modern art adorn the walls. Hyung-Ja's daughter, Juseon-Choi, has contributed a number of these pieces, which her mother proudly displays. Plaques honouring Dr. Lee's contributions from all over the world stand on the pieces of antique furniture. This quiet sanctuary, protected from the hustle and bustle of the Torch Center activities, exudes Dr. Lee's love for oriental culture and art, for beauty and serenity.

But the real core of power of the Torch Center lies several stories below the open plaza in the middle of the complex. A round carpeted room, bare of furniture except for a few mats on the floor, is the central prayer room. Surrounding this room and down a circular corridor are dozens of doors opening into prayer cells. Some days the hallway is lined with shoes, as intercessors leave them outside while they pray. Hyung-Ja Lee began her journey into ministry at another Prayer Mountain many years earlier, and she has made sure Christians in Seoul have a 'prayer mountain' available to them right in the heart of the city.

While she and her family enjoy the rewards vast wealth can bring, she comments, 'I think stewardship is more than giving a correct tithe. I personally feel uncomfortable being greedy.' And the many who have experienced not only the assistance of the Korean World Mission Trust, but her personal generosity, know that she lives by that creed.

It's not easy being a wealthy Christian for she receives many requests from all over the world. Though they touch her heart, she cannot possibly respond to them all. In order to make wise decisions and protect herself from undue pressures, she has asked the executive committee to set aside a 'generous budget and plan to help needy people.' For example, they have given scholarships to hundreds of orphans, and provided winter heating oil for 46 orphanages during the last 18 years.

Hyung-Ja believes that women in Korea have a clearer focus than men when they want to work for the Lord. 'We are more diligent in obeying his Word. Practically . . . we can devote more time than men since our jobs are more flexible. . . . I am not saying that we women have less work to do, but that our zeal to serve the Lord makes it possible to give more generously.'

She is especially concerned about poverty among women around the world. She believes the Torch Center should work harder to help them as it works hand in hand with missions. But Dr Lee is quick to add, 'my main interest is soul-winning; mercy ministry is secondary to that.'

When asked what obstacles women face in giving, Lee Hyung-Ja makes two observations. One, 'husbands can become an obstacle if they are not happy in giving. A Korean woman is more dependent on her husband for her source of income. She should not use it without her husband's consent.'

Secondly, 'sometimes the church itself can be an obstacle too. They often require the members to give their offerings, tithes, mercy offerings etc. only through the local church.' She even believes that churches could be wiser in the use of their finances by cutting some of the marginal expenses and turning those into offerings for the needy and missions.

Korean churches, however, have been a model of sacrifice and giving. Koreans gave out of their intense poverty brought on by the Japanese occupation and the Korean War. The first buildings to be rebuilt after the war were churches, paid for by the paltry resources Christians had salvaged. Hyung-Ja recognizes this virtue: 'Even when we were a poor country, we used to have good hearts to share among our neighbours. We think of others and are not afraid to face poverty. It is not good to grasp only for oneself. For then the Lord gives constant poverty, since he does not like selfishness. When you give generously as he gave himself to us, then he gives you something constantly to offer.'

Six

Reaching Out to the Poor and Abused – Gladys Acuna, Guatemala

Is not this the kind of fasting I have chosen: to loose the chains of injustice and untie the cords of the yoke, to set the oppressed free and break every yoke? Is it not to share your food with the hungry and to provide the poor wanderer with shelter – when you see the naked, to clothe him, and not to turn away from your own flesh and blood?

Then your light will break forth like the dawn and your healing will quickly appear: then your righteousness will go before you, and the glory of the Lord will be your rear guard. Then you will call, and the Lord will answer; you will cry for help and he will say: Here am I.

Isaiah 58:6–9

This fictional account based on a true story will introduce you to life on the rubbish dumps of Guatemala City where Gladys Acuna works:

Margarita lived in a tiny shack on the edge of the dump, where the foul odour of rotting garbage hung thick and heavy. Her Poppa, Jose had built their shack out of large cardboard cartons and sheets of tin. Ever since Margarita was a very little girl, she'd been helping her father dig in the dumps. She could hardly remember her mother, who had died after they came to live at the edge of the dump. Some days Poppa and Margarita dug for hours under the hot sun which rotted the bits of food so fast Margarita couldn't find anything to eat. One day Poppa found a dead cat, and stopped right then and there to cook a stew in the pot he carried tied around his waist. How good it tasted! Margarita hardly ever ate meat! On cooler days Margarita often found edible crusts of bread, cabbage leaves or overripe fruit from the market. But most of the time she and Poppa looked for rags and bottles, which they separated into bags and boxes to be sold at the end of the day. Once Poppa found a watch whose hands were still moving. 'Oh Poppa, can I keep it?' she begged, imagining how she would hold her arm out proudly for her friends in the other shacks to see. But Poppa shook his head, and stuffed the watch deep into the pocket of his grubby overalls. 'This will bring enough for a week's supply of kerosene for our lamp.' But Margarita knew he would also buy a bottle of the strong-smelling whisky peddled on the dump, and then he would become very angry and fight with the other men. Margarita would slip across the road to Aunt Isabella, who lived with her three small children in a shack not much bigger than theirs. Like Margarita and her father, Aunt Isabella (she wasn't really her aunt, but she was the next best thing to one) had moved to Guatemala City from the country. When her husband died, there was no other work except digging in the dump.

This morning Margarita and her father started out for the dump earlier than usual. It was Christmas, and if they were lucky, they would be able to find food and bottles thrown away after Christmas parties. 'You start digging here, Margarita,' Poppa instructed. 'Get as many bottles as you can, and keep them in a pile until I collect them. But,' he warned, 'keep your eye on them. Those street kids are up here today.' Then Poppa moved up farther where he thought the digging would be better.

Margarita knew the street kids were dangerous. They slept on the streets, rather than living in the shanty town near the bottom of the dump, and often came to dig in the dumps. Their gangs had stolen her whole day's pickings more than once. That's why Poppa stayed nearby – unless he had a bottle of whisky with him. Then he would go where she couldn't see him. Poppa always said she looked just like Momma when she caught him drinking. Poppa must have loved Momma very much to remember her face for more than ten years!

As Margarita poked around, she found a lot of crepe paper and tinsel among the broken bottles. Someone had a party! Bettina, one of Aunt Isabella's daughters, joined her, and the two girls worked together excitedly. Margarita found a crumpled paper angel. 'Look Bettina,' she shouted as she held the shining angel on her head and danced around their growing pile of bottles and brightly coloured paper.

'Girls!' a voice called. They both turned to see a stranger struggling up the dump. She was holding out a paper to them. When she reached them panting, she said, 'If you'd like a free blanket, we're giving them away at the church at the bottom of the dump.'

Margarita had never heard anything like this before. Why should anyone give her a free blanket?

'Don't you know it's Christmas?' the kindly-looking woman went on. 'We've brought you presents because it's Jesus' birthday. Come down in about an hour.

We're having a little programme and then will give blankets out.'

As the girls gingerly accepted the papers, pretending they could read the black marks on them, the woman turned to go down the dump. 'Hang on to those tickets. You won't get a blanket without them.'

Excited, the girls began putting their day's finds into a sack. 'I'll have to take my sack over to Poppa so he can watch it for me,' Margarita explained. 'If I leave it here someone will be sure to steal it.'

Dragging the heavy sack behind her, Margarita climbed to the top of the dump, where she'd seen her father disappear. He always wore a big-brimmed straw hat with a red flower she'd found and tucked into the band. Usually she could recognize him halfway across the dump. But today Poppa was nowhere to be seen.

'Poppa – Poppa,' she called. Some of the men working nearby stood up and pointed. 'He's down there.'

So Margarita dragged her bag, which was getting heavier all the time, up and over another pile of rubble. And then she almost stumbled over him.

Poppa was lying on the ground, an empty bottle clutched to his chest.

'Oh, Poppa,' Margarita cried, and she dropped down beside him and tried to shake him. 'Poppa, wake up. Somebody is giving away blankets down at the church, but I can't leave you here like this. They'll steal everything I found today.'

She pushed the heavy bag of bottles closer to Poppa, noticing that even the shovel he always carried was gone. The dump thieves had already been here once.

Trying to hold back the tears, Margarita felt the crumpled ticket in her pocket. By the time Poppa wakes up, the blankets will all be gone, she thought. How nice it would be to roll up in a clean warm blanket at night. She'd never owned a new blanket – just a rag, when she could find one. And this was a Christmas blanket, the lady had said – and Margarita had never had a Christmas present in her whole life.

She laid her head down on Poppa's chest, trying to keep warm as strong gusty winds blew across the dump.

Then she heard Bettina calling, 'Margarita.' Bettina climbed up the dump toward her, wrapped in a beautiful blue and white blanket. 'Look Margarita – look at my Christmas blanket. Why didn't you come down for yours? The lady kept calling for people with tickets.'

When Bettina heard Poppa's snore, and saw the empty bottle roll off his chest, she understood. She pulled Margarita to her feet. 'Go on, run – the crowd is still waiting around the door of the church. I'll watch your things.'

Margarita's feet flew across the dump – hopping over a plastic bag which had burst open, kicking aside a broken bottle, avoiding a dead rat, its feet curled upwards over its bloated stomach, not bothering to stop for a yellow mug that had lost its handle.

Within seconds, she'd reached the crowd. But as she tried to push to the front, angry voices complained, 'The blankets are gone. We've been waiting for nothing.'

Margarita's heart sank. Gone! She was too late. She began to crumple the tattered ticket she'd been holding in her hand.

Just then a lady came out of the building and climbed on a ledge so she could look over the crowd. 'Does anyone have a ticket? We've found one more blanket.'

Margarita pushed under the elbows of those in front of her, and held out the ticket toward the lady. 'Here,' she called breathlessly. 'Here's my ticket.'

Climbing back up the dump, her beautiful red and white blanket wrapped around her, Margarita held the colourful papers that the lady had given her in her hand. She didn't know what they said, but she could see the picture of a man holding some children on his lap. And she remembered that the lady had told her, 'Here's a picture of Jesus. We want you to know that Jesus loves you – that's why we've brought these blankets on his birthday.'

Margarita hurried back to Poppa. It would help to keep him warm until he woke up. And then she'd ask him to read the paper about Jesus to her. Maybe Poppa would find out that Jesus loved him too.

*   *   *   *

As Gladys Acuna and Lisbeth Piedrasanta gathered their belongings together to leave the dump that Christmas Eve in 1986, they were strangely silent, each wrapped in her own thoughts. The vision of the many disappointed faces they had to turn away filled their minds. Even the utter joy on the face of the last little girl to receive a blanket couldn't make up for the many who returned to their homes empty-handed.

Gladys and Lisbeth had seen those 'homes' as they'd wandered around the edge of the dump earlier in the day, handing out the tickets – inviting people to a Christmas service and offering one blanket for each ticket. Shacks of tin and cardboard held each other up around the rim of the dump. The dirt floors would turn muddy in the rainy season. Bare wires were strung haphazardly from one shack to another, a basic necessity for the TV's they could see inside many doorways. This must be what kept them from going mad, thought Gladys.

Through the haze of burning refuse, Gladys could see wild pigs rooting for food, and bony dogs scavenging in packs. Flies swarmed everywhere, rising from the putrid vegetables and animal carcasses rotting in the sun. Gladys frantically waved them away from her face, trying to protect herself from the deadly germs they carried.

Walking past the communal latrines, it took her all her strength not to hold her nose. Women with buckets and basins crowded around water taps found here and there along the edge of the dump, waiting for the moment when the water would be turned on for a short time. Everywhere across the wide open valley people scrambled in the refuse for something of value, plastic, bottles or glass they could sell or barter.

But hardest of all was to look into the children's faces. There was a hollow deadness about their eyes which peered out from pinched, grubby faces that looked as though they hadn't been washed for weeks. Nor had a comb touched their dull, lifeless hair, matted and no doubt riddled with lice. Gladys could not believe so many children lived in such hopeless conditions on this stench-ridden place. I'm glad I won't have to come back here again, she thought to herself.

Gladys and Lisbeth returned to their own comfortable homes to celebrate Christmas with their families the next day. But somehow as they looked at the table laden with tempting holiday food, all they could see or think of were the sad faces of those children digging in the rubbish for a crust of bread. What hurt even more were thoughts of the hundreds who hadn't received a blanket and didn't know anything about Jesus' love for them.

This unusual Christmas project had started when a group of Californian Christians had visited Guatemala the previous summer. They'd seen the plight of the dump people and sent money to Lisbeth and Gladys to purchase as many blankets as they could for the people living there. Though Guatemala is in the tropics, Guatemala City is over four thousand feet high and nights can be cold. Inside each blanket they had wrapped a tract, a New Testament and a package of food.

Though the young women had no intention of returning to the dumps after they had fulfilled their mission, they could not forget the requests of many there. 'Won't you come back and teach us more about the Bible?'

Gladys struggled with this request for she had never seen such hopelessness and despair in her life. She had grown up in a Christian Spanish/Indian family. She had felt the call of God upon her life from her youth. However, her mother had died when Gladys was fifteen, and suddenly she had the care of the home and three younger brothers and sisters. 'I had to mature very fast,' she recalls.

Yet her father saw something special in Gladys and encouraged her to make something of herself. It was not common in the early seventies for Guatemalan women to attend university. Their families expected them to marry and bear children and believed that education was a waste of time and money. But Gladys's father seemed to have a God-given perception that his daughter could do more. Even though he struggled as an electrician to provide adequately for his family, he wanted them to be the best they could be.

While in university, Gladys began working with Campus Crusade, and it was through this ministry that she met Lisbeth Piedrasanta. Lisbeth studied Christian counselling in the United States. When she returned the two young women spent a lot of time talking about the value and need of counselling. There were no Christian counsellors willing to help people with limited funds in Guatemala City at the time. As Gladys learned more and more from Lisbeth's training, she realized God had given her a gift of counselling as well, and the two began dreaming about opening up a counselling centre especially for poor women and children with learning disabilities. The opportunity came when Virgil and Bea Zapata, the leaders of the Instituto Evangélico America Latina asked them to become part of their organization. With the help of the school they opened a small clinic and their days were full counselling people who could not otherwise receive professional help.

But after their experience with the Christmas blankets, Gladys and Lisbeth could not put the faces of the dump children out of their minds. They decided to go back on Saturday afternoons to start a Bible class for them. The children gathered around them, shyly touching their shiny hair or clinging to their arms. Gladys found herself hugging these dirty urchins so hungry for affection. Often their mothers came to listen, and soon the two women started a class for them.

But they needed so much more – teaching on hygiene, simple medical treatment, skills-training, food, clean water. The heart-wrenching needs of the people went far beyond the smells and ugliness of their surroundings.

By the next Christmas Gladys and Lisbeth received funds to buy many more blankets and Christmas treats, and they found themselves spending more and more time with the dump people. A Christian medical doctor joined them to help treat some of the more obvious ailments – ringworm, diarrhoea, scabies. To do this they needed money for medication, and a place for a permanent clinic. A Christian friend in the United States gave them enough money to purchase a piece of property on the edge of the dump, and in 1990 Casa Del Alfarero (The Potter's House) was born.

Probably no one else in the world would have considered the piece of property next to the dump 'prime.' But for Gladys and Lisbeth this was the beginning of a project that had been growing in their hearts for two years. With the help of volunteers they put up a simple corrugated iron building for a clinic, and watched with joy as the first medication arrived from an organization in the USA. Two Guatemalan doctors offered to visit the clinic each week and several nurses joined them. When Gladys talks about the clinic her dark brown eyes sparkle with joy, 'We can supply all the medication [the doctors] need.

Even our national hospital doesn't have some of the medication we received.' Most of the medicines are supplied through Compassion International, a USA-based Christian organization that sponsors children around the world.

Once the two women had given up their counselling programme and spent their full time at the dump, they implemented other new developments. They opened a small trade school and hired Alex to teach carpentry and masonry. They started a class for women to learn to sew, visualizing that the women could find jobs in the city and get their families out of this hopeless situation. They constructed simple buildings, just basic shelters, so that they could serve a hot lunch at noon to children. They installed a shower and insisted that the grubbiest children shower before coming to lunch. What must it have felt like for children who had never seen water in any quantity larger than a bucket, or mud puddles on the dump, to stand with clean fresh water running over their bodies?

But in the middle of all this progress, a serious blow fell on Casa Del Alfarero. In drawing up the deed of sale, the owner of the property had miscalculated the dimensions of the lot. His family took Gladys and Lisbeth to court, accusing them of stealing their land. Since the dump ministry had paid for the land, the women decided to contest the case. However, in a shocking turn of events, the judge ordered Gladys and one of her board members to be jailed until the case against them could be settled.

On the advice of her lawyer, Gladys stayed hidden in her home, where she lived with her father, for two months. During this time she and the board decided to drop the case and let the relatives have the land. 'And when we did that,' Gladys explains, 'very suddenly the Lord gave us another piece of land just behind us at a very good price.'

Gladys doesn't look at finances as an obstacle to the ministry, even to meet the needs of 27 full-time and part-time staff. 'I don't need money first,' she says. 'If God calls me to serve, he will provide the money. If God says "Do it," he will give me the money to do it.'

From the beginning, the dump ministry has tithed its income sending the tithe to other ministries. 'For example,' Gladys explains 'if someone gives us a hundred toys, we give ten toys to someone else. Since we've been doing that, God has been giving us more.'

The ministry's donor-base is small but very faithful. A church in Auburn, California prays and gives regularly. Gladys estimates they have a donor-base of about 33 individuals. They have attempted to involve more Guatemalans, especially for their camp sponsorships. The annual camp now draws as many as two hundred dump children.

Sometimes inviting a child to camp takes more than explaining all the fun they will have. One day Gladys visited the shack of a little seven-year-old who had been coming to Casa Del Alfarero from time to time. She found Claudia preparing a bottle for her baby brother, heating the milk over a gas burner. Two smaller brothers clung to her skirts when they saw Gladys at the door. The 'little mother' reached down to hug the youngest one to reassure him.

When Gladys asked Claudia if she would come to camp Claudia told her to speak to her mother when she came back from working on the dump. 'No, No,' the mother asserted vehemently. She explained that Claudia had to stay with the smallest children while she collected refuse on the dump. How else could she buy food? Gladys had a brilliant idea. If she paid Claudia's mother what she would earn for three days working on the dump, would she allow Claudia to go to camp?

Thus Claudia had a never-to-be-forgotten experience in the fresh country air, running and playing with other children, sleeping on a comfortable bed with clean blankets, and eating food she'd never tasted before. She listened to stories about God the Father who loved her and sent His Son Jesus to die for her. Claudia had never known any father's love. Gladys saw such longing and responsiveness in the little girl's eyes that she determined to see that she received special attention and teaching after the camp. Maybe here was someone she could rescue from the dump's clutches before it was too late.

Gladys has tried to change the direction of other young people's lives. For example, Minor is a fourteen-year-old waif, without parents or home. He sleeps where he drops, and wears his clothes until he finds something else in the dump to replace them. Minor's growth has been stunted by lack of food and by his long-term glue-sniffing habit. Though the Guatemalan government has outlawed the sale of glue to children, the dump children know where to find it easily.

Common shoemaker's glue has destroyed the minds of dozens of children and young people on the dump. Like Minor, their eyes become glassy, their skin sallow, and their thought-processes slow down. It has the wonderful side effect, however, of reducing hunger. For though on occasion children can find MacDonald's hamburgers or discarded airline meals on the dump, the pickings are very scarce for them and they are hungry most of the time.

Minor is old enough to scavenge on the dump, and he drags a burlap bag with him everywhere to collect glass or plastic. As soon as he has enough to sell, he exchanges it for his next bottle of glue. He also appears regularly at Casa Del Alfarero for a noon meal, and like it or not, must take a shower before he is given food. As Minor was a dump child without parent or home, Gladys attempted to ease his suffering by providing a tiny room for him to sleep in. She discovered, however, that he almost immediately rented it out to someone else so he could use the proceeds for his habit. Gladys closed the room to him. When Minor complained that he didn't have a place to sleep Gladys simply told him, 'God gave you a place to sleep, but you didn't take it, so I don't know what you're going to do.' On another occasion Gladys tried to place Minor in a foster family, but he wouldn't stay because he didn't want to obey the rules.

Life on the dump has a culture all its own. Many of the 600 or more families living there have been there for four or five generations. They've never known anything else, and feel insecure off the dump. A woman asked Gladys to go and buy a cake for her. 'I asked her why she didn't go herself,' says Gladys. 'It's only four or five blocks away. But the woman said she was afraid that they would refuse to serve her.'

In the ten years that Gladys has worked on the dumps, no one has ever willingly left the dump to work or live somewhere else. Instead more and more people try to come and make a living there. Some find squatter areas in other parts of Guatemala City and come each day to scavenge on the dumps. Gangs have also found this to be a lucrative business. When individuals come to the dump with their pickups or vans filled with refuse from their homes, the gangs are waiting for them, and rob the driver of his watch and money. Gladys almost forgets the robbers and gangs on the dump. She declares, 'I feel comfortable here. But sometimes the children will say, "Senora Gladys, come with us very close because there are robbers around." So they take care of us and tell us when we can't go for a walk.'

Why would a young woman spend the prime of her life in this dirty smelly, hopeless environment, when she sees so little change in the lives of the people? Perhaps it's in obedience to the words of Isaiah,

> *Is not this the kind of fasting I have chosen: . . . to share your food with the hungry and to provide the poor wanderer with shelter – when you see the naked, to clothe him, and not to turn away from your own flesh and blood? Then your light will break forth like the dawn and your healing will quickly appear: then your righteousness will go before you, and the glory of the Lord will be your rear guard. Then you will call, and the Lord will answer; you will cry for help and he will say: Here am I.*

Isaiah 58: 6–9

Gladys believes there is hope. She's seen it in the women as she's taught them the Bible way to live. She tells them, 'You've inherited alcoholism; you're an alcoholic; so are your son, your grandson. Now it's time to say no. You have to apply God's principles.

'I've been teaching the Gospel of John and I talk about the Samaritan woman. So I teach them to be emotionally thirsty,' Gladys explains. 'This woman had four or five men, but she was emotionally thirsty. I tell them that I am single and that when I feel thirsty for love I just say "God I am thirsty for your love." '

Most women on the dumps move from man to man without marriage. One day Gladys visited a woman who showed her pictures saying, 'This is John's father; this is Andrew's father.' She didn't know who was the father of her youngest child. Sometimes Gladys teases the women by saying it's not fair they have two or three men, and she's never had one husband. But seriously she tells them she doesn't really need a man to be happy, especially when she sees the way men beat their wives and children. And at forty-two her smiling face, gentle disposition and loving attitude prove she is speaking the truth.

On the other hand she teaches the women to be loving, caring 'wives' – to serve breakfast and to iron their men's clothes. After one such session a woman told her, 'I began treating my husband differently and he asked me "What's happening with you? I need to meet this lady that is teaching you because you have been changing so much." '

Gladys loves to relate the stories of success, like Estelita who has lived on the dump all her life. As a child she learned to fight for her rights. She started coming to Casa Del Alfarero to receive Christmas gifts, and became a Christian. Somehow she had learned to read and write, so Gladys asked her to work as a receptionist at the medical clinic. Estelita's first reaction was, 'I can't do it.' But Gladys reminded her, 'Remember what the Bible says. "I can do all things through Christ." Do you believe Jesus can help you?'

Estelita loves her job at the medical clinic and is now learning to type. Even more encouraging, her family has seen the change in her. When her daughter first heard her praying out loud, she exclaimed 'Mom you're crazy talking alone. Who are you talking to?' Estelita explained that she was talking to God.

Not long after that she saw her daughter talking by herself. 'Who are you talking to?' Estelita asked. 'I'm talking with God, telling him that my father should stop drinking.' Miraculously, the father, who had been violent and destructive at home, asked for forgiveness and has stopped drinking.

Fernando, a 28-year-old paraplegic, is another encouraging example of what can happen on the dump. Fernando had been raised by an abusive grandmother who forced him to find his food on the dump. Fernando wanted go to school, but his grandmother tied him up so he could not leave the house. Eventually he escaped and lived on the streets becoming a drug addict and a gang member. One night he was shot by the police in a street battle, and returned to his grandmother's home in a wheelchair.

Gladys recalls, 'I learned about Fernando, rebellious, destitute and in a wheelchair living on the dump. I went to see him to see how I could help him.

During our second visit Fernando received Christ as his Saviour. His family also came to Christ through his testimony.'

Fernando's longing to study has been partially fulfilled, as he attended Bible studies. Gladys encouraged him to draw pictures illustrating each chapter of the book of John he was studying. She saw an artistic gift that needs to be developed. But until that happens he is learning a practical skill, typing, and works part time in the ministry's office.

While the visible results of her ministry on the dump may be few, Gladys admits that God has produced many changes in her life. She told an audience of four thousand world leaders meeting in Korea in May, 1995, 'Many leaders are leaving their ministries because they have not understood that God sends brokenness as a transforming tool in their lives and not for destruction. We complain about our circumstances because we do not believe that God uses trials to make us more like Christ.'

One of the trials Gladys has faced is the discovery that she is a diabetic. She says, 'God took away my natural energy and replaced it with his supernatural strength to accomplish my daily tasks. With diabetes I must be careful of infections and cuts because I do not heal easily. Therefore when I go into the dump I am in danger from broken glass, garbage and contamination.'

Yet this does not keep Gladys from visiting people in the hovels on the edge of the dump. Each shack has a character of its own filled with precious treasures rescued from the discards of those who live in relative affluence outside. Gladys marvels at their ingenuity in repairing broken chairs and tables, tying together bed frames which skew on three legs, and mending cracked enamel basins and leaking buckets. Even more amazing are the ancient television sets that have been 'jerryrigged' to work; the radios held together with bits of tape and wire. She tries to ignore the dangerous electrical connections and the bare electric wires. But they provide light from a forlorn bulb hanging from the roof, casting dismal shadows into the dark corners piled high with 'collections.'

In the midst of the debris and clutter, Gladys's heart is moved when here and there a woman has made a colourful patchwork quilt for a bed, or hung a picture on the wall to bring a touch of beauty to a dark and hopeless environment.

Gladys no longer sees the ugliness, nor fears to accept a cup of coffee offered her from a broken mug. She remembers that Jesus said, '*If anyone would come after me, he must deny himself and take up his cross and follow me*' (Mt. 16:24). 'Working at the dump, I have had to deny myself the pleasure of wearing pretty clothes, high heels and jewellery. I have learned to live with the smells, the lice and the misery caused by the millions of flies,' she states.

As the ministry has grown in scope, so has the staff. But Gladys finds that few people can take the pressures and hopelessness for long, and so there is a constant turnover of workers. Gladys and Lisbeth also felt that they needed more men on the staff to deal with the men and teenage boys who were coming for training and Bible studies. When Edgar Guitz came on the staff it was clear that he had a special call to the ministry and a much-needed gift of administration. Gladys had long realized that she works with her heart. 'When I see a need I want to help everyone and I don't use more of my brain,' she says laughing. So Edgar's skills were much appreciated.

The year that Edgar joined the ministry, Lisbeth was given a sabbatical by the board, and during her time of rest and recuperation felt God was moving her out of the dump ministry. With Edgar on the staff the timing seemed to be right. Gladys appreciated this young man's ideas and spiritual insights; they worked together well and soon became good friends.

It was about this time that Gladys' young nephew began praying for a husband for Auntie Gladys – 'one who will love her and love children.' But Gladys had always felt God had given her the gift of celibacy so she could more fully do God's work, and she had long since given up the idea of marriage. Just before she left for the Global Congress on World Evangelization in Korea in May, 1995, Edgar said 'I have something to tell you when you come back from Korea.'

Gladys put the thought out of her mind. However, while she was in Korea a friend told her that God was going to give her a husband. Gladys laughed off the suggestion. 'I haven't met anyone in whom I'm interested,' she told her friend.

Shortly after she returned from Korea, Gladys told her friend Edgar about the strange word she'd received from the woman in Korea. And Edgar confessed that what he was going to tell her was that he loved her and wanted to marry her. Though Gladys had discounted Edgar as a prospective husband because he was younger than she, she realized that indeed she could return his love. Gladys and Edgar were married in August, 1996.

What is the future for Casa Del Alfarero and the seemingly hopeless people it serves? Gladys believes the future lies in the children. With Edgar now directing the ministry, Gladys feels she must concentrate on the children. A school is on the drawing board, to be built on the property God provided after they lost the court case. After ten years on the dump Gladys realizes it is almost impossible to change the people. They have never known any other culture; they are afraid to leave and find it difficult to conform to the rules of normal society. The dump children do poorly in the local schools, and drop out very early.

Gladys believes if she can start with the children, teach them discipline and the Bible and expose them to the outside world gradually, there is hope for them. At the same time she dreams of a 'parents' school' to teach parents how to love and train their children, and to end verbal and physical abuse.

Her motivation remains clear. 'God designed a specific ministry for me in order to fulfil his perfect plan that I become more Christlike. He gave me a dump. There is nothing respectable in being called to a dump. It is not the place where many servants of God would like to work. But I believe this is the place God has called me, and he has used it to change my life.'

Seven

A Soap Opera With a Happy Ending – Kay Arthur, United States

Deborah, a prophetess, the wife of Lappidoth, was leading Israel at that time. She held court under the Palm of Deborah between Ramah and Bethel in the hill country of Ephraim, and the Israelites came to her to have their disputes decided. She sent for Barak, son of Abinoam from Kedesh in Naphtali and said to him, 'The Lord, the God of Israel, commands you: "Go, take with you ten thousand men of Naphtali and Zebulun and lead the way to Mount Tabor. I will . . . give him into your hands." '

Judges 4:4–7

As a teenager, Kay Arthur volunteered to teach Sunday School in her local church. She knew almost nothing about the Bible but she felt sorry for the children in the class who seemed so bored. So she taught them a new song. Even then, Kay could act and hold an audience with her antics as she sang:

I had a little chicky and it wouldn't lay an egg
  so I poured hot water up and down its leg.
So the little chicky hollered, and the little chicky begged,
  and the little chicky laid a hard-boiled egg.

The children responded with peals of laughter and Kay felt a thrill of satisfaction that they were no longer bored. At that point in her life she had absolutely no idea that she could have had them sitting on the edge of their seats with stories from the greatest Book ever written, because she didn't know the Author. But for the teenager, holding her Sunday school class spellbound with 'The Little Chicky' back in the late forties, that was the farthest from her mind.

Kay was born in 1933 in the heart of the depression years. She saw her parents struggle financially. Her father started out as a grocery clerk, diligently working his way up in the company. But every promotion meant a move. Kay attended twelve elementary schools and four high schools. She lived in a romantic dream world, longing for a handsome Prince Charming who would shower her with attention and security.

Kay had seen such a happy marriage in her own home. Though her father had never been able to get much education or follow his heart into religious work, he was a loving husband and father. Kay remembers her parents dancing in the kitchen to a hit tune on the radio, and she doesn't recall them ever raising their voices to each other.

Having grown up in a formal church without any gospel teaching, Kay was sure she was a Christian because she'd been baptized as a baby and confirmed at the age of twelve. She tells of attending church wearing a huge picture hat and gloves, genuflecting piously towards the altar and sliding onto the kneeling bench, all the while slyly looking to see if the boys had noticed her as she prayed.

Kay recalls, 'I wanted to get married more than anything else in the world.' As her father saw his lovely young daughter maturing beyond her years he warned her, 'Honey, men will date bad girls, but they won't marry them.' So Kay determined to remain a virgin until she married, though Satan was already beginning to build a fortress of immorality in her mind, as she dreamed of romantic men like Tyrone Power falling at her feet in adoration.

After Kay finished high school she went to train as a nurse in Cleveland, Ohio. She was very attractive and mature-looking, and older men began taking her out. 'What I was on the inside,' Kay admits, 'began to show on the outside. My appearance shouted "available." '

However, Kay still remembered the standards of her parents and though she dressed provocatively and flirted outrageously with the men she met, her philosophy was, 'You can look, but you can't touch.' She learned later that she had developed a reputation among the Phi Del boys at the nearby engineering school as a girl with whom you couldn't get to first base.

And then Kay met her Prince Charming. Tom Getz was everything she could have dreamed of. He was an outstanding athlete who had offers to pitch for leading baseball teams, but his father felt he would make more money in business. Tom came from a wealthy family who belonged to the country club; he drove a nice car and could take her to expensive restaurants. She was impressed with his brilliant mind – they spent hours talking about serious issues; even about God (but not Jesus Christ). The first time he kissed her, he gave her his Phi Del pin, and shortly afterwards they were formally engaged. How she loved the huge diamond ring he placed on her finger, and all the promises it held of living 'happily ever after'. She finally had the one and only thing she wanted in life.

On their fairy-tale honeymoon to Bermuda, however, the bubble burst. Tom sat Kay down and said, 'You are now Mrs. Frank Thomas Getz Jr. These are the things I don't like about you and I want changed.' Kay felt trapped as she saw her handsome and gifted husband sink into an angry depression, and a niggling fear whispered, 'You've made a mistake.'

After the honeymoon Tom entered officers training school to earn a commission in the Navy. Within a year he was posted to Europe, so Kay travelled across the Atlantic on the *US Constitution* with their infant son Tommy and her eleven-year-old sister as companion. But the military changed Tom's orders and Kay ended up stranded alone in Europe for nine months.

She saw Tom for only forty days out of that whole time, and every time he came off the ship he was depressed. During this period of loneliness Kay found herself enjoying the attention of other men. Her dark eyes sparkled as she listened attentively to their stories and her vivacious personality made her the centre of attention at social gatherings. Kay confesses that during those months she became involved with another man, enjoying the flattery and flirtation. 'But I kept my standards, though I did everything short of falling into adultery.'

Tom went into flight-training, but his depression worsened and he dropped out of the Navy to enter seminary. Kay joined him in Alexandria, Virginia, where he began studying for the priesthood. Instead of finding riches in Scripture and the truth to set him free, Tom spent his time questioning the authorship of the Pentateuch. 'He was in a seminary that didn't teach the Bible as the word of God. We never heard teaching on being saved or anyone giving a testimony,' Kay remembers sadly.

With the arrival of their second son, Mark, Kay hoped that Tom would take a greater interest in his family. But nothing seemed to help his depression and after a year in seminary he announced to Kay, 'We're dropping out.' Kay had made many friends at the seminary, especially among some of the men who found her very attractive. So she threw a cocktail party for them the night before they left. Some of their guests got very drunk and had to be helped to their cars. One student called her the next day to say, 'That was a great party last night. I could hardly preach this morning.'

By now the marriage was a shambles. Tom got a job as an engineer, but came home from work each day only to go to bed. Kay begged to be able to go back to college herself, but Tom refused. She wanted to go back to nursing, but Tom wouldn't let her. Instead he demanded that she keep an account of every penny she spent.

One night she hurried home to tell him she'd got a job as a model – and that seemed to please him. He liked to brag to his friends that his wife was a model and Kay felt like a 'charm-bracelet' dangling on his wrist. When she asked permission to buy a dining-room suite, he refused. But now that she had her own money she told him she would do as she pleased, and went out and bought it.

After one very successful modelling job she came home feeling more cheerful and excited about her career than she had in a long time. She found Tom sitting in the living room in his shorts, miserable and dejected. Angry words followed as he lashed out at her. Kay shouted back that she didn't care about him any more. He followed her upstairs into the bedroom. Kay remembers, 'I let him have it verbally. My tongue was "set on fire from hell". I provoked him so badly that he backhanded me and I fell on the bed.'

Tom, the officer and gentleman, had never struck Kay before. Shocked, she screamed, 'That's it,' and threw her wedding ring and gorgeous diamond across the floor. He got down on his hands and knees looking for the rings, and as she grabbed her pillow and blanket to move to the couch downstairs she shouted, 'You care more about those rings than you care about me.'

The marriage was over. Kay needed help and the only person she could think of going to was the minister at the seminary they had recently left. As she recalls the visit now, she feels shame, 'I forgot my cigarettes so we both smoked his pipes. He never opened the Bible and explained what marriage is all about. And when we stood up to say goodbye, he took me in his arms and kissed me in a very unpriestly way and said, "Kay, you sure are a good-looking woman." ' Kay went home to pack, collect her children and end her marriage, then returned to the seminary town to be close to the man who had held her in his arms. 'I did everything short of adultery,' she sighs.

The months that followed were a nightmare of despair and depression. The seeds of immorality and rebellion now flourished. Kay remembers standing in her apartment shaking her fist at God and saying, 'To hell with you God. I'll see you around town. I'm going to find someone to love me.' She became what she thought she would never be: an immoral woman. She went from one man to another. After introducing her two little boys to her date, she'd sit them in front of the TV and go out. When she returned they would ask wistfully, 'Is this going to be our daddy?' The boys loved their dad and she often took them to stay with him, driving with her current lover to Tom's, where they'd find him with another woman.

For two years Kay had an affair with a married man. At first she didn't know he was married. When she found out she was so desperately in love with him, she couldn't leave him even though she discovered that his wife was pregnant with their sixth child. Today she understands that she had become a slave of sin. Much as she tried she couldn't free herself from the kind of life she was leading. Over and over again, she'd say 'I'm not going to do this any more,' but again and again she found herself back in the clutches of evil. Eventually she broke off the adulterous relationship, but her inner turmoil and disgust left her pain-racked and helpless.

One day as she was coming out of John Hopkins University Hospital where she was working, she recognized an old friend driving by. She flagged him down saying, 'George, what are you doing here?' Only later would she realize that this had been a meeting arranged by the God of the universe who was giving Kay another chance.

Kay and the children began visiting George and his wife Carol. There seemed to be a peaceful, wholesome attitude about them and their friends. People talked freely about God and Jesus Christ as if he were a personal friend. One night a man attending a party at George's confronted Kay. 'Why don't you quit telling God what you want and tell him that Jesus Christ is all you need?' he asked.

Kay was furious. 'I'm sorry,' she retorted, 'I don't need God. I need a husband.' She turned on her heel thinking, 'How uncouth can you be!'

But the piercing question had gone to her heart. She spent a restless night, and the next morning could barely drag herself down to the kitchen to prepare breakfast for the boys. When Mark tugged at her skirts with a question, she looked down at that innocent upturned face, and all she could see was the mess she'd made of her life and her failure as a mother. Sobbing she responded, 'Mark honey, I've got to be by myself for a while,' and ran upstairs.

Throwing herself down on the floor beside her bed Kay cried out to God. She didn't know that he loved her unconditionally. No one had told her that his love was personified in his Son Jesus Christ, who died for her. She had no idea that God was willing to forgive the immorality, the anger, the deceit, the terrible example she'd set for her boys. She cried, 'God I don't care what you do to me. I don't care if I never see another man as long as I live. I don't care if you paralyse me from the neck down. I don't care what you do to my two boys, if you'll just give me peace!'

God gave her the Prince of Peace instead. Kay admits that she didn't fully understand what happened to her that day, July 16, 1963; she didn't have a complete understanding of the plan of salvation. She didn't know 'We all, like sheep, have gone astray, each of us has turned to his own way, and the Lord has laid on him the iniquity of us all' (Is. 53:6). But she knew that God had met her and cleansed her. From that moment she knew innately that she couldn't wear the clothes she'd been wearing or talk the way she'd been talking. She was different – she had a new escort, Jesus Christ – and everything had become new.

The next day one of George's friends, Dave, came to pick up Kay and the boys to take them to a Christian camp. Just when she was ready to forget about men, God put a wonderful Christian man in her life – a man who loved to talk about the Bible and to answer her questions. Kay and Dave began spending time together talking about the Lord. Kay was full of questions.

Dave had given her a J.B. Phillips translation of the New Testament, and as she started reading it she kept saying, 'I didn't know that was in the Bible!' She couldn't put it down. She would prop her Bible up on the steering wheel as she drove her car to work. (She realizes now that her guardian angels must have been putting in overtime.) She bought records of Scripture reading so that she could listen while she was working around the house. She attended a church where the word of God was taught and sat on the edge of the seat, her hands gripping the pew in front, eager to drink in every word the preacher said. She would lie on the floor in the evening after the boys were in bed reading the Scriptures aloud, uncharacteristically happy to be alone.

Dave became her spiritual mentor. He had a way of applying the truths of the Scripture to nature and life. They shared communion together by the side of the road. And Kay fell in love again. Here was the kind of man who would not only nurture and care for her, but shared her love for her new found Saviour.

But it was not to be. One night at the end of a wonderful evening together David shared that though he cared for her very much, he could not marry her. He had been seeking counsel from several pastors who were close friends, and they had strongly advised against it because of her divorce.

Anger surfaced once again. Was she now to go without dating or any male friendships because marriage was out of the picture? She flew out of the car and ran up into her bedroom, throwing herself on the floor and weeping uncontrollably. Suddenly it seemed as though God was saying to her 'Am I not enough for you?' In an instant she thought, 'You are'. And she blew her nose and stopped crying. As she lay on her bed she wondered what God had in store for her next. As she prayed he seemed to be saying, 'Go back to Tom.'

That thought had never crossed her mind. She didn't love Tom, nor did he love her. He had telephoned several times before her conversion, threatening suicide. Trained in the school of thought that anyone who threatened suicide was just trying to get attention, Kay hotly responded, 'Be sure you do a good job so I get your money.'

But since her conversion Kay had on occasion told Tom about her new life in Christ and suggested he might want to consider this. Tom expressed his happiness for her, but denied that such a personal relationship with God held an interest for him. Now as she prayed she realized that if God could change her, he could change Tom, and they might be able to start again.

But life was busy. What with her job and the boys to care for, fellowship with Christians and time for Bible study, Kay put off writing to Tom. She was going into hospital for back surgery after an accident which had damaged her vertebrae and Tom phoned to wish her well. But even then she didn't bring up the question of reconciliation.

On the day she was to check into John Hopkins for surgery she received a call from the hospital, where she also worked. She was given a message to call a number in Cleveland. She recognized it as her former in-laws' number and expected Tom to answer the phone. Instead her sister-in-law answered, 'Just a moment Kay, Dad wants to talk with you.'

Kay had no premonition of what she would hear. 'Kay, Tom's dead – he hanged himself.' Stunned, she hung up and made arrangements to fly to Cleveland for the funeral. When she walked into the house she found her in-laws drinking heavily to drown their sorrows. 'My great brain is dead,' her father-in-law cried. When she tried to comfort him by reading from the Bible, he moved his hand defiantly, 'Get that – Bible out of my sight.'

Kay went up to Tom's room where he had hanged himself. Later when she viewed his body in the coffin at the church she saw that his hands were broken and blue and swollen. Evidently he had changed his mind, but could not release the knot, breaking his hands in the attempt. As she stood there it struck her that this was the very spot where she and Tom had stood to promise their eternal love to each other. A sob caught in her throat for she felt that she was guilty of putting that rope around Tom's neck. She hadn't understood his depression; she hadn't tried to be the loving, helpful wife he needed; she had loosed her vindictive tongue against him, driving him to this!

But she was not bearing that guilt alone. Now she had peace knowing that Jesus had paid for all her sins, and that if she confessed and forsook them he was merciful and faithful and just to forgive those sins. He had cleansed her from all unrighteousness. And she would go on with her life.

After Tom's death Kay felt strongly that she should go to Bible school. She didn't know much about Bible schools, but met some friends who were going to Tennessee Temple and they invited her to join them. She sold much of her furniture, packed the rest into a trailer, and she and the boys set out for Tennessee with $250 in her pocket.

With the beautiful faith of a new Christian, Kay simply expected God to provide for all her needs. Tennessee Temple didn't know she was coming, but they accepted her. That was a miracle in itself, for though she appeared very conservative in relation to her 'old self' she was far from the Tennessee Temple type. These were the days when fundamentalists referred to John R. Rice's book, *Bobbed Hair, Bossy Wives and Women Preachers*, when identifying threats to Christian standards.

Kay purchased a house with $250 down, in spite of the fact that five other couples wanted it, and she didn't have a job or a husband as security. But she had God and he continued to prove his sufficiency for her. She soon found a night nursing job. Husbands were a little scarce, even on a Bible school campus, so Kay began asking God to bring one to her.

One day a friend asked her if she knew Jack Arthur. Her church had been praying for him because they had learned that he had been stoned in South America for handing out New Testaments with the Pocket Testament League. Kay had never heard of Jack and didn't think anything of the conversation. Some months later however, Kay was praying and it seemed as though God put the thought in her heart, 'You're going to marry Jack Arthur.' She was puzzled. She'd never met Jack, didn't even know what he looked like. But she told two of her closest friends 'I want to tell you about this strange revelation I had from God, just in case it comes to pass. You'll never believe me afterwards.'

Kay went to the missions office of the school to look up his prayer card so that she would recognize him if he ever came to the campus. She thought about writing him a letter saying the church was praying for him since he was facing opposition – and just casually mentioning that she was a widow with two children. Then she decided against it. If God had indeed put this thought in her mind, he could also arrange for them to meet without her help.

She had little time to give much thought to marriage. Her schedule at school and work kept her busy. But she lost her night-shift job at the hospital because the head nurse wanted her to stop witnessing to the patients. The patients weren't complaining, she discovered, but the other nurses were. So rather than stop witnessing, she left.

She soon found a job working at weekends in a 12-bed diagnostic hospital, but one night the supervisor rang to say they had no patients in the hospital so Kay need not come in. Kay was upset at first for she needed the money. However, since she had a free weekend night she decided to take the boys to a concert at school. After the concert they all went to the Happy Corner for ice-cream cones. As she was paying for the cones she heard Mark say, 'Mr. Arthur, would you sign my Bible?'

Kay whirled round to see that indeed the man from the prayer card, the man from God's revelation, was standing beside her talking with her son. For a moment she was flustered, thinking, Do I look all right? Is my hair too short? Then she handed the melting ice-cream cone to her son, and introduced herself to Jack Arthur. They talked for a few minutes, and Jack told her he was returning to South America by the end of the year. Kay thought, 'You don't know it yet, but I'm going with you!'

However, the next morning he left the campus and didn't come back. She had been very impressed with this tall, vibrant young man who exuded confidence and a clear sense of his call to serve God. She wanted to get to know him better – she wanted him to get to know her better. But now he was gone.

Confused and yet still confident of God's word to her, Kay stayed on to finish her Bible school training that summer. With no other leading, and still hoping for Jack's return, she enrolled in Tennessee Temple college that fall.

One day early in September, 1965 she was crossing the street, and there was Jack Arthur. She learned later that he had come home and told his mother he wanted to get to know the young widow with the two little boys he'd met the previous year. Kay and Jack began dating and in November he asked her to marry him. Kay's response was swift and positive, but she said, 'I've got something to tell you. God told me eleven months ago that I was going to marry you.' Jack's response: 'I didn't have a chance, did I?'

Within a year of their marriage Jack and Kay and the two boys were in Guadalajara, Mexico where Jack did what he loved best – holding open-air meetings, showing Christian films, distributing New Testaments, and sharing Christ with people who didn't know him. Their son, David was born during that first year. As a trained nurse, Kay fully expected to use her medical skills, but found there were many other unmet needs on the mission station. Someone was needed to minister to the missionaries' teenage children, and Kay volunteered. She knew enough to share the words of life, and many of the young people accepted Christ. Now they needed teaching and discipling, but everyone on the station was too busy. Feeling totally inadequate she prayed, 'Lord I don't know how to teach but if you will teach me, I will teach them.' To her surprise, the young people flocked back week after week, as many as seventy-five crowding into the small mission house. Even with three little boys to take care of, she threw herself into her new teaching role with the young people, only to have it cut short by illness.

In 1969, after only a few years in Mexico, Kay's health forced the Arthurs to return to the United States. When the doctor told Jack he should take Kay back to the United States where she could get better treatment, both of them were heartbroken. Neither of them had any idea that this disappointment would mark the beginning of a worldwide ministry.

Jack soon found a job as manager of a new Christian radio station in Chattanooga, Tennessee. Once Kay was fit for some kind of ministry herself, she began teaching a class of young people in her home. Though she'd had only a year of Bible school, she found herself drawn to studying the word of God, and looking forward to sharing its exciting truths with the young people in fresh new ways. She demonstrated her points by tapping her feet and making strange animal noises – and the young people loved it. Without publicity or fanfare, the numbers of teens grew and grew until the small Arthur living-room couldn't hold them and they had to move to a local warehouse for their meetings.

Kay also began a weekly women's Bible study around her kitchen table, for which she diligently prepared her own lessons. It was during the preparation of an inductive study on Romans that the concept of her teaching gift overwhelmed her. She explains that experience, 'I came to Romans 12 – since we have gifts that differ . . . let each exercise them accordingly: . . . if service, in his serving; or he who teaches, in his teaching . . .' (NASB) I thought, "Oh my goodness, I'm supposed to stay within the realm of my gift." ' Under the conviction of the word of God and with the rapidly growing classes, now including men who asked to attend her Bible studies, Kay realized God had given her a unique gift to teach his Word – a gift that is recognized today by the thousands of women and men around the world who listen to her teach and study her books.

Grace Kinsler, a wealthy Christian in Atlanta, heard about Kay's growing teaching ministry, and when the Bible teacher who had been teaching in her home had to leave, Grace invited Kay to take over the class. Soon her home was overflowing with women drinking in Kay's unique ability to bring the word of God to life for them.

Though she has not completed college or attended seminary she has an insatiable thirst to understand and interpret God's word correctly, and a profound gift for remembering and bringing truth together from the whole of Scripture. Today in honest humility she admits, 'I know the Word; I've paid my dues . . . God is responsible for providing the audience; I am responsible for doing my homework, for knowing the word of God and praying.'

Jack left his job at the radio station to take care of the property and administer all the business aspects of the growing classes. The study at Grace Kinsler's outgrew her home and moved to the Roswell Street Baptist Church where it grew to more than seventeen hundred every week. Men asked to join the class after they saw the difference the Bible studies made in their wives and children.

However Kay realized that the weekly treks to Atlanta would eventually have to end because of the growth of the work in Chattanooga. What would happen to her students? Would they be able to continue studying in-depth for themselves? It was because of this concern that she began writing inductive Bible studies. In 1975 Precept Ministries was born, with the first inductive course on Romans. In 1981 when Jack and Kay stopped going to Atlanta, three thousand registered for the autumn classes led by teachers trained in the leadership methods of Precept Ministries. Videotapes and books began pouring out of the ministry, and later offices opened in Hong Kong, Australia, Mexico and Korea.

Precepts Ministries' home base in the green rolling hills of Chattanooga now includes administration buildings, a dining area, dormitories, a television studio and the Grace Kinsler Memorial Training Center which can accommodate 320 students. Kay's artistic touch is everywhere on the beautifully designed campus. Hundreds of men, women and young people come here each year to complete the required leadership training for them to serve as Precepts teachers across the country and the world. Kay also teaches on a daily 15-minute radio broadcast which is carried by over one hundred stations, and hosts a live weekly talk show with Jan Silvious, a long-time friend. She teaches several times a year overseas, and has spent much time in Israel where she based her only novel, *Israel, my Beloved.*

Kay has served on the board of several organizations including the National Religious Broadcasters and the National Day of Prayer. She has also participated as the only woman on a special think-tank at Dallas Seminary to consider questions of eschatology.

In the early days of her ministry people often asked how she dared teach men. She recalls speaking in a church in Florida where she gave an invitation at the end of the service. The pastor and his wife took her and Jack out to dinner afterwards and bluntly asked, 'What gives you the right to teach men?'

Kay's response rests on her interpretation of 1 Timothy 2:12 which states, 'I do not permit a woman to teach or have authority over a man.' She explains that the word for woman in Greek can mean either woman or wife, while the word for man can be either man or husband. Since the chapter goes on to speak about childbearing, she believes the word must mean 'wife' since only a wife should bear children. The word for man or husband is possessive, and so must refer to a husband.

Therefore Kay believes that the verse should read 'I do not allow a wife to teach or exercise authority over her husband.' This means she is not to take the role of teacher to her husband. However when asked to explain how this is true when Jack frequently attends her classes, she says 'He sits under my teaching voluntarily because he enjoys it and critiques what I say. But I don't usurp his authority in our marriage.'

Kay is adamant that she would not take this interpretation of 1 Timothy apart from other Scriptures. She refers to Old Testament history – Miriam the prophetess, Deborah who was raised up by God and served as a judge all the days of her life. She points to Huldah the prophetess who taught King Josiah what to do and what was going to happen, and to the four daughters of Philip who were prophetesses. Since Paul defines prophecy in 1 Corinthians 14 as 'edification, exhortation and comfort' she believes this is clearly a form of teaching.

Kay admits there are other valid interpretations of this verse, but this satisfies her and frees her to teach other men, including Christian leaders and pastors. Though criticism about her role as a teacher has decreased, she tells those who have a problem, 'If you do not believe I should be teaching you, then don't sit here, because "whatever is not of faith is sin" and you see the Scriptures differently from me.'

Many people do not realize what a strong role Jack plays in Precept Ministries. He serves as the president and Kay is executive secretary. He admits that the change in their roles has had its ups and downs for him. He was a well-known missionary with a public ministry for many years. But as Kay's unique gift of teaching became evident, he knew he needed to encourage her. 'She must be in her gifting and it is my responsibility to give her support and permission to teach,' he says.

There were times when he used to feel, 'Hey, I could be up there teaching'. He even questioned his own gifts. But today Jack is very comfortable in their respective positions. He is responsible for the management and administration of Precepts, which has grown into a $6.5 million organization with more than 125 staff based in Chattanooga, and another 60 around the United States. Jack often travels with Kay, especially when they lead Bible-teaching tours to Israel with as many as three hundred people.

Jack believes that at present Kay is so driven to obey God's call on her life, that she doesn't take enough time for personal relaxation. However, their three sons live in Chattanooga so times with the family are important – especially for Kay to be a grandmother to her eight grandchildren. And she's quite happy to send Jack off on his deep-sea fishing trips without her!

Since 1975 Kay has written and published more than 20 books and 25 inductive Bible studies. Her passion is to see Christians become the 'pillar and support of the truth' (1 Tim. 3:15) by studying the Word of God for themselves. In the introduction to the International Inductive Study Bible which Kay edited she writes:

> *If you want to satisfy your hunger and thirst to know God and His Word in a deeper way, you must do more than merely read Scripture and study what someone else has said about it. Just as no one else can eat and digest your food for you, so no one else can feed on God's Word for you. You must interact with the text yourself, absorbing its truths and letting God engrave His truth on your heart and mind and life.*
>
> *That is the very heart of inductive study: seeing truth for yourself, discerning what it means, and applying that truth to your life. In His inspired Word, God*

has given us everything we need to know about life and godliness. But He doesn't stop there. He gives every believer a resident teacher – the Holy Spirit – who guides us into His truth.

(International Inductive Study Bible [Eugene, OR, Harvest House Publishers, 1992], p. 7)

Kay is spending her life and energy making sure Christians know that truth.

Eight

To be or Not to be Ordained? That could be Rejection! – Yolanda Eden, Cuban-American

There is one body and one Spirit – just as you were called to one hope when you were called . . . . It was he who gave some to be apostles, some to be prophets, some to be evangelists and some to be pastors and teachers, to prepare God's people for works of service so that the body of Christ may be built up.

Eph.4:4,11,12

There is neither Jew nor Greek, slave nor free, male nor female, for you are all one in Christ Jesus.

Gal. 3:28.

Yolanda would never forget the day her father came home from their farm in the Cuban countryside with the shocking news that everything was gone! The sugar plantation, the herds of cattle, the house – everything.

Angrily Yolanda's father explained what the workers had said when he'd arrived for his usual visit to oversee the running of the farm, 'This isn't your business any more. It belongs to the government.' They literally threw him off his own property.

Initially Fidel Castro hadn't revealed his true colours. But shortly after the revolution which catapulted Castro to power in 1959, Cuban intellectuals and business people began to feel the pinch of his policies. For nineteen-year-old Yolanda Concepción, life would never be the same.

The sixth of nine children, she had grown up in the lap of luxury in Oriente across the island from Havana. Her musical gifts were encouraged and she had planned to go on with her studies after high school.

From early childhood Yolanda had dreamed of serving the Lord, following in the footsteps of her mother who was a lay preacher in the Church of God. Their spacious home was always open to pastors and missionaries passing through. When Yolanda was only ten she accepted Christ as her Savior. She was born cross-eyed, but remembers hearing a radio evangelist pray for healing. Her mother asked, 'Do you believe God is going to heal you?' Yolanda said 'Yes,' and took her glasses off. She never had to have corrective surgery and her eyes are perfectly normal. Several years later Yolanda's older brother Vincente developed tuberculosis and had to be sent to a sanitorium in Havana. While there he too was miraculously healed.

But now just as Yolanda had completed high school and looked forward to furthering her studies, the communist government had taken everything. Her father's bank accounts were confiscated. Two of her older brothers had gone to the United States to study and were working there. Rumours were rife that Castro was closing churches and harassing pastors. In spite of the dangers involved, her mother willingly offered accommodation to a young evangelist, Adib Eden and his team, while they held evangelistic meetings in their area.

Yolanda remembers that the first time she met the twenty-one year old evangelist she was not at all impressed, and thought he was arrogant. As his interest in her became obvious she prayed, 'Lord I don't want him prideful.' But it didn't take long for the dynamic young evangelist to capture her heart. While Yolanda's mother believed that Adib was the man for her daughter, her practical father fumed, 'Do you know what you're doing? We've got money and he has nothing to offer. You're going to live like a gypsy!' In the end, however, he capitulated and gave his blessing. Adib had already made plans to leave Cuba; many pastors had been imprisoned and he knew it was only a matter of time before the authorities caught up with him. It was becoming virtually impossible to carry on a public ministry. He felt that he should leave Cuba until freedom was restored. Therefore his offer of marriage had a sense of urgency. Two months later, on August 26, 1961, Adib and Yolanda were married.

Adib's parents certainly didn't approve of the marriage or of his plans. His father was a Lebanese Muslim who'd attempted to bring up his only son in the Islamic faith, reading the Koran to him every day. Adib's mother was a nominal Catholic, but she was also upset when at twelve years of age, Adib came home from a local Baptist church to announce that he had become a Christian. It was many years before they were both reconciled to Adib and his Saviour. No amount of shouting or threats of being ostracized could change the young man's mind, and by the age of fifteen he was already travelling from place to place as an evangelist. By the time Adib met Yolanda he'd completed seminary and was in full-time evangelistic work.

Within a month of their marriage the young couple managed to flee to Miami. Yolanda's sister remembers the difficulties of leaving Cuba even in the days when it was still legal. 'The Cuban authorities took everything. When we came to the United States, we couldn't bring clothes or any jewellery. We weren't allowed to bring money. When Adib and Yolanda got here, they had the clothes they were wearing and their luggage. And then the US government held them because they were refugees.'

Adib was allowed to enter the US because he had a job with a Baptist church which provided an apartment so that they could work with Latin-Americans in Miami. However, within a short time doctrinal differences led to a breakdown of the relationship, and he was back on the road as an evangelist.

Yolanda became pregnant almost immediately with their first child. Nevertheless she travelled to New Orleans and other places with Adib, but managed to get back to Miami to deliver their son Adib. The Hispanic community was generous and open-hearted to the young couple, though churches were small and an average offering might come to just $20. Sometimes they would have just enough money to fuel their old car to get to their next appointment. A Puerto Rican church gave Yolanda a 'baby shower' providing essentials, but she was often stranded without funds while Adib was on the road.

In the first eight years in the United States, Yolanda and Adib had four children: Adib followed by three sisters, Yolanda, Priscilla and Lizzie. One daughter was born in Connecticut, one in New York, and the third almost arrived in California but Yolanda made it back to Miami in time. Often Yolanda was asked to speak or give greetings to the congregations where Adib ministered.

'I was very timid,' Yolanda remembers. 'Often they would introduce me in church services as the wife of the evangelist and ask me to say a few words. I would only say, "God bless you," and sit down. Even though I didn't say much, I was always interceding for my husband, because I felt that was my ministry.'

Priscilla recalls that these years were especially hard on the older children because their father was away so much. Adib must have realized this too because he settled down in Miami and opened a Christian bookshop. He was such a good businessman that it frightened Yolanda and she prayed much that his 'Lebanese business sense' wouldn't deflect him from the ministry she was sure God had called him to. She almost hoped the business would fail, yet it was wonderful to have him at home instead of in California or Latin America on campaigns.

But Adib had another idea. So many Hispanic people were coming into Miami that there weren't enough daycare centres to care for the children while their mothers worked. So he opened the Childhood Development Centre, which eventually provided care for over five hundred children in three locations in Miami.

At this point Yolanda threw herself wholeheartedly into the children's ministry. She cooked and drove a bus, served as Adib's secretary and taught the children. Every day she brought her four little ones to the Centre with her. Lizzie remembers sitting in the office 'playing secretary and clacking at the typewriter' when she was just a toddler. Meeting a great need among the Spanish-speaking population, the Day Care Centre received government subsidies and the Edens were able to provide scholarships for new immigrant families. The Centre also provided their family income for the next fifteen years.

Ever an entrepreneur, Adib constantly stretched his capacities to new horizons. Over the years he started a Christian grammar school and high school, and purchased a Christian radio station which Adib Jr. eventually directed. But his greatest achievement grew out of the needs of the parents who brought their children to the Day Care Centre each day. Many of them had fled communist Cuba and were suffering the pain of separation from families and the loss of respect and position. Others from Haiti and Puerto Rico had come to the USA to escape the poverty of their homelands and were finding it difficult fitting into their adopted country. They were spiritually hungry.

As Adib and Yolanda befriended the parents of the children in the Day Care Centres they realized God had put a new burden upon their hearts. They invited parents to attend a Bible study and in 1974 formed the International Christian Community Church, the Catedral del Pueblo, with a congregation of 20 people. Over the next few years the congregation outgrew its facilities and in 1980 they purchased their first building in the suburb of Highleah. Even this was soon too small, and over the next five years they rented school buildings and halls, moving furniture and equipment every Sunday.

In 1985 the Catedral del Pueblo purchased an old roller-skating rink. The renovated rink provided seating for more than two thousand five hundred people. Adib was fast becoming one of the best known Hispanic evangelists in the country, and the church attracted to its pulpit leaders from all over the Spanish-speaking world. Sunday after Sunday new immigrants from Central and South America were welcomed to the services. At one point it was estimated the congregation was made up of people from more than 20 countries.

The church offered job placement programmes, English language classes, food and used clothing for those in need, as well as a Bible institute, 5 a.m. daily prayer times, a daily midday prayer and fasting meeting, counselling plus day care and a Christian school. Services were broadcast over Adib's radio station, and he dreamt of starting a TV programme and even a home for the elderly.

For Yolanda these were days full of responsibility. In 1983 their fifth daughter and sixth child, Rachel, was born. After a hiatus of seven years since their fourth daughter, Rebecca's, birth, this took some adjustment, especially with the constant flow of visitors. Lizzie recalls, 'We were always having people to stay. We grew up often sleeping on the couch or the floor because a guest had our bed. But I enjoyed it. It wasn't always easy but it was very nice growing up the way we did.'

While Yolanda still preferred to stay out of the limelight, Adib often asked her to sit on the platform with him. He enjoyed the peace of her presence and the knowledge that she was his constant intercessor. Yolanda did not hesitate to voice her opinions about his plans, and they shared the concerns of the church together, but she shied away from any leadership position. She was happy to visit the sick and counsel those who came to her.

In 1982 Yolanda had the opportunity to attend a School of Ministry in Miami Beach which changed the direction of her life. 'I had a new revelation of Christ. I truly saw the desire of Christ to live in us. I sensed a direct call to be not only a helper to my husband, but something more,' says Yolanda. 'No sooner had I shared this with Adib than he said to me, "You need to begin to preach." '

When Adib suggested that Yolanda begin teaching a Bible study she resisted, feeling inferior and out of place. But he persisted and she began leading the daily prayer and fasting service and soon shared a radio programme with him. 'But I avoided the platform,' she says. 'For me, that was my husband's responsibility, and I was content interceding for him.'

By 1987 the church had grown to fifteen hundred members. The whole family had thrown themselves into the life of the church in one way or another. Adib, Jr. directed the radio station which broadcast the morning services; Priscilla, a gifted pianist and vocalist, directed music and worship. The family was busy and happy enjoying the constant interaction with Christian leaders as Miami became the Hispanic crossroads of the USA. They took raucous, fun-filled holidays together when Adib and Yolanda managed to relax and leave their heavy responsibilities behind.

Yolanda did her best to maintain Adib's blood sugar level since he'd been diagnosed as diabetic, and gave him his insulin injection every morning. But he blithely disregarded the dangers, and enjoyed nothing more than strong Cuban coffee in the Cuban cafes and restaurants in the neighbourhood of the church.

Thus in May 1990 when he began feeling weak and ill, he refused to consider it as anything serious, even though the family saw him deteriorating quickly. 'For a whole week we knew there was something wrong with him,' Priscilla recalls, 'but we couldn't get him to go to the hospital.'

When they finally took him to the hospital that Saturday, the doctors said that he had suffered a massive heart attack, the pain camouflaged by his diabetic condition. Stunned, Yolanda heard the doctors tell her that his heart was so badly damaged, it was functioning at only 16 percent capacity. A heart transplant was out of the question. They told her he had only ten months to live at the most.

While Adib recuperated at home, Yolanda's responsibilities at the church grew. In their hearts they both believed that God would miraculously heal Adib, and indeed as the months went by he seemed to get stronger. In fact, he began to voice to Yolanda the deepest desire of his heart – to travel as an evangelist again. Astounded she listened to his plans – she should take over the pastoring of the church so that he could be on the road!

With fourteen-year-old Rebecca and seven-year-old Rachel still heavily dependent upon her, and the care of an ailing husband who didn't seem to realize how precarious his health really was, Yolanda had her hands more than full at home. Yet she stepped into many situations at the church that needed her input during Adib's convalescence. The idea of pastoring this growing megalith seemed preposterous.

Yet Adib persisted and after a few months called the elders together to propose that Yolanda be appointed as his successor. The church leaders had seen her spiritual growth and leadership potential develop over the years, and recognized the wisdom of Adib's request. Adib had often referred to himself and Yolanda as a leadership team. Perhaps some elders recognized that Adib's time with them would be short. The board agreed to Adib's request and drew up a formal document naming Yolanda as his successor.

August 26, 1990 was to be the big day. Adib and Yolanda planned to preach together in the Sunday morning service – her first message to the whole congregation. It was also their 29th wedding anniversary and the women of the church planned a celebration with refreshments following the service.

Yolanda was understandably nervous, but comforted by the fact that Adib would be standing right beside her. But it was not to be. On the Saturday morning Adib suffered another massive heart attack. The whole family gathered at the hospital to hear the doctor's ominous words, 'He's not going to make it.'

Yolanda didn't want to leave Adib's side; she felt in her spirit that God was telling her he would die. But Adib urged her, 'Go Mama, the church needs you – the people need you.' Yolanda couldn't think about going to church or participating in the service that had been planned with such enthusiasm and joy. Yet in the night God wakened her to confirm that she should go to church the next morning and share with the congregation words of encouragement.

As she took the platform, she could see the sorrow and shock in everyone's eyes. They loved Adib almost as much as she did. She did her best to share how God was dealing with her, and to encourage their hearts. As she finished speaking the elders surrounded her on the platform to pray for her.

To the doctors' surprise, Adib seemed to rally the following week, though he remained in intensive care. The following Sunday Lizzie and Yolie stayed with him as Yolanda returned to preach a second time. Adib listened to the live radio broadcast, his eyes beaming, 'That's your mom – she's preaching.' he whispered. When she returned to the hospital he confirmed her calling, 'The staff is already in your hand.'

Adib wanted more than anything else to officiate at Yolanda's ordination. Even in his weakened condition, he planned every detail. Omar Cabrera, a well-known pastor from Argentina would be holding a crusade in the church in the last week of September, so Adib asked him to preach along with a visiting pastor from Puerto Rico and Panama. As an object lesson he arranged for a live sheep to be brought down the aisle, representing the need for a shepherd – the pastor.

On September 28, 1990, Adib saw his dream come true. Even though he was suffering from pleurisy and so weak that he had to have an oxygen cylinder and be supported by one of the other pastors, he was able to stand before the congregation to present Yolanda as a candidate for ordination. There was not a dry eye in the audience, as they realized that this was probably the last time their beloved leader would stand before them. It was particularly hard since it was also his 50th birthday. But as he passed the baton to his precious partner and soul-mate, they committed themselves to uphold her and pray for her in the difficult days ahead.

Yolanda felt stunned through all the proceedings. 'Better than anyone else, I was aware of my limitations,' she says. 'Even though my husband taught me how to be a teacher, I was definitely not developed as a leader.'

Even more she wanted confirmation from God himself, that he had called her to minister, and that it wasn't just Adib's idea because 'there wasn't anyone else.' Sometime earlier she had taken a three-day retreat on Key West to seek God's direction. She told the Lord, 'I want to be sure that it was you who called me.'

As she studied the Scriptures God brought her to the passage about Moses' call to the ministry and how God had become angry because Moses refused, saying he wasn't capable. But God told Moses that he would provide and lead if Moses simply obeyed. Yolanda recalls, 'God said to me, "I want you like that. You aren't going to do it: I am going to do it." ' And Yolanda responded 'If you are going to do it, then here I am.'

God then gave her the promise he gave to Joshua after Moses' death, 'As I was with Moses, so I will be with you.' Yolanda clung to this promise as a clear revelation from God that if she had to take Adib's mantle, God would be with her.

With Adib back in hospital, now suffering from kidney failure, Yolanda kept vigil beside his bed. She knew he would soon leave her, but she hardly dared think of the responsibility that would fall on her shoulders. Even over these last weeks, despite his weakness Adib made sure that the church schedule was laid out for the following year. He still talked of his dreams – a television station, a Christian Hispanic university, a home for the elderly.

On Friday evening November 9, 1990, he asked Yolanda to read the Bible to him. She struggled to retain her composure, for somehow she knew this would be the last time .

Softly she read: ' "My thoughts are not your thoughts neither are your ways my ways," . . . declares the Lord. 'As the heavens are higher than the earth, so are my ways higher than your ways, and my thoughts than your thoughts" ' (Is. 55:8,9).

She was back in the hospital the next morning when the nurse came to take him for his dialysis. Quietly weeping alone in the room she heard 'Code Blue! Code Blue,' and knew Adib had made his heavenly journey.

In the weeks following Adib's funeral, three different pastors filled the pulpit at Catedral del Pueblo. Without knowing how God had confirmed his call to Yolanda, or what the others had spoken about, each one spoke on God's call to Moses, giving her even greater assurance that she had heard his directions correctly.

A month later Yolanda stood before the congregation as their pastor. Who could fathom the grief that welled up within her as she stood behind the pulpit where her husband had delivered such powerful evangelistic sermons? She stood almost lost on the huge platform which stretched from one side of the old skating rink to the other, a grandmother figure – short and a little overweight – simply dressed in a dark suit and sensible shoes with a string of pearls around her neck. The reddish-brown hair casually combed back framed her pale face. Only those sitting near the front could see the deep anguish in her dark eyes. No one could see the heavy burden pressing on her heart.

To have lost a beloved husband in the prime of life; to be left with a seven-year-old and a fourteen-year-old daughter at home and another in college; to have the care of a ninety-year-old father-in-law living with her and an elderly mother in a nursing home would be enough for most people. But before her lay one of the heaviest responsibilities thrust upon any woman – a vibrant, needy group of people who were looking to her as their shepherd and leader.

'As I was with Moses, so I will be with you,' the Holy Spirit reminded her. There was no question now that he had called her. She would need all the help she could get in the months ahead.

Adib's business acumen had enabled him to juggle all the branches of the church within a very loose organizational structure. But on the day of his funeral his faithful secretary broke her leg and Yolanda found herself administrator as well as pastor. Every day she wearily carried her briefcase bulging with papers back and forth between church and home. Lizzie finally left her job to relieve her. 'I really felt the Lord calling me to come and help my mom,' she says. 'I needed to be here. She lacked a lot of the business sense my dad had.'

In spite of her confidence in God's call, and the agreement the elders had made with Adib about his successor, the transition was not easy. Priscilla clearly remembers how men in the church tried to take over. 'Problems came up,' she recalls. 'From day one after my father died there were men who were trying to minimize her and take over. Because she didn't know what to do; because she'd gone through grief and was left with this church and the schools and the radio station, there were men who tried [to take the leadership]. It was not normal for a woman to be a pastor in a Hispanic community. I had never known a woman pastor either.'

A lot of people left the church. They felt Yolanda didn't fit her husband's shoes, didn't have his charisma – after all she was just the pastor's wife! Some said she wasn't knowledgeable enough or well enough trained. And many resisted the idea of a woman pastor. But Yolanda persisted, 'I was sure in my heart that God had spoken to me,' she says. 'God makes no exceptions of people – neither Jew nor Greek, slave nor free, male nor female' (Gal. 3:28).

The first time she attended the association of Hispanic pastors of Greater Miami, she sensed their coldness and rejection. Over the years many of the pastors had feared and resented Adib's powerful personality and influence. Now instead they saw a humble woman who listened quietly and seemed to move above the gossip and criticism swirling behind her back.

Yolanda continued to attend the pastors' meeting in spite of their rejection. She longed to see the unity of the body of Christ grow and she didn't want to quit just because of their attitudes. Gradually the other pastors began to appreciate her spirit and her contributions. After the first year they put her on one of their committees. In 1995 Yolanda was appointed vice-president of the association of Hispanic Pastors of Greater Miami and wields a great deal of influence in bringing churches together.

The more public rejection by radio pastors cut her deeply. Some said, 'The church won't last six months without a male pastor.' While this hurt, she determined not to use her own weekly radio programme to hit back. When pastors confront her face to face about her role she simply tells them, 'It's not my fault God called me.' And in time some of these pastors have become her greatest allies.

Gradually Yolanda began functioning more and more in her pastoral role, serving communion, officiating at weddings, occasionally baptizing, though she isn't very comfortable doing that. She also made changes in the board of elders. As several elders left the church she appointed women so that men and women are equally represented. The church now has a staff of fifteen, including a Panamanian worship director and a Korean youth pastor. The prediction that the church would fold proved false. By 1995 Catedral del Pueblo, with two thousand three hundred members, is one of the largest Hispanic churches in the United States.

Of course her leadership style differs drastically from Adib's. While he was primarily an evangelist, Yolanda is a teacher and discipler. Adib never lost his vision for new outreach and developments, even on his deathbed. Yolanda has a pastor's heart. She thinks nothing of visiting a sick or troubled church-member, sitting into the small hours to comfort and counsel.

Yolanda realizes that it's necessary to make difficult decisions. This hasn't been easy for her, but now that she is in a leadership position she knows she must be stronger. She is also broadening her horizons, as Adib did. He read avidly and kept up with what was happening in the world. Yolanda's interest in reaching out to the world for God has put missions high on her list of priorities.

Her eyes sparkle and she can hardly keep a smile from her face as she talks about the couple the church has sent to Honduras, and the church they have helped to build. Other missionaries have gone from the church to Spain, Brazil, Guatemala. The church held its first missionary conference in May 1996, and Yolanda prays this will be the beginning of a greater involvement in fulfilling the Great Commission. She serves on the committee of the Hispanic Missionary Congress of North America (COMHINA) which has sponsored major united missions thrusts in Miami. Because of its facilities Catedral del Pueblo often hosts these joint efforts.

Catedral del Pueblo has not only accepted her leadership but it is obvious to a visitor that she is much loved and respected. When the elders gather around her before the worship service, the prayers reflect their confidence that God has anointed this woman to present the word of God to her people. The worship service is lively and lengthy, led by a black Panamanian brother who has the ability to focus on the presence and power of the Holy Spirit in the service. Even the parakeets who have their home in the sanctuary join in the songs of praise.

When Yolanda finally gets up to speak she carries a large Bible – and it is the word of God she preaches. Her message is clear and to the point. Speaking on Phillipians 1:27 she reminds her people that the damage done by bad testimonies is often irrevocable. People don't want to hear the gospel because we are the blockage. The morning she preached that discipleship message, a young man came forward to give his life to Christ at her invitation, and many went to the prayer room for counselling and prayer.

Through the difficult transition from pastor's wife to pastor, Yolanda's major concern was how her children would cope. It was not easy for them either for they had grown up under the dynamic leadership of their father. Priscilla admits, 'I can't lie, the first few years were hard. I think when my dad died I was in deep denial, and their leadership styles were so different.' But she continued to serve in the church music programme and now helps part-time in the office.

It seems the change was most difficult for the older three, perhaps because they had grown to adulthood working under and with their father. Adib Jr., who now owns the radio station, drew back from his mother, especially after she had to stop broadcasting over his station. But the girls seemed to be more supportive – each in her own way. Rebecca, studying at Pensacola Christian College, didn't tell her friends that her mother was a pastor. She didn't want to be the subject of ridicule. On the other hand, Lizzie, who has since become the church administrator, admits, 'We're all very proud of her. We are in awe as we see what God has done with her. She was always the virtuous woman the Bible talks about, and I guess that is why the Lord has lifted her up because she never looked for position or glory.' Rachel, who was only seven when her father died, struggles like all preacher's kids under the magnifying glass of the congregation. A teenager today, she is very conscious of what her friends say and think. But she shyly admits, 'If they found out [that my mom is a pastor], I'd tell them that I'm real proud of her.'

And I have a feeling that Adib, watching from his heavenly mansion, is too!

Nine

Leadership Becomes Her –
Judy Mbugua, Kenya

*For the horses of Pharaoh with his chariots and his horsemen went into the sea, and
the Lord brought back the waters of the sea on them; but the sons of Israel walked
on dry land through the midst of the sea. And Miriam the prophetess, Aaron's sister,
took the timbrel in her hand, and all the women went out after her with timbrels and
with dancing. And Miriam answered them, 'Sing to the Lord, for He is highly
exalted; the horse and his rider He has hurled into the sea'*

Exodus 15: 19–21. (NASB)

I sent Moses to lead you, also Aaron and Miriam.

Micah 6:4

Calm and self-assured Judy Mbugua stood behind the six foot long pulpit of
the largest Presbyterian church in the world. She was later told that she was
the first woman to preach from that pulpit. Her warm brown skin contrasted
with the white, embroidered, floor-length gown and cape, designed and made
for her back home in Nairobi, and carefully chosen for this occasion. But her
appearance was far from her thoughts as she gazed into the colourful sea of
faces filling the cavernous sanctuary.

When asked to give the plenary address for the AD2000 Women's Track
during the Global Congress on World Evangelism in Korea in May 1995, her
biggest concern was what she could say to the four thousand delegates to help
them realize the unused potential of the women in churches around the world.
Even during the conference she'd been writing and rewriting the message she had
prepared. But now she was at peace. God had given her the word she was to share.

Referring to the passage in Mark 11 where Jesus told his disciples he needed
transport to ride into Jerusalem, she urged, 'Every donkey qualified to carry
someone should be out in the field and not tied up! This donkey was not
productive because it was tied.'

Judy likened the plight of women around the world to donkeys – haltered,
restricted and unable to move freely to serve the King of Kings. 'If Jesus

chooses to use women, often seen as lowly and humble as a colt, no one should continue to tie them and force them to be unproductive. He needs every available resource to be released.'

'Untie the donkeys and release them into His service,' she pleaded with the world leaders listening to her entranced. The humorous analogy struck home and she moved off the platform to thunderous applause. For the rest of the conference people talked about 'untying the donkeys.' Judy hoped and prayed it would become reality.

Judy knew about donkeys – tough little beasts of burden that could carry heavy loads for hours. She'd seen them patiently plodding along so loaded it seemed their backs would break, and she'd also seen them baulk in the hot African sun when no amount of cajoling or beating could make them move.

Growing up in rural Kenya Judy saw women just so overburdened. Working from sunrise to sunset in the fields, often with babies on their backs and others in their wombs; walking miles to gather firewood; gracefully balancing heavy pots of water on their heads as they carried them across the fields to their huts. Even today some rural Kenyan women walk three hours a day to fetch water, putting in a thirteen to fourteen hour work day.

Her father, Mwalimu Hosea, had a stroke of good luck when colonial white farmers in his district insisted that some of the Kikuyu boys, herding cattle on the lush green hills, should go to school. Kikuyu boys had always herded cattle and the local clan leaders saw no need to disrupt their traditions so the boys could learn the 'white man's propaganda'. But the British settlers were determined to educate the 'natives' working on their farms and they simply abducted some of the boys and forced them to go to school.

Mwalimu couldn't comprehend the good fortune that befell him the day he was rounded up to attend school. He was later sent to one of the most the prestigious high schools in Kenya. He became a teacher and then a school inspector in the Limuru district in eastern Kenya. Their home compound in Ngecha was a cut above the average Kikuyu homes. In fact Mwalimu was one of the first men in his district to own a car.

Judy remembers a ride in that car when she was nine years old. She'd been asked to be a flower girl at a wedding and needed a pair of shoes. Her father took her to neighbouring villages calling out, 'Does anyone have a pair of shoes we could borrow?' Someone finally offered a pair of boy's shoes, several sizes too large, which had to be stuffed with paper so she could keep them on her feet. Never having worn shoes before, Judy struggled the whole day of the wedding to walk normally – but she was so proud!

When she was older she asked her father, 'Why didn't you just take me to town to buy shoes?'

Her father responded that during the 'emergency' unnecessary traveling wasn't allowed – and certainly they wouldn't have been given a permit to go to buy a pair of shoes for a little girl.

The British colonial government declared a state of emergency in Kenya in 1953 as the 'Mau-Mau' terrorists led by Jomo Kenyatta organized an insurrection against the white settlers. The spirit of independence was beginning to sweep across Africa. To join the Mau Mau one had to take a blood oath, drinking blood and eating raw meat. Frustrated and bitter over many years of domination and loss of dignity, the Mau Mau or 'Hidden Ones,' mainly from the Kikuyu tribe, slipped into rural farm homes slaughtering whole families in their beds. Servants betrayed the masters and mistresses for whom they worked in the city by arranging for terrorists to enter and kill.

Local Mau Mau leaders began putting pressure on Judy's father to take the oath. As a Christian he did not believe this was right. The Mau Maus continued to pressure him, threatening the family. In desperation Mwalimu arranged to sleep at the local government post while the family hid outside in the maize fields at night. Judy remembers how they feared their baby sister's cries would give away their location.

Though Judy was then just a small child, the memories of atrocities on both sides are still vivid. 'I saw a man said to be a Mau-Mau gangster tied to a colonial government vehicle driven at full speed. The man died a miserable death with his body torn to pieces as he hit the stones on the rough road,' she recalls. 'Another time I saw a woman who had been stripped naked and whipped severely for being late getting to her house after the 6 p.m. curfew.'

She was often reminded of the danger her father was in when she heard of human heads hung from trees by the Mau-Mau to remind people what happened to government sympathizers. However by late 1953 the British had imprisoned Kenyatta, later exiling him until he returned as the first president of independent Kenya in 1963.

During these years Judy knew little of the developments in her nation. She grew up in a small village as the sixth in a family of nine children with parents who loved her and could provide the basic necessities of life. She attended Sunday School every week and could rattle off her testimony like a 'pro' – but knows now it was a shallow exhibition without any reality. She just loved being put up on a table in front of the church so all could see her when she repented of a list of sins. 'I used to steal sugar; I used to tell lies. Now Jesus has come into my heart . . . I have come completely clean.'

Her parents faithfully took the family to church every Sunday. At home she learned to pray, but Christianity was lived out in legalistic do's and don'ts. 'My daddy told us it was wrong to wear trousers or short skirts or to plait our hair or wear earrings,' she says. She recalls a day when she had defiantly braided her hair, then covered her head with a scarf so her father wouldn't see it. 'However, that turned out to be my unlucky day,' she remembers. 'As I bent down to sweep the floor my headscarf fell off just as Dad came through the room. I think he realized that if he said anything I would collapse . . . his look was enough to destroy my mischievous spirit.'

One of the benefits of her father's education was his desire to see all his children educated. 'In my family there was no gender discrimination – sons and daughters got equal opportunity,' says Judy.

So in January, 1954 Mwalimu entered his sixth child, Judy, in school. Though Judy, now seven years of age, was quick to learn, she hated the discipline of getting up in the morning and walking barefoot through the rough grass. 'I was in trouble many times for getting to school late.'

Judy was an apt student and especially loved arithmetic and science. She completed intermediate school in 1961 near the top of her class and fully expected a place in one of the more prestigious high schools. For some reason this did not happen, and in her disappointment and resentment, Judy dropped out of school to take a teaching job in Limuru. Little did she know that this detour would cost her heavily in the years ahead.

At sixteen Judy was a romantic and devoured any love story she could lay her hands on. A hit love song was her favourite:

> She was only sixteen
> Only sixteen and I loved her so
> She was too young to fall in love,
> And I was too young to know.

One day she took her class out on a field trip, but instead of going to the gardens for nature study, they ended up at the railway station. The young station master filling in for the regular one was the epitome of Judy's romantic dreams – tall, handsome, charming – and interested in her. While the children asked questions about trains and scampered around the station as children do, the young man introduced himself as Richard Mbugua. The chemistry between them was electric and before she gathered the children together to leave, they had arranged to meet again.

Judy admits now it was 'love at first sight'. The relationship developed rapidly as Richard visited her school as often as he could. When Judy discovered she was pregnant she had mixed emotions. She had been taught that sex outside marriage was wrong; she knew that her parents and church would be disappointed and condemning. In fact, her family had been warning her about this relationship with a man seven years older than herself. But she consoled herself that at least they would now have to allow her to get married.

But this was not the case. Instead her father continued to urge her to go back to school, even after the baby was born. He saw her potential and realized that once she was married it would be virtually impossible for her to study. So her parents denied their permission and blessing.

Judy and Richard could not stop seeing each other however. They loved each other and their new daughter deeply. Judy continued to live at home, hoping that her family would change their minds. But when their second child was born, Judy and Richard took matters into their own hands. They decided that she would go and live with Richard in Muranga where he was now station master. Though they paid no dowry, and did not have the feasts at the homes of both parents that generally accompany a traditional African wedding, in Judy's and Richard's eyes they were now married.

Happy as they were together, they both missed the affirmation and security of the extended family that binds together so many African marriages. Judy's parents were still sceptical of Richard's ability to care for her, and Richard's mother was not sure that a girl from a well-to-do family would settle down in this kind of marriage.

In 1965 when Judy was heavily pregnant with her third child she received word that her father had suffered a heart attack and was very ill. Though her delivery date was close, she felt she must go home and see him once more. The rift between them hurt her deeply for she loved her father very much, and as the eldest daughter of her mother and father (her father's first wife had died leaving four small children) they had been very close.

The bus ride to Nakuru was uneventful and the visit joyous. Her father seemed much improved, and in spite of the doctor's dire predictions, lived to be eighty-six. Judy's parents could see that she was thriving under Richard's love and care, and seemed to accept the marriage. They urged her to take back vegetables and grain from their farm, and she took as much as she could, even though she had her year-old son with her.

Going back to Muranga Judy had to pass Kabete, Richard's family home. She had met his family once, but had never been to their place. She decided to stop and leave some of the home-grown vegetables and grain her family had pressed upon her, as a conciliatory gesture. She was sure this would please Richard.

Exhausted, Judy struggled off the bus, with one child in her arms and another in her womb. She knew she couldn't carry the bulky load of produce on her head the two kilometres to her mother-in-law's house, and so found someone to watch over her things and began the long walk in the hot sun. Fortunately she found her mother-in-law at home. All the other women were out working in the fields. Leaving baby Alex with one of the children, she and her mother-in-law trudged back through the heat to pick up the things she'd left behind.

Just as she lifted one bag to balance it on her head, a sharp pain took her breath away. This couldn't be the baby yet! She sat to rest for a moment, hoping it was just a strain from the long ride. But another pain attacked, and she knew she was in labour. Her mother-in-law urged her to get up and head for home, ignoring Judy's plea that she be taken to the hospital. After all, most rural babies were born at home, and she saw no reason why this newest grandchild should not be.

In agony Judy retraced her steps to her in-laws' home stopping to rest as each pain convulsed her. By the time they arrived at the farm, Judy was desperate. She lay down in the shade of a large tree, the pains gripping her with such intensity that she pulled grass out by the roots. It seemed like hours as she lay there alone, and when finally her mother-in-law reappeared, she seemed unperturbed by Judy's condition. Older Kenyan women have served as village midwives for centuries and take labour in their stride. When Judy asked her to get a car to take her to the hospital, her mother-in-law indicated she would be all right there. It wasn't until Richard's sister arrived some time later asking, 'What's going on here?' that the family rallied with a sense of urgency. 'What if she dies here because we didn't send her to the hospital?' the sister asked.

Someone sent for a car, and when it arrived several tried to help Judy get in. Deranged by pain and angered by what she felt was callous treatment, Judy shook them off and got into the back seat on her own. Fortunately her mother-in-law followed her into the car since five minutes into the drive to the hospital the baby 'fell' and her midwifery experience was all that was needed to complete the job.

Judy admits it was many years before she could forgive her mother-in-law's treatment of her. But before she died, they had accepted each other and become good friends.

Judy's romantic dreams were shattered once she began taking care of Richard and the babies which followed one after another. She knew nothing about handling money; her parents had been able to provide everything she needed while she lived at home. But now she had to stretch Richard's small salary – and by the middle of the month the money was gone. Richard struggled to ensure that his family had food on the table, but it strained their relationship. 'He felt I was careless and I felt he was uncaring,' Judy says.

Simple household tasks became an obstacle course. In her own home Judy had not had to take much responsibility for there was always a helper in the house to do this. Just ironing her husband's white trousers became a challenge. The first time she tried she ironed the folds on the side instead of the sharp creases down the front Richard demanded. Fortunately he burst into laughter when he saw her effort and showed her how to do it correctly.

Judy was only twenty when her fourth baby was born. She'd never had to manage by herself before. She spent days crying, wondering 'How are we going to raise these children with my husband's salary?' She confesses, 'I even wished I'd listened to my parents and waited until I finished school.' Finally she and Richard came to the conclusion that Judy should go back to school to gain skills so she could take a job. She would return to live at his home place in Katebe. From there she could travel into Nairobi, eight miles beyond, for secretarial training.

This was no easy decision. It meant that Richard had to withdraw all his life savings to put up a two-bedroom wooden house on the family property. It had no running water but was adequate for Judy and the children. The hardest part for her was returning to live at Kabete where she still did not feel welcomed as a daughter-in-law. She determined she would stay only long enough to complete her training.

In July 1967 Richard put his little family on the bus for Kabete, and was alone once again. For Judy, it was the first time she had ever lived alone without husband or parents. Nights were frightening. One night a thief pushed a stick through the window and tried to manoeuvre her sewing machine within reach. Judy and the children shouted until a neighbour came to frighten the thief away. These experiences unnerved her, but Judy was resolved to accomplish what she had come for.

She enrolled in a morning secretarial course in Nairobi and left the children in the care of a young girl she had hired to look after them. Her inability to handle money continued to plague her, and by the middle of the month she no longer had bus fare to go into town and missed many classes. At the end of the third month when Richard came to see her, he found a weeping, frustrated wife. Coping with four children alone, two of them in diapers, while expecting a fifth did not make it easier. She was so tired by the evening when the children were finally asleep that she would put her feet in a bucket of cold water to keep herself awake in order to study.

She wept as she told him how she had had to take two of the children to the hospital when they were seriously ill with measles. She could not manage both of them on the bus when she could barely get herself there. 'In the end I took one to a neighbour about half a mile away, carrying one on my back and the other on my shoulders. Then I took one to hospital and came back for the other later,' she explained.

Richard recognized that she was at the end of her tether. He suggested that instead of going into town she purchase a typewriter and manual and teach herself how to type. Judy threw herself into this with vigour. 'All this suffering enhanced my resolve to be somebody, and I knew the way out was by getting more education and professional training, which I did with determination,' she writes in her memoirs.

But in 1967 a new force erupted in Judy's life. She had been attending the local church, and was always ready to confess and pray, but without any sense of assurance of salvation or spiritual reality in her life. During an evangelistic campaign a visiting evangelist spoke on Ephesians 5:14, 'Awake, sleeper, and arise from the dead, and Christ will shine on you.' (NASB)

The preacher's words pierced her heart as she listened to him speaking as if to her, 'If your expectations have not been fulfilled; your dreams not realized; your plans not met; the shell of your body could be moving but inside you are dead.' He went on to say, 'Only Jesus can fulfil your life and give you peace by establishing his plan in you.'

Judy felt the Spirit of God tugging at her heart, but she knew that Richard would not want a 'saved' wife and she could well lose him. So she decided not to be saved. The next night the call was even stronger. She started to go forward and something whispered, 'Go ahead, but that is the end of your marriage.'

She returned the third night and became so convicted of her need of Jesus that she said to herself, 'Husband or no husband, I would rather have the light of Jesus shining on me than anything else.' Walking home that night looking up into the starry skies she prayed, 'Oh God take me home to heaven before I fall back into sin. Lord, I feel so clean, so fresh. Please take me home to you now.'

Instead God began slowly but inexorably to unfold the plan he had had for her all along.

Her first step was to draft a letter to Richard trying to explain what had happened in her life, and apologizing for any inconvenience this might cause him. She wrote, 'I hope you will not find it impossible to stay married to a "saved" person.'

When his letter finally came, she opened it fearfully, dreading his response. Instead she read, 'I do not mind your getting "saved" as long as you keep it private.' Judy was so happy she started telling everyone she met how happy she was and why.

Her greatest joy now was to read the Bible and pray with her children. She loved to tell them of answered prayers. Now that she was part of the family of God, many experiences in the life of her parents took on new meaning, and she realized that God had answered many prayers for them. All her children came to know and accept the Lord as Saviour at an early age.

In the little church she attended, however, she sensed a strain between herself and the older women. When she hugged them in greeting, they would pull back. One of them finally told her that her plaited hair offended them. Torn between disappointing her husband, who always wanted her to look attractive and did not want her to be a fanatic, and offending her new sisters in Christ, she sadly cut off her hair. Since then Judy has discovered that 1 Peter 3:3 ('Your beauty should not come from outward adornment such as braided hair') refers to what takes priority in a Christian's life rather than the actual plaiting of hair and wearing of jewellery, and she encourages women to look beautiful for Jesus.

Now more than ever Judy wanted to formalize their marriage. Her parents agreed to her request, and in 1969 Richard and Judy were married in church. She wore a lovely pink dress in the church, but for her wedding pictures she wore the traditional white gown which had always been her dream. What they had committed to each other privately almost seven years earlier was now public and permanent before God and man.

Judy passed her typing exam in 1970 and started working in an insurance office in Nairobi. Not satisfied with the meagre salary she was receiving, she continued studying. She earned several certificates in shorthand and finally was able to take it at a speed of 180 words per minute. As her speed in typing and shorthand increased, so did her upward movement in the company. She was soon working for a senior official in the Ministry of Finance. She will never forget the day she picked up the phone in one of the offices and a voice said, 'This is Jomo [Kenyatta], can I speak to Mheshimiwa?' Judy continued studying while working, taking pre-university courses and management training. In 1977 she resigned from the Ministry of Finance and joined an insurance company. She received generous salary increments. It was during this time that she learned the importance and value of tithing – a lesson she has never forgotten.

By 1984 Judy had risen to the top of her profession. A news article described her appointment as the company's administrative officer with three hundred employees. 'How many women do we know in a number of professions who were given a small opening and have gone ahead and used it advantageously and are now top-notch professionals in a number of occupations? Judith Mbugua is such a woman.'

Judy enjoyed the use of a company car, generous leave and ample secretarial help. She even spent a month in England and Scotland as the guest of her boss's mother and later made a visit to Israel. By this time Richard had also done further training and was working in the civil service. They had built their own home on the outskirts of Nairobi and were able to send their children to the best schools.

Judy's daughter, Njeri, who studied for her PhD in the USA, would later write, 'While other Kenyan families devoted their meagre incomes to the exclusive education of their sons, my parents, despite financial difficulties, educated all five of us. In retrospect, I know this was very difficult for them. I am indebted to them for going against my country's norms and valuing me highly – reflected in their availing me equal access to education as my brothers. My mother's influence built in me a reliance on God, self-confidence, and personal direction. I know I have come this far in my education due to the influence of my mother.'

The family was now attending the Nairobi Pentecostal Church, one of the largest churches in Nairobi, where Judy had found the teaching on the Holy Spirit especially meaningful. Even though Richard attended the Sunday services with her, he did not get involved in other church activities. Judy found that in attending alone she did not fit in the married couples class, or the widows group or the singles. Realizing there were other women in the church with unsaved husbands she invited a group of them to her home. There were twenty-five women at their first meeting in February, 1980, and the fellowship grew and grew. Six months later they numbered a hundred and within a year two hundred women were gathering once a month to pray for their families and learn how to be better wives and mothers. Called Homecare Fellowship, the group outgrew every home available. They even put up a tent – and finally Judy asked her church if they could use the sanctuary. Women came from many churches around the city; such was the longing to see husbands and children become Christians that as many as a thousand women came together.

Over the next few years Judy experienced a stirring in her heart to full-time ministry. Even though she still loved the responsibility and prestige of her job, she was finding it difficult to do both. People came to her office for counselling and phoned her about plans and she was often travelling.

Opportunities to participate in international conferences began to come to her. At first her boss willingly gave her time off to attend Haggai Institute in Singapore and the Women's Aglow conference in the United States, but after several years he told her she would have to cut back on her 'religious involvement' during work time.

Judy approached the church board about joining the staff to undertake women's ministry. Their response was devastating. One reason given for their refusal was that funds were not available. But Judy was deeply hurt to hear them say that she should be spending more time with her family and that she should wait until her husband was saved before taking on a full-time ministry. Some even warned that the rapid growth of the Fellowship was no indication of her calling. They said, 'Things that grow so fast also break very fast.'

'I cried a lot after that meeting and asked the Lord to remove the burden since nobody seemed to understand me,' Judy explains.

The vibrant growth of Home Fellowship could not be stopped however. Women's lives were changed; husbands were accepting Christ.

The entry for August 13, 1985 in Judy's diary reads: 'I have made a final decision to follow the Lord wherever He leads. I have decided to trust him for daily bread. I am waiting for his directions for full time, but my mind is finally settled.'

The need to expand Home Fellowship had precipitated that decision. With women coming from churches all over the city, Judy saw that they were not able fully to participate in Home Fellowship's leadership because it was so closely connected with her church. Women in other cities were asking to start groups. It became very clear that the only way Home Fellowship could meet these needs was to register as a separate, interdenominational organization.

But this decision was to cost Judy pain and misunderstanding. When the registration was miraculously granted, even though government policy was against any more new religious organizations, the accusations and misunderstandings came pouring over Judy like an avalanche. The church leaders felt betrayed that she was now taking this powerful ministry out of their control. Some of her friends believed she was doing this for personal gain. In fact, rumours circulated that she'd gone to the United States to raise money for a car for herself. She could not seem to stem the rumours and finally resigned.

These were the most heartbreaking times in her life. So many of her best friends did not accept that she was guiltless. How grateful she was for Richard's and the children's support during these painful days. She recalls how her oldest daughter Susan challenged her to determine who had called her. 'If you are called by God then [you know that] he who called you is faithful and will supply.' But even though the family defended and supported her, they also encouraged her not to resign her job.

As the criticisms and rumours continued, Judy received messages from friends all over the world, who though they did not know her exact situation, gave her encouraging words from the Lord. In spite of the lack of confidence of her church leaders, God showed her she should not leave the church but continue to support it. The church asked her to wait for six months before participating in this newly-registered ministry, now called Homecare Fellowship and she complied. This submission helped heal the rift.

But on May 17, 1987 the question of whether she should take up the full-time ministry was still not resolved. She wrote in her diary, 'I read this message in my devotions: 'If we are to obey God's call, we must make sure that we are not overly influenced by statements and criticisms of other people. We must develop a strong character so that, once we have made a decision in the light of the revelation of God, we will not easily be swayed away from our goal by what people say." '

'I shared with a church leader that I had definitely decided to resign and do full-time ministry with Homecare. By this time people had restored confidence in me. I had decided I would not leave my church but would continue serving there should need arise. I was getting "peace." '

With this decision God began to set things into motion that would forever change Judy's life and ministry. It all started with a simple invitation by Dr. Tokumboh Adeyemo, leader of the Association of Evangelicals in Africa and Madagascar (AEAM) to the General Assembly in Zambia in August 1987. At first she decided to decline; she'd taken all her leave and would have to go without pay. But for some reason she felt she should go and asked for unpaid time off. Her long-suffering boss seemed to be a tool in God's hands, for no one else would have allowed an employee so much freedom and outside distraction.

At the meeting in Zambia Judy found twenty-six key women leaders from all over the continent who had been brought together to discuss the need of a women's commission to deal with women's issues in Africa. The AEAM had never had such a commission. But the leaders realized that women made up the majority of the evangelical congregations in Africa, they were the most committed and active members, and they had been largely ignored and marginalized. It was time for a change.

For a week the women met together without male input or interference to wrangle over the issues that needed to be dealt with, and how the church could best help them. Early in their discussions they chose Judy as chairperson. In her heart Judy felt inadequate when she looked at the educated leadership calibre of these women. She vehemently refused, but finally under duress agreed to serve, 'only while in Zambia.'

The meetings were productive. The new women's commission would be called the Pan-Africa Christian Women's Association – PACWA as it is best known today. The theme – 'Our time has come.' They planned to call a continental congress in 1988 – and they urged Judy to accept the chairmanship of the conference committee which would be based in Nairobi.

Not daring to take time off during the day, Judy held all the planning sessions after hours. Richard and the children, now grown up and in college or working, saw little of her. She was still determined to quit her job, but somehow couldn't force herself to write the letter. Though she was again the leader of Homecare the prospect of a full-time position didn't seem to fall into place. Perhaps the uncertainty of what 'full-time' would mean, or the convenience of resources and contacts through her office kept her from cutting the umbilical cord.

It became obvious that the conference would have to be postponed until 1989, primarily because communications across the continent were so slow. In some places it took three months for a letter to reach its destination, and faxes and phone calls were still being routed through Europe.

Money was an issue as well. Dr. Adeyemo commented to a visitor, 'This is the most gifted group of women you could find. But when it comes to fund-raising, I have to write the letters over my name, because donors won't take women seriously.' Fortunately, Dr. Adeyemo took them seriously and made every effort to help Judy's committee find the funds to help women attend the conference.

One day Dr. Adeyemo called Judy into his office and asked her to consider accepting a position with AEAM as co-ordinator of the women's commission. Her first response was a vehement 'no.' How could she lead highly educated women around the continent when she did not have university training? Dr. Adeyemo pointed out her professional training and nearly twenty years in a highly successful job in the secular marketplace. Yet she begged for time to pray and they decided that they would both seek God's leading.

By now Judy was utterly confused. She knew God had called her to full-time ministry. But WHAT ministry? She'd always thought it was Homecare but somehow that door had never opened. She had to know in what direction the Lord was leading her.

Shortly after the meeting with Dr. Adeyemo, Judy and two of her children went to a conference at Kanamai. 'I went to Kanamai with one resolve. Like Jacob of old, I cried, "Lord I will not leave unless you bless me." '

During the week she shared her dilemma with only one person, her pastor, who was also at the conference. She did not even tell him the specific issues she was dealing with, simply that she needed guidance.

One night a young woman stood up to say she had a prophecy for Judy. Tearfully she told how she had resisted giving this prophecy in public, fearing it might be wrong or might embarrass Judy. Judy herself stiffened as she listened, wondering why God would expose her life so publicly in front of her family and friends.

But the prophecy spoke to the very heart of Judy's question. Judy was to head a women's ministry. 'When the hard times come, for they will surely come, she must not be moved,' Lucy shared.

Later Lucy told her privately, 'My first reaction was, "But Lord, there is the Homecare Fellowship, and nobody will take it seriously. Even if it is another ministry, how do I know it will come to pass? Suppose it is my flesh and I am imagining all this. It will be disastrous and I will have spoken in public. Lord, please let me go and tell Judy in her room after the meeting." But the Lord said I had to speak publicly and in front.'

In spite of the initial embarrassment, Judy was deeply grateful because God in his wisdom had revealed his purpose before her family and friends. That night the pastor and leaders prayed for her and commissioned her to go to 'whatever' women's ministry the Lord wanted her to have.

The following months were a whirlwind of activity as Judy attended planning sessions and pre-PACWA meetings in preparation for the conference. On August 6, 1989 PACWA was launched at the Jomo Kenyatta Conference Centre with more than two thousand women from 42 countries. The hall was a flamboyant picture of colour and design as women from every nation arrived in their traditional dress. The air was filled with singing and clapping, and women danced joyfully in the aisles expressing the excitement of the moment. His Excellency the president Daniel Arap Moi arrived with great pomp and fanfare to open the conference. When Judy saw her picture on the front page of the newspaper the next day, standing with the president of Kenya, she began to weep. It was as though a video flashed across her mind of the pain and struggle she had gone through to get into the ministry; the heartbreak and disappointment; God's faithfulness and prophecies fulfilled.

The PACWA conference was more than celebration, for throughout the week women looked at family and social problems and how they as women could make a difference. Over the next few years as PACWA branches were formed in more than 20 countries, women seriously confronted the issues of AIDS, abuse, poverty and skills-training.

The delegates spelled out PACWA's objectives:

1. To carry the gospel light to people who are yet to be reached.
2. To stop the tide of ungodly secularism and materialism.
3. To assert the true dignity of women as found in God's word.
4. To inject into African society biblical morals and values through women who are the mothers in all societies.
5. To educate women on matters of justice, equity and socio-economic development.
6. To deliver Africa from moral decadence and ultimate collapse.
7. To foster effective co-operation of all Christian women's ministries in Africa.

Near the close of the conference the executive committee met. One of the main items on the agenda was to recommend that a woman be appointed to represent women's concerns in the AEAM office. The question was posed – where should the office be and who should be appointed?

As the women began reading through the agenda, a low rumble of laughter began filling the room. Eva Sanderson, the chairperson of the council saw the puzzled look on Judy's face. She explained, 'We're laughing because we don't need to pray about this item. We already know where the office will be and who the co-ordinator is.'

Judy was still in the dark, and felt a bit piqued. When the laughter ceased she asked, 'How did you manage to locate a co-ordinator without informing me, since I'm the chairman of the executive?'

There was another burst of laughter. When the room settled down Eva explained that everyone on the committee had already agreed wholeheartedly that Judy was the best person for the position.

In her heart Judy saw the pieces falling into place, though the very thought of leading this august body of women terrified her. She still thought that all the months of anguish and experience were preparing her for Homecare. Yet God had given every indication of his leading, and when next she met with Dr. Adeyemo she accepted the position as continental co-ordinator of PACWA.

Judy wrote in her diary, 'In October, 1989 I resigned my job and found myself in the AEAM office to take up the co-ordination of the ministry. . . Was I ready to go by faith, foregoing some of the conveniences and prospects that I had in my old job? The answer was a quick "yes." The Lord already dealt with me on that.'

In the intervening years Judy has crisscrossed not only Africa, but the world. She continues as leader of Homecare Fellowship which has now expanded to fourteen branches. She loves to tell the stories of women whose lives have been totally transformed through the touch of Homecare. Women in desperate situations often come for help – sometimes even for help they are unwilling to receive.

'Wanjiru came to us so that we could help her with money for an abortion,' Judy wrote. 'She had consulted a doctor and was told the cheapest one would cost fourteen hundred shillings. She had only eight hundred. When she came to us we explained that we do not destroy life. She was very disappointed. In the end, after much talk and argument, we agreed that we would pay her to carry the pregnancy through, and after the baby was born we would be responsible for the baby. The committee contributed sacrificially for her upkeep and two days before the baby came she accepted the Lord. She is keeping him, and has named him Paul, hoping this boy will be a preacher.'

In 1990 Luis Bush, international director of the AD2000 & Beyond Movement, approached her to serve as the chairperson of the AD2000 Women's Track. The goal of the movement – 'A church for every people and the gospel for every person by the year 2000.'

Once again Judy felt overwhelmed and inadequate, but after weeks of prayer and consultation with her leaders, and encouraged by Dr. Adeyemo, she felt that God had given her a green light. The AD2000 Women's Track now serves as the prayer and evangelism arm of PACWA, and at the same time mobilizes women from churches and organizations which may not belong to AEAM. With her greater global visibility through AD2000, PACWA and others, Judy is asked to speak in other parts of the world.

Judy has become a vocal advocate for women in ministry. In her plenary address at the PACWA conference she said, 'It is a challenge to Christians to lessen the tension between sexes, to loosen chains that have bound women in the area of ministry and simply to recognize their potential. Working together in harmony will bring glory to God. But it is also time for men to realize that we are God's latest model of creation – the model with least problems. So we are asking men to give us a chance, an opportunity to use our God-given abilities.'

Her unabashed promotion of women's dignity and abilities is a clarion call to church leaders to change attitudes and 'release the donkeys.'

Notes

1. Judy Mbugua, ed., *Our Time Has Come* (Carlisle, U.K.: Paternoster Press, 1994), 8.

Ten

Twenty Years in the Wilderness –
Juliet Thomas, India

. . . we travelled to Philippi, a Roman colony and the leading city of that district . . . On the Sabbath we went outside the city gate to the river, where we expected to find a place of prayer. We sat down and began to speak to the women who had gathered there. One of those listening was a woman name Lydia, a dealer in purple cloth from the city of Thyatira who was a worshipper of God. The Lord opened her heart to respond to Paul's message. When she and the members of her household were baptized, she invited us to her home.

Acts 16: 12–15.

Juliet Thomas deftly pleated the white and gold sari, tucking it in at the waist and draping it gracefully around the body of the slim dark-haired girl standing in front of her. How many times had she been called to 'dress the bride'. Though most Indian women wore saris, Juliet could pleat and fold the shimmering silk with special finesse and was often asked by the bride's family to 'do the honours'. But today Juliet's heart was filled with joy as she dressed her own beautiful daughter Isobel for her wedding day.

She'd watched Isobel grow up into a self-confident young woman, an accomplished pianist and a glowing Christian. She and Edison her husband had prayed much about the selection of just the right husband for her, and they were secure in the fact that God had directed them to a good Christian man of character.

Even in the joyful anticipation of this union, Juliet couldn't help thinking of the women of India who had become the focus of her life in recent years. Far too many of them were still bargained off for whatever dowry the family could pay. Wealthy families often paid hundreds of thousands of rupees in cash, gold jewellery, and household goods to their son-in-law's parents. A poor family looked on a daughter as a burden from the moment of her birth, knowing they could never pay an adequate dowry for a good marriage. Almost daily, newspapers report a 'dowry death' in the major cities – where greedy in-laws pour kerosene over the hapless bride and set her alight, claiming it to be an accident or suicide. Seldom brought to justice, these parents can then seek another bride and more dowry for their son.

It grieved Juliet to know that the practice continued in spite of the fact that the Indian government had outlawed dowry as it did sati, where a widow threw herself on her husband's funeral pyre. Hinduism teaches there is no salvation for a woman until she is reborn as a man. Her religious duty lies in serving a man – her father in childhood, her husband in her middle years and her son in old age. Her husband is like a god – and after he dies her life has no value.

Juliet was very aware of the inferior position of women in India. One writer has described it this way: 'Smothered or poisoned at birth, given away in marriage at a tender age, bargained over like some commodity by dowry-hungry in-laws, secluded in the name of chastity and religion, and finally burned for the exaltation of the family's honour, or shunned as inauspicious widows, the burden of oppression took different forms at different stages of a woman's life, from birth to death in a chain of attitudes linked by contempt for the female.'[1] Added to the low position of women in India is the degradation of the caste-system which stratifies people from the highest Brahmin caste to the lowest outcaste.

When William Carey, the eighteenth-century missionary, came to India, he observed, 'Besides being oppressive, caste cut off all motives to inquiry and exertion and made stupid contentment the habit of their lives. Their minds resembled their mud homesteads, devoid of pictures, ornaments and books. Harmless, indifferent, vacant, they plod on in the path of their forefathers'[2] Believing that their 'karma' (retribution for the accumulated good and evil of each mortal lifetime which determines whether a soul migrates up or down) must be fulfilled in this lifetime, the outcastes doggedly accept their fate, allowing the powerful and dominant to deprive them of dignity and self-worth.

The caste system has been declared illegal in India, but its painful ramifications are still felt by millions. About 47 percent of Hindus are in the backward and outcaste strata, and are still socially stigmatized, causing tensions even in the church. At its root is a basic attitude of discrimination.[3]

As Juliet put the final touches to the sari, making sure that every pleat and fold hung perfectly, she was grateful for the true freedom her daughter enjoyed as a woman of God. Isobel had suffered none of the degradations so many Indian women face. In fact she had even written a song to be used in Juliet's meetings with women that expressed that freedom:

Praise the Lord I am a woman,
With a part in His great plan;
Filled with His strength, touched by His grace
And led by His own hand.

Chorus:
All that we're meant to be in Christ,
Complete, fulfilled and free,
Fear and weakness changed by His pow'r
And all-sufficiency.
When pressures seem to crush my soul
And bind and fetter me,
His presence lifts my spirit high
In radiant victory.

How many times had Juliet taught this song to women in the seminars which she held all over India – in North India's desert heat; in the towns of Bihar, once known as the 'missionary's graveyard'; in mass meetings in the megalopolises of Delhi and Bombay. Everywhere the women of India were hungry to know more about God, to learn to pray and study the Bible. And everywhere she nurtured their fragile wounded spirits with the good news that Jesus had created them in his own image, and loved them with an everlasting love.

Juliet's father worked as a manager on a rubber plantation in Malaysia. Her mother followed Indian custom and returned to India for the birth of her first child. She left in the seventh month of her pregnancy and it was several months before she returned to Malaysia and Juliet's father saw his daughter.

Juliet grew up in a nominally Christian middle-class home, well cared-for and loved. But she grew up with a sense of inferiority because very early in life she was aware of her dark skin. She especially recognized the difference between herself and a very fair-skinned cousin. She recalls, 'I landed six months later [than my cousin] in the same place, but so dark and so ugly. The family told me later that they looked at me wondering what was going to happen to me.'

Under such circumstances it's not surprising that Juliet developed poor self-esteem. 'As I grew up in Malaysia I was very conscious of my bad looks,' she admits. 'The Chinese in Malaysia are very fair-skinned, and in school and everywhere I was the darkest, and this created in me a great sense of inferiority.'

In spite of this, Juliet excelled in everything she did in school. She majored in math and sciences, took part in drama and did very well in sports. Hockey was her favorite. When her school team won a very important match, the editor of the school magazine planned to put a picture of the team on the front cover. But when Juliet heard that, she ran to her room and hid.

One of the team members came looking for her to tell her everyone was waiting for her. But Juliet responded, 'No, I am so ugly, I would just spoil that picture. Take one of the reserves. She will look much better.'

Juliet ruefully remembers, 'I never came out of my hiding place. The photo was taken without me as I refused to be in it. I was stubborn.'

When Juliet was thirteen she was sent to boarding school on the island of Penang and later to Madras, India for her college education. Once again she excelled, not only in her studies, but in leadership. Girls living in the hostel had divided themselves into rival gangs who would do anything to outdo each other, or put each other down. To be part of one of these exclusive cliques gave prestige and power; to be excluded meant you were shunned by the leaders and looked upon as inferior. Juliet's strong will and leadership qualities soon took her the top of her gang.

But another powerful force was at work in the school. A small group of Christian girls met regularly for prayer and Bible study, and Juliet was one of their prayer targets. They often invited her to attend, but she wasn't interested.

However her brother, Sitther, just a year younger than she, had become the first born-again Christian in her family. Whenever they were together, he would talk about faith in Jesus Christ, but Juliet thought he was just a fanatic. Once when she was at home in Malaysia, she went through an old trunk containing school mementoes, pictures and books, and came across a brand new Bible, still in its original wrappings, which had been given to her as a child by an uncle. She loved the smell of new books, and took pride in keeping her books as neat and new as possible. She took it to Sitther to show him in what good condition this Bible was still. He took it and flipped through its pages, noting it had never been read or marked and reprimanded her, 'This shows how little you have used it.'

'It was like a slap in the face!' Juliet writes in her devotional booklet, *You Can be the Woman God Uses*. 'Stabbed to the heart, I turned from him and crept to a quiet corner, and for the first time in my life opened my Bible and began to read it. This was the beginning of God's exciting work of grace in my own heart. The Bible became my constant companion.'[4]

But it was several years before Juliet was willing to show more interest in knowing Jesus Christ. The Christian girls continued to pray for her and invite her to join them. One night she agreed to attend a meeting in Madras where she was deeply convicted. The next time they invited her to a prayer group she went and received Christ as her own Saviour.

'When I accepted the Lord Jesus,' she recalls 'I became turned inside out in the sense that my colour didn't matter to me any more. All of the sense of deep inadequacy didn't matter . . . I had such conviction of the blessedness of being in Jesus Christ. It gave me such a relief within me and after that, the people around me would note the glow on my face. It was the radiance of Christ within me. It can be that way for any of us when we come to know the Lord and hold that position in Christ. We are the daughters of the King. We may be very ordinary . . . but we are very special to him.'

Juliet was full of enthusiasm to share her new-found faith. She invited all her friends to the chapel meetings. 'I was so on fire for him I wouldn't talk to anyone for more than five minutes without telling them about the Lord Jesus Christ.'

Juliet spent much time praying for her friends, and about her own future. At nineteen she already had plans for a teaching career. She wanted to be completely obedient to God, and serve him in whatever way he showed her. But her prayers seemed to hit a wall. She felt she wasn't getting through to God, and she couldn't understand it. Finally she went to one of the Christian lecturers at the college to ask for help.

The teacher's immediate response was, 'Have you talked to Ariamalar?'

Juliet was shocked. She couldn't imagine herself talking to the leader of the rival gang, much less asking her forgiveness for the way she had treated her.

But the teacher persisted, 'Because you are in Christ you are to forgive and you are to be cleansed. There's no other way if you are to become clean [so God can hear your prayers and use you.]'

On her knees in her own room Juliet struggled with God, promising him that if this is what he wanted she would obey. But each day as she sat in the classroom with Ariamalar or passed her in the hall, she could not find the courage to confront her.

After three weeks of agonizing indecision, Juliet heard that Ariamalar was ill. This is my chance, she thought. I'll go to her room and express my concern, and maybe we can become friends.

Juliet spent time in her room on her knees asking God for the strength to face her former rival. Her legs trembled as she climbed the stairs to Ariamalar's room and knocked gingerly on the door. As the door opened Juliet looked into the eyes not just of Ariamalar, but her whole gang sitting around the room. This was not at all what she had expected; she had had in mind a quiet private chat, one to one, away from prying eyes and ears.

'Instead,' Juliet tells it now, 'God made me take on the full load of them together, alone. I could have sunk through the ground when I saw them and they were equally shocked to see me standing there.' She thought, 'When God deals with me, he deals with me thoroughly.'

But once in the room Juliet blurted out her apology – for her hostility and anger; for the things she'd said about Ariamalar and her gang; for the way she had turned others against them; for her exclusiveness and pride. 'Will you forgive me?' she pleaded.

After their initial surprise, one of the girls asked, 'Why are you doing this?' And Juliet was able to tell her that her new faith in Christ prompted this change. The stunned girls recognized that something truly remarkable had happened to this girl, once the proudest in the college.

Juliet still remembers the importance of that lesson learned so soon after coming to Christ. 'If I want to go on with the Lord and have a relationship with God, no matter how hurt I am, I must fix it.' But she admits it's a lesson she continues to learn over and over again.

Two years later Juliet completed her college course in Madras and returned to Malaysia. She loved math and science and looked forward to doing advanced studies and then beginning her teaching career. How good it was to be home with all the family; to eat the curry her mother had prepared; to unpack her things in her own room. Juliet could sense how proud her parents were of her accomplishments, and how her younger brother and sister were eager to hear her stories. But that first night home, after the rest of the family had gone to bed, her parents told her they had an important matter to discuss with her.

Juliet was not surprised when her parents began explaining that they had received a letter from her uncle who had been her guardian while she was studying in Madras. He had been in contact with a very fine religious family looking for a wife for their son. The uncle felt this was an excellent match. He had checked the background of the young man whose name was Edison Thomas. He had a good character, was well educated and had no evil habits. Furthermore, since the family was Christian, they would not require a dowry – an issue about which Juliet's family felt quite strongly.

Juliet's heart sank. Marriage was the last thing on her mind right now. She wanted to study more and teach, to use all the things she'd been learning for so many years. But she was also a respectful, dutiful daughter who felt honour-bound to obey her parents. In Indian culture parents are expected to arrange suitable matches for their children, believing that the perspective of experience and maturity is a far better basis for choice than the inexperienced and frivolous emotions powered by a nascent sex drive as in the West. The more Indian Christians heard about the divorce rate in the West, the more convinced they were that common sense, reason, prayer and mature evaluation led to better and more long-lasting marriages. While in the West couples fall in love and then marry, Indians believe love will follow if everything else is in proper balance.

So Juliet was not upset that her parents had made such an important choice for her, but rather that the timing was all wrong. She tried to explain her position, and they listened sensitively for they did not want to force her into a decision. Through the long night they debated back and forth, her parents pointing out over and over again that this was a good proposal which she should not turn down. They had great confidence in the uncle's opinion, and knew that he had Juliet's best interests at heart.

From her perspective, Juliet tried to show them how much it would mean to her to have the opportunity to teach at least for a year. Once married, her in-laws and husband might not approve of her working. It is customary in India for a daughter-in-law to come under the authority of her mother-in-law in the home. In fact, Indian girls are often reminded as they grow up, 'This isn't your home. You're going to be the daughter in another home.'

So Juliet pleaded for one year of independence and opportunity to use what she had learned. After many hours of discussion, her parents agreed that if Edison's parents had no objections, she could stay in Malaysia to teach for a year, after which they would get married.

Juliet was ecstatic when the letter finally came from her uncle saying the Thomas family agreed to the delay, and she began teaching math and science in a local high school. During that year she and Edison were not allowed to correspond. Juliet explains, 'My father was very strict. In our community people would talk if they saw any girl talking to any boy unless they were relatives or family friends.' The lack of correspondence didn't bother her; she'd grown up with that expectation. But curiosity about what her husband-to-be looked like certainly grew.

She remembers the day when Edison's photo arrived. Her mother opened the letter with a passport-size picture inside. Juliet heard her mother call out to her, 'Come and see, praise God. You have such a good-looking young man.'

In December 1961 Juliet and Edison were married in her parents' home town of Nazareth in the state of Tamil Nadu, India. Juliet wore a lavishly gold-embroidered sari, the gift of the groom and his parents. Juliet and Edison did not meet until their formal engagement party in Madras just before the wedding. Even then they went through the service without speaking.

A few weeks after the wedding her parents returned to Malaysia and Juliet left for Bangalore with her new and unknown husband and his elderly parents. Now in her role as daughter-in-law, wife and eventually mother, Juliet's ideas of teaching or serving God had to be set aside. For twenty years God tested and moulded this wilful young woman into a prepared servant that he could use.

Looking back Juliet understands what God did in her life. 'God has to prepare his servants. There are things in us that will not be good in the ministry. God will have to have time to knock those things out of our lives. If I'm obedient and I'm willing to learn; if I'm not pigheaded and hard, then maybe God can do that in a little time. But you see, God took a long time with me. I was a very hard nut to crack. To knock things out of my life was very difficult. And so God had to break me. I went through a terrible breaking time for almost twenty years of my life.'

The marriage was not easy at first. Having grown up in South India, Edison was more conservative and orthodox in his expectations of a wife, while Juliet's independent spirit had been fanned by life in Malaysia. It was a cross-cultural family, and Juliet, who found adapting difficult at best, was the one who had to conform. It didn't make it any easier that Edison, though a formal Christian, was not yet born-again.

Early in their marriage Edison began working for the Ministry of Defence as a research scientist. His parents lived with them from the beginning until Edison's father died in 1981 at ninety-four years of age. Isobel and Peter were born within the first three years of their marriage. Juliet's brother and sister came to India to study and also lived with them. At times ten to twelve people lived in the house and Juliet was responsible for their well-being, trying to make ends meet on one income. Many nights she cried herself to sleep, exhausted and physically weak. She had developed large fibroids which should have been removed immediately after Peter's birth, but with so many people to care for, she could not afford the time for surgery. She nursed her mother-in-law through terminal cancer, and then finally went in for surgery when her parents came from Malaysia to stay with her. Several years later her father also died in her home of a heart attack.

Though she sometimes must have felt as though God had put her in a box with no way out, Juliet admits that those twenty years were the crucible God was using to prepare her for ministry. In spite of the hardships she is thankful that she was able to care lovingly for her aged parents and in-laws. And more importantly she looks back with thanksgiving that everyone that came to live with them went away with Jesus Christ.

While the pressures of family cares were heavy, the inner turmoil was almost unbearable. For Juliet, like a caged bird, wanted her intellectual freedom. She wanted to be able to go places and do things as she'd been used to before marriage. In the church they attended, Juliet found many opportunities to attend prayer meetings and Bible studies, and though Edison disapproved, she went whenever she could get away. More and more she was being asked to teach a class or speak to a group of women. She relished the opportunity to study and use her training.

But deep within her heart she knew her actions were exacerbating her already difficult marriage. Yet she feared losing her identity, becoming a non-person. She feared becoming a puppet, saying and doing what someone else wanted her to. There was no desire to gain greater freedom to go into public ministry. In fact, God was convicting her that her children needed her at home, and that she must give them greater priority if she was to be a good mother. But she did not want to lose her own identity. She wanted to be herself and make her own decisions.

And then one day as she was reading the Scriptures again it became forcefully clear that God wanted her to be a more gentle and quiet person and to submit to her husband. She was displeasing Edison with her attitude of independence and rebellion and didn't meet his standards for a wife.

Juliet struggled with God. 'All the reasons the secular feminists give, I gave to the Lord,' she recalls. 'I asked him, "Aren't I equal before you in worth? Haven't you given me equal privileges? Even you don't force yourself into my life; why should I have a man doing that in my life?" '

But all those arguments availed nothing. Things were so bad between her and Edison that one morning she sat before the Lord and said, 'Lord, I don't agree; I don't think it's fair, but I accept that you want this for us. I don't feel I can submit my will to my husband, but I will submit to you. And for your sake I will submit to my husband.' God was convicting her that she had to be first and foremost a good wife and mother.

A few days later a friend asked her to speak at a women's meeting. Instead of saying yes, as she would ordinarily have done, she told her friend she'd let her know in a few days. Juliet went to Edison and asked him if it was all right with him if she accepted the invitation. At first he didn't reply – he is a man of few words – and she had to ask him two or three times. She expected him to get angry, but instead he quietly told her, 'Go.'

This was the turning point in Juliet's life. What she had attempted to gain through independence and rebellion, God gave her through submission and gentleness. 'It was not an easy thing to do,' Juliet admits, 'but I became a totally different wife. My husband saw the difference, and God began to work in his life. I used to pray, "Lord change him." If only he would change then everything would be OK. But after I submitted my will, God began to help me see that it was not him; it was me. I needed to change. Within months he became the man that he really is – kind, understanding, helpful. Today he releases me and stands with me. We walk together in what I have to do. But I praise God that he held me to my priorities even through my rebellious years.'

By 1981 the 'wilderness' sojourn seemed to be over. Her responsibility towards parents and in-laws had been fulfilled. Isobel and Peter were completing high school. At last Juliet was able to begin teaching again, this time in a mission school.

During her involvement in a city-wide programme organized by the Evangelical Fellowship of India (EFI), she visited a local slum for the first time in her life. Though she lived less than a mile from the slum, she had never seen the utter degradation and poverty millions of Indians suffer.

She saw children squatting to relieve themselves in open sewers, while a few feet away women washed clothes in the filthy water. Muddy alleyways were turned into foetid quagmires by the monsoons, and rats scurried through the rubbish. Shacks made of burlap bags, cardboard and tin housed families of ten to fifteen people. The summer heat turned these windowless cells into virtual ovens.

But the women – the women were what tore at Juliet's heart. How could they look so regal carrying on their heads a platter of cow pats for fuel? She looked at the love shining from their eyes for the baby suckling at their breasts, even as two or three toddlers tugged at their skirts, their swollen bellies belying their constant hunger. Who would pay dowries for these hapless little ones? No wonder she'd heard stories of a desperate mother forcing scalding broth down her newborn's throat to end her miserable existence! Who cared when a drunken husband, his spirit destroyed by drudgery and hopeless poverty, cruelly beat his wife to vent his frustration? Perhaps it was here in the slums of Bangalore that the seed of her abandoned love for the women of India was first planted.

From her first visit to the slums Juliet felt a compassion for the women whose lives were a constant drudgery of mindless work, constant child-bearing and abuse from their husbands. Many were suicidal – they had nowhere else to turn.

Juliet formed a team of women to visit the slums each week, sharing the love of Christ and caring for medical needs as they could. 'We used to fall sick often, as we were exposed to many diseases and in the early years our team had a rapid turnover,' Juliet recalls.

The team continues to minister in a part of Bangalore's largest slum where forty to fifty thousand people live in huts without electricity, running water or sanitation. One of the major projects is adult literacy classes. 'The women are excited that they can write their names,' says Juliet. 'They don't have to sign anything without knowing what it is about. They can read the numbers and destinations on buses. And best of all, they can read God's Word.'

Then in 1982 God opened up an unbelievable opportunity. Through the Evangelical Fellowship of India, Juliet was sent to Korea to attend a church seminar. What amazed her was to see how active women there were for the Lord. She commented to the Korean women, 'Our culture is such that our women can never have such teaching and training, nor such freedom to serve as you.' But the Koreans told her, 'We were called the "hidden women" before the Gospel came to us. We were not even meant to be seen. In Christ alone, the church has equipped us and set us free to serve.' Juliet was particularly impressed that 90 percent of Korean house churches are led by women.

Juliet returned to India with a new view of what women could do for Christ. Later that year Evelyn Christenson, a well-known writer and teacher in the

USA, came to Bangalore to hold a seminar. Juliet helped organize that meeting which was attended by two hundred women.

The morning before Evelyn Christenson was to leave, she invited Juliet to her hotel room. Though the two women had never met before the seminar, God had bonded their hearts in an unusual way. Evelyn had seen leadership and spiritual insights in Juliet that convinced her God was going to use her in a special way among women. 'She prayed, commissioning me for women's work in India' Juliet relates.

'That night when I went home I just wept. I told God, "I love to teach and I don't know what you want me to do, but if you want me to resign from my job, I will." ' When Juliet explained this new development to Edison he encouraged her to resign and follow God's call. Even the school principal did not seem surprised. In fact she said, 'I knew it was coming. God has special purposes for you.'

Juliet agreed to stay on until they found a new teacher, but in three weeks she was free. Free to do what? She had no ministry in mind; no organization to turn to. She was simply waiting for God's next step.

Within weeks she met Dr. John Richard, head of the Evangelical Fellowship of India, at a Bible Society meeting. Over lunch Dr. Richard dropped a bombshell. 'We want to open a department for women and we want you to head it up.' Shocked and yet aware that God might be pulling the pieces of her life together in a totally different way, Juliet spent several days praying. She remembers the sense of fear and inadequacy, but also the deep sense from God that this was what he wanted her to do.

In January 1983 Juliet became the first Secretary of the Women's Commission of the Evangelical Fellowship of India, an organization with a high profile. Evangelical churches all over India belong to this fellowship. EFI leaders didn't really know what they were asking her to do. They simply told her, 'You pray and feel what God is leading you to do.'

'That's how it all started,' Juliet explains. 'I was challenged, but I began to pick up prayer groups and work with them. I saw how women were touched and how great their hunger for God was. As I began to know their needs more, I began to talk about family life and how God had brought me through a lot. We talked about the word of God because the word had changed my own life. Out of the things I had suffered, the Lord taught me and I began to share with them, one step at a time. That was how the prayer ministry began.'

For five years Juliet served with EFI, organizing women's seminars all over the country and working with pastors to incorporate women into the ministries of the church. Then in 1988 Operation Mobilization asked Juliet to head their women's department. Having learned something from the struggles she had

had as a woman working with a male organization, Juliet openly discussed the terms under which she felt she could work. 'Women don't function like men,' she told them. 'We think differently. We need your guidance, but with gentleness and sensitivity.' OM's leaders gladly assented to her requests, and have been fully supportive of her ministry from the beginning.

Once again Juliet prayed for direction. She simply started with small prayer groups near her home in Bangalore, and went to teach wherever she was invited. Evelyn Christenson's second visit in 1990 was a godsend. Evelyn made her materials available and also helped Juliet start a radio ministry over Trans World Radio.

Juliet organized city-wide prayer networks and informed the city prayer co-ordinator of prayer requests. Evelyn Christenson wrote *A Study Guide for Evangelism Praying* for the AD2000 Women's Track which Juliet has used as a prayer tool. She has had it translated into several Indian languages. The Guide trains women to pray for the lost and encourages them to form prayer triplets to pray for three unsaved friends or relatives and an unreached people group.

India has an estimated three thousand ethnic groups, of which only 100 have been evangelized. Thousands of Indian women are now praying for these unreached people. As they catch the vision for prayer they are also planning to visit local tribal groups to find ways to share the gospel with them.

Early in 1995 Juliet formed this loosely knit, but powerfully effective network into the Arpana (Dedicated Women) National Prayer Network. Its goal is 'to motivate, build and network women of prayer all over the nation so that we can pray unitedly, powerfully for the unsaved and unreached people in our communities and our nation.' By the end of 1995 these prayer groups were active in 102 cities in 23 states of India. Juliet has also been able to appoint nine state co-ordinators to relieve her of some of the burden of travel and supervision.

From the beginning Juliet realized that she had to gain the co-operation of pastors in order to have the key women leaders of the churches attend. When she planned one of her early seminars in Calcutta, she visited pastors of the local churches for recommendations of the women who should be invited. As soon as she mentioned the meetings, she could sense a shutter coming down. She learned that in the past when women participated in women's programmes, they came home hostile, fighting with pastors and husbands over women's rights. Juliet had to explain carefully that her women would be learning the word of God and she would be teaching them how to have a closer relationship with him. Reluctantly the pastors agreed to co-operate. But when the women came back changed and marriages at the point of divorce were reconciled, the pastors rang Juliet to say, 'Why are you teaching only the women? Get the men also and come back for a long time.'

Juliet has found that many pastors and Christian leaders in India want and need help in teaching and training women. They realize that in this culture it is only women who can really teach women. Juliet loves to tell the story of a seminar she held in Bihar which is very remote and backward. The pastors were so eager to have their women trained that they formed a committee to do all the work, not only preparations and travel arrangements beforehand, but the shopping and cooking for the conference so the women would be totally free to attend all the sessions.

The joys of seeing women grow in Christ are lessened by the pain and suffering she sees as she travels all over India.

Once World Vision asked her to visit a project in a village where the people worship the fertility goddess, Yilma. Juliet wept as she saw the squalor of the women with six to eight children living in one-roomed huts, without running water or electricity. Every woman in the village is virtually a prostitute, having been given to the temple priest by her parents when she was a child of eleven or twelve to bring good fortune to her family. Following an elaborate marriage celebration, the girls become Deva-Dasi's, or women who belong to the goddess. After a few weeks in the temple they are turned out to live in camps where their only livelihood is prostitution, for they are ineligible for marriage. Any man having relations with a Deva-Dasi believes he is blessed by the goddess. Older women who are no longer attractive to men become pimps for the younger women.

One hundred and fifty women attended the first morning of Juliet's retreat. She was told not to hold evening meetings because the women 'are working'. One woman testified that she had seen a vision of the Lord Jesus who had told her he was the only God. A few nights later he reappeared telling her to throw away her idols. This young woman brought 25 other women to faith in Christ.

World Vision has set up a rehabilitation centre and provides a hot meal for mothers and their children in the village where Juliet was speaking. A pastor with a compassionate heart for the plight of these women works with them.

During the retreat the pastor invited Juliet to come with him to visit the women living on a street where he had never been before. As they walked between the hovels, Juliet suddenly felt a sharp sting in her toe. She looked down to see a large black scorpion scrambling away. Within minutes her leg had swollen to the groin with excruciating pain. Her friends helped carry her back to the place where she was staying and offered to take her to the nearest hospital. But in this backward area, Juliet knew that AIDS was rampant. Though the pain was agonizing she felt she would rather put herself in God's hands. She knew that death could occur within the first twenty-four hours. By morning the pain had become so terrible she was willing to do anything for relief. Then a villager came to remind her friends that a Christian woman doctor lived in the next town. They bundled Juliet into a rickshaw to be taken there. Within the next twenty-four hours the pain had subsided and Juliet knew that her life had been spared.

Over and over in her travels she meets young women like Shyamala who belongs to a high-caste Hindu family. Since her conversion her family and relatives persecute her. They treat her as an untouchable, which means she may not eat with or even touch her own children! Or Ranjani who must hide her Bible from her family and can read it only in secret.

In spite of the dangers and taxing demands, Juliet continues to maintain heavy and horrendous travel schedules all over India. Travelling into small towns and cities across India takes unusual stamina especially in the hot summer months when temperatures soar above 100 degrees. When she travels by train, she rides long hours in crowded, dusty coaches, often without even a place to put her luggage. She may be gone for three or four weeks at a time, teaching one seminar after another in places far from her home.

In addition, Juliet has been asked to serve internationally as a member of the executive committee of the Lausanne Movement, a position which requires at least one overseas trip a year. She also serves as vice-chairperson on the World Vision board in India, as well as regional representative for the AD2000 Women's Track, and speaks in the USA and Europe and in other parts of Asia.

Sometimes physical and emotional weariness overwhelm her. She wrote in a recent Arpana newsletter, 'I was feeling very tired – tired of travel, tired of battling against insidious jealousies and rivalries; tired of trying to pull together those that are so divisive. Then I went on to minister the Word and encourage prayer in a few cities in . . . northeast India. My heart broke and I wept as I saw their tremendous hunger for God and the desperate needs all around. The Lord laid on my heart again that very heavy burden to reach and touch women in India for Christ.'

And Juliet Thomas will continue to carry that burden until the Lord tells her to put it down.

Notes

1. Sakuntala Narasimhan, *Satin* (New Delhi: Viking Press, 1990), 150.

2. S. Pearce Carey, *William Carey* (London: Hodder and Stoughton, 1924), 140.

3. Patrick Johnstone, *Operation World* (Carlisle, U.K.: OM Publishing, 1995), 274.

4. Juliet Thomas, *You Can Be the Woman God Uses* (Bromley, U.K.: Pilot Books, n.d.), 26.

Eleven

The People's General – Eva Burrows, Australia

But to each one of us grace was given according to the measure of Christ's gift . . .
And He gave some as apostles, and some as prophets, and some as evangelists, and
some as pastors and teachers, for the equipping of the saints for the work of service,
to the building up of the body of Christ

Eph. 4: 7, 11, 12.(NASB)

And since we have gifts that differ according to the grace given us, let each exercise
them accordingly . . . he who leads, with diligence

Rom. 12:6,8b. (NASB)

There is a peaceful ambience about the tenth floor apartment overlooking
downtown Melbourne. Simply but elegantly furnished, it exudes an old world
charm with its copies of Van Gogh and French Impressionists gracing the
walls. The music of Mozart filling the room and the bookshelves lined with the
writings of such well-known authors as John Stott, Richard Foster, Charles
Swindol and Helmut Thielicke – and an occasional Agatha Christie – reveal
something of the traditional tastes of its occupant.

Here in her homeland of Australia, General Eva Burrows has retired from
the highest position in the Salvation Army. After forty- three years of demanding leadership responsibilities around the world she finds more time for
developing her spiritual life as she 'relaxes in the Lord.' She loves to sing old
Army songs, like the 'sacramental' song written by General Orsborn:

> *My life must be Christ's broken bread*
> *My love His outpoured wine,*
> *A cup o'erfilled, a table spread*
> *Beneath His name and sign,*
> *That other souls refreshed and fed,*
> *May share His life through mine.*

Eva acknowledges she has a 'big intercessory prayer programme,' as she
prays for people and global ministries. Her phenomenal memory can recall the

names of hundreds of leaders around the world with whom she has worked. During her tenure as general she was known to remember the names and faces of her 400 executive officers around the world, including the difficult Korean names – and people whom she hadn't met for years. Now she relishes the time she has to pray for those she's met and ministered to over the years.

Yet this impressive woman with her beautifully styled silver-grey hair conveys an authority and enthusiasm that belies any talk of 'retirement.' Her dark eyebrows outline her penetrating brown eyes, which can melt with compassion or burn with anger.

Her boundless energy has just turned to new outlets as she serves as chairman of the board of an Australian insurance company which ploughs its profits into education for drug- and alcohol-abuse. She is also governor of a foundation which is seeking to establish programmes for the poor in the Third World.

After so many years of serving in top leadership positions Eva admits, 'I knew that I would miss the camaraderie around the table, because I love debate and dialogue and coming to decisions in consultation.' So her role on these boards is mutually beneficial.

But she declares that she was ready to relinquish the position of general after serving seven years (including a two-year extension of the normal five-year term). She still enjoys travel and turns down more invitations to speak globally than she accepts. The advantage now is that when she goes to speak she can stay on and have a little holiday as well. 'There are no fax machines, no telephones asking what we should decide about this new big problem,' she explains.

Sometime, if she gets time, she's going to learn to paint in oils and study theology at the university – and read all the books she's been wanting to read! But right now the work of Christ and the Salvation Army continues to fill her days.

The Salvation Army, founded by William Booth in 1872, has grown to more than two million members in 97 countries. Its fifteen thousand local corps (or churches) and more than four thousand institutions, schools and hospitals are led by some twenty-seven thousand officers and cadets. Military terminology permeates this far-flung ministry which started among the poverty-stricken residents of the East End of London in England.

Over time a hierarchy of leadership has developed. Those with obvious leadership gifts move through the ranks of Cadet, Soldier, Lieutenant, Captain, Major, Brigadier, Lieutenant Colonel, Colonel, and Commissioner. From the top leadership of the Army a new general is elected to serve a five-year term. As in a national army, soldiers are trained as officers; appointed to fields of service; provided with quarters (which are inspected by officers from time to time). From the beginning women were allowed – even encouraged – to preach and hold positions of leadership. Catherine Booth, charismatic and dedicated wife of the founder preached and worked to extend the usefulness of women. 'It will be a happy day for England,' she once observed, 'when Christian ladies transfer their attention from poodles and terriers to destitute and starving children.'[1]

It was into a poor but strongly committed Army family that Eva Burrows was born in 1929, the eighth of nine children. Life focused on the Army and the children were expected to attend services and open-air meetings with their parents. They distributed the *War Cry*, the Army's magazine, learned to play instruments and participated in all the age-regulated children's programmes. 'My father was a bit "Army barmy," ' says Eva.

Even at six years of age Eva was organizing other children and demonstrating leadership qualities. No wonder she spread her wings and flew in her own direction for a while in high school. She refused to wear the Army uniform or to attend what she called 'boring' meetings. She was tired of always putting God and the Army ahead of her own desires.

Her godly mother saw the potential in her young daughter. Because of the family's poverty each child in turn had to go to work after completing high school. But Ella Burrows insisted that her gifted daughter go on to university, and though her husband Robert grumbled at first, he acquiesced as the other children urged him to allow her to go. Eva received a small scholarship because of her excellent grades, and since she could live at home, gave it to her mother, who secretly hid it away for some future need.

At Brisbane University a friend invited Eva to a Christian Union (Inter-Varsity Fellowship) camp. She heard the Scriptures in a fresh way and realized that she had been rebelling against not only the Army but God himself. After the camp she returned to a Salvation Army meeting where she went forward and knelt at 'the mercy seat' to ask forgiveness and cleansing. She describes that step, 'It was salvation in its fullest context, total consecration of all of myself. That moment was the most crucial of my life. After we prayed, I felt a great sense of release and peace, thoroughly glad to have given God everything.'[2]

With her renewed commitment to Christ Eva returned to the Army, knowing that in spite of hardship and sacrifice, she had to be an Army officer. Once again she donned her uniform. One Sunday morning when she was nineteen, her father suffered an asthma attack just as he was about to preach. As he left the service clinging to the arm of his wife he managed to gasp out, 'Eva – you finish.' Drawing on some studies she'd done at a Bible camp, Eva preached a sermon on the Israelites and the salvation they received by sprinkling blood on the doorposts of their homes. As she shook hands with the congregation at the door, an old Salvationist thanked her saying, 'Eva, always preach the Blood; preach the Blood.'

With the end of World War II General Albert Orsborn called a youth congress in London, inviting Salvationists under thirty from around the world to join in a great celebration. When Eva heard of the congress, she longed to go, but she didn't have the money. It was then her mother revealed that she'd put aside her scholarship funds all these years for just such an opportunity. For the next few months Eva worked at every kind of manual task she could find to make up the difference.

In July, 1950, forty young Salvationists sailed on a dilapidated passenger liner, the *Otranto*. What an exciting moment as the bands played and colourful paper streamers drifted across the water as the liner pulled from the dock. Little did Eva know as she waved and blew kisses to her family, that she would not return to live in Australia for many years.

In London the congress more than met her expectations – twelve hundred young people from many countries of the world in their distinctive international uniforms. The Aussie timbrelists, including Eva, took the congress by storm with their unusual choreography and precision.

Eva had already informed the Army that she would like to serve in Africa in the field of education. Leaders suggested that rather than return to Australia she should stay in London, studying at the Salvation Army's International Training College for a nine-month course in doctrine, Bible study, Army history and regulations and leadership-training. At the end of the course she was commissioned a Lieutenant and was appointed to serve for five months of practical work – preaching, visitation, and evangelism – in Portsmouth.

In 1952 Eva completed an additional year of study in cross-cultural subjects and teacher training at London University to prepare her for her work in Africa. Eager to go home to see her family before heading off for what was then a seven-year term in Africa, Eva worked her way to Australia as a children's worker on a passenger ship.

When Eva offered herself to serve in Africa, which she believed would be a lifetime ministry, she knew her opportunities for marriage would be limited. From the time she had committed her life to Christ and to serving as an officer, she had accepted the possibility of celibacy as a gift from God. On several occasions during her university days she developed relationships with young men to whom she was attracted. But their commitment to Christ and his ministry was not the same as hers and she broke off these relationships before they became too serious.

In looking back on women's roles in the Army when she was young, Eva admits that single women had more opportunities than married women, especially if they demonstrated leadership gifts. All her role models as a young woman were single women. 'Married women were not allowed to teach in those days. The matrons of hospitals were single women. In my generation it wasn't a second class thing to be single.'

Today she says, 'I know that marriage is a beautiful thing, but the gift of singleness is beautiful too. God gives more than enough back to you when you give up something for him.'[3]

Howard Institute in Southern Rhodesia (now Zimbabwe) didn't quite know what to make of the exuberant, lively young missionary who fell in love with Africa at first sight, and tried to draw its people, music and language into her heart all at once. Teaching the elementary students was just the beginning. Eva loved sports and coached netball and athletics. She sewed her own uniforms, supervised the planting of a school lawn and garden, and led scout programmes. She flew around the compound on a co-worker's yellow Lambretta scooter. When everyone was ready to go to bed at the end of a long hot day, Eva would often tap on the window of one of the other teachers and ask, 'Would you like to play Scrabble?'

Eva loved the joyous African music and the way Africans put new rhythm and harmony to old tunes. She defended their dancing as part of worship, as long as it had no connection with witchcraft.

Paradoxically, it was in the heart of Africa that classical music became one of Eva's lifelong obsessions. Her housemate had a radiogram on which they played their only record – Mozart's Haffner Symphony – over and over again. Eva also kept up with the world by ordering *Time* magazine and mail-order library books from the capital city of Salisbury (now Harare).

Often at the end of the day she would end up in a nearby village, sitting around the fire with the elders, absorbing their culture and language. She became fluent in Shona. She didn't let the criticism of an older missionary, that she was too familiar with the Africans, keep her from identifying with them and loving them. As a result her students excelled in their subjects. When she moved to the teacher training side of the school, her students' results were so high that the department re-checked them to make sure there was no mistake.

Howard Institute put a high priority on the spiritual life of its students. 'We were not only training them intellectually; we were also training them to be good Christians. When they went out to teach they would be the most educated and respected people in the village. We wanted them also to be spiritual leaders and good Christian models.'[4]

After five years (the term had been shortened) Eva returned to Australia for a furlough. She stayed on an additional year to earn her 'Master of Education' in Sydney. Now Captain Burrows, she was appointed vice-principal of Howard, the first woman ever to hold this position, and developed an advanced teacher training programme for the school.

Political tensions were mounting as the Rhodesian prime minister announced a Unilateral Declaration of Independence, separating the country from British colonial rule. Eva found restrictions and discrimination against Africans by the white settlers difficult to accept. She feared guerrilla warfare would be inevitable. In spite of these circumstances, Eva continued to receive deep respect and love from her African students. 'I definitely felt for the African,' she says. 'Even in the church in those days the Africans were second-class citizens . . . it hurt me that white Rhodesians did not appreciate the capacities of the Africans.'[5]

At thirty-eight years of age and advanced to Major, Eva was appointed principal at Usher Institute, a well respected girls' secondary school and teacher training college in Rhodesia. Once again she threw herself into bringing new ideas and improvements in the curriculum to the school. However only a few months after her appointment, her brother phoned to say that her mother had suffered a severe stroke. The family provided her air ticket and she flew home. She walked into her mother's hospital room and whispered softly in her ear, 'Darling, here's Eva.' Her mother opened her eyes wide in recognition, breathed her name, and lapsed back into a coma until her death a few weeks later.

Eva's extraordinary leadership abilities and relational skills did not go unnoticed by the Army hierarchy. When General Frederick Coutts came to Rhodesia he was duly impressed with the young principal. Upon his return to headquarters in England he remarked in his usually taciturn manner, 'perhaps one should . . . er . . . think of . . . er bringing her to . . . the international centre.'

Soon afterwards Eva received her Army orders to come to England to serve as vice-principal of the International College for Officers (ICO) the school she had attended more than seventeen years earlier. Farewells were not easy, for Eva truly loved Africa, and the Africans loved her. Yet, as an obedient Salvationist, she knew the time had come to move on, little realizing that she would now be on the fast track without any brakes.

Except for one – stopping off at home in Australia for a short furlough, she found her father on his deathbed with terminal cancer. Eva was able to take him from the hospital and care for him in his little retirement cottage. When he went through doubts and depression, Eva helped him through the crisis. She would often sing one of his favourite Army songs:

> *I have no claim on grace; I have no right to plead;*
> *I stand before my Master's face condemned in word and deed.*
> *But since there died a Lamb who guiltless, my guilt bore,*
> *I lay fast hold on Jesus' name, and sin is mine no more.*

Eva was able to care for her father for two months until his death. Then completing her furlough in Australia, she turned her face to new responsibilities in London.

The proprieties and hierarchy of the London headquarters demanded as much cultural adaptation for her as life in the African bush had. No doubt Eva shocked the reserved British as she rushed up the stairs whistling, or stopped to chat with the domestic staff. At General Wickberg's farewell meeting, all the officers sat in order of the their rank and position, observing proper protocol. But when Eva saw Commissioner Catherine Bramwell-Booth, granddaughter of the founder, sitting in front, she went up to greet her, chatting cheerfully as with an old friend.

On another occasion Burrows, now a Brigadier, did remember protocol. She and several army officers were invited to a royal garden party at Buckingham Palace. One of the Queen's attendants introduced her to the Queen making mention that Eva had served in Zimbabwe. The Queen asked, 'How does this group get on when they come from so many national backgrounds and cultures?' For once seemingly a little tongue-tied, Eva responded that they were a very happy family. She later told her colleagues that she was sure the reason the Queen had spoken to her was because the uniform always 'gets you noticed.'

Eva loved the interaction with international students at the ICO. She felt the school offered her a window on the world, and she made a great effort to become acquainted with the different cultures and appreciate their national traits. After almost two years as vice-principal, Eva was appointed principal of the ICO, and given the rank of Colonel. Even though she had turned prematurely grey, at 44 she was the youngest Colonel in the Salvation Army.

Then one day Eva was called into the general's office. She had no idea what it was about, but she knew it had to be important. Nothing could have surprised her more than to hear that she was being appointed as the head of Women's Social Services in Great Britain. She gulped and responded as politely as she could, but admitted 'in my mind I questioned their wisdom.'

So did some of her co-workers in the Social Services who felt that other more qualified people had been passed over. They didn't appreciate her rather high-handed manner of making changes, and she finally realized that in order to accomplish her purposes she needed to apologize to her fellow-workers, who'd been working among the poor and abused far longer than she had.

However, as Eva moved among the homeless and destitute, she felt something of the compassion of her mother who had worked among down-and-outers all her life. She found areas that desperately needed updating, such as the outmoded barrack-like accommodation in the women's hostels. She worked towards greater efficiency by recommending that the men's and women's social services be combined.

Eva reinforced the concept that evangelism and social work had to go hand in hand. 'I have no problem that we are in social work to meet the needs of people,' she said, 'but the spiritual is one of their primary needs as well. I do not see any dichotomy in this area.'[6] Throughout her years of service in the Army, Eva emphasized evangelism – she never failed to 'preach the blood.'

Why did the Army appoint this gifted cross-cultural educationalist to a position so far out of her realm of experience? Today Eva believes it was in preparation for the future leadership role that those in top leadership recognized would fall on her shoulders. 'They no doubt felt that this would be a helpful experience for me and it proved to be so.'

'I remember once reading an article in the *Officer Magazine* series called "The Appointment I Didn't Want." Many people contributed and most ended up saying, "I didn't want it but it proved to be the best appointment I ever had." I often end up saying the Salvation Army can never put us anywhere where God can't use us . . . In that post I got a feeling for the lost and lonely.'

Yet now in her retirement General Burrows will admit that the Army has changed a great deal since the early days when people used to say that everything was under one hat and that hat belonged to William Booth.

'We have changed to what we call consultative leadership. Even military generals say that soldiers fight better when they understand why they're fighting and what they're fighting for. People don't move now just by command. That sort of immediate obedience belongs to another era. I certainly found that in my style of leadership which though strong is very much in the consultative mode. I always work better if I talk things out with people.'

In 1977 Colonel Burrows received a new assignment as Territorial Commander for Sri Lanka. Once again she threw herself into learning a new culture, a new way of life, even a new language. The Army was a source of life and help for thousands of Sri Lankans. Dressed in the traditional sari, Eva travelled the difficult roads in the humid heat to visit each of the corps scattered across the island. Even in the day-to-day ministry, Eva was there. On Christmas morning she was one of the first to arrive to help distribute food to the hungry. Yet she never lost sight of the big picture. She made sure that Sri Lankan officers were integrated into the headquarters staff. She launched a building project to replace the dilapidated headquarters in Colombo and before leaving the island in 1979 had a cheque in hand of US $1.3 million for the project.

One of her greatest challenges came when she was asked to give a series of Sunday morning meditations over the radio. How could she speak about

Christianity in this Buddhist and Hindu country without offending her listeners? As she agonized in prayer God seemed to say to her, 'Preach Christ, not Christianity.'

'Christ is the difference,' she says. 'The Buddhist presents a noble path, saying "Walk in that path." But in our Christian faith Christ says, "I am the path." He does not merely tell the way but he walks with us, supports and strengthens us, and is our living Saviour. And so I spoke about Christ.'[7] Later when she was elected general, she verified this truth which had become so profound during her time in Sri Lanka, 'I preach Christ, not Christianity.'

Shortly after she assumed her appointment in Sri Lanka, Eva attended the first of three High Councils to elect a new general. Though the youngest member of the High Council, which is likened to the College of Cardinals which elects the Pope, Eva was overwhelmed when she was asked to serve as Council chaplain, to give the devotions each morning before this body of highest leadership in the Salvation Army.

Back in Sri Lanka the pressures accelerated. In 1979 she became a Commissioner, the highest rank next to the general. There are only about 30 in the entire Army. But rank had nothing to do with her fervent sense of achievement and her demand for excellence from herself and everyone around her. Her office door was always open to anyone who wanted to see her. Night after night she took unfinished work home with her. The plans for the headquarters building demanded hours of committee meetings as well as fund-raising efforts. While in India for a regional conference, General Brown asked Eva to draw up plans and curriculum for a regional officer's college for the region. The Sri Lankans had learned to pace themselves in the heat and humidity, but Eva continued to work long hours as though she were in London. The pace was taking its toll.

In September, 1979 Eva was given another appointment as Territorial Commander of Scotland, and with barely a few weeks break between assignments she moved to Glasgow. On January 11, 1980 Eva awoke with a crushing pain across her chest and shoulders. She knew it was a heart attack.

For the first two days in the hospital Eva didn't know what was going on around her. But when she woke she saw a familiar black face. One of her students from the Usher Institute in Zimbabwe was leaning over her, 'It's all right, Commissioner you're going to be all right.' The young woman had finished her nursing training in Zimbabwe and was doing postgraduate studies in Scotland. 'You did so much for us in Africa and looked after us there,' she smiled encouragingly, 'and now I'm going to look after you.'[8]

The nurse's prediction came true – Eva was all right. She spent two weeks in the hospital and three months recuperating at home. The doctor gave her a clean bill of health – if she would learn to pace herself and follow instructions. Later she would write, '[The heart experience] made me more sympathetic to people with health problems. Probably in the past I was not understanding enough in this area. I would tend to say, "Come on, you can get over this, you'll be all right." '[9] Eva bounced back, and over the next three years made many changes in the Army's impact on Scotland. In fact the provost of Glasgow gave her a nickname which stuck all over the territory – 'Effervescent Eva.'

In 1982, thirty-two years after Eva had first left Australia, she went home to serve as Territorial Commander. As the first woman to head the territory, she presided over an all-male board and a headquarters staff of 160 people. At fifty-three the new Commander was trim and smart in her impeccable navy blue uniform and her perfectly groomed silver hair. She knew she would have to prove herself to the somewhat chauvinistic Aussies in this male-dominated society.

'There had never been a woman in charge of the Salvation Army in more than a hundred years. The men in Australia probably knew I had plenty of experience, but I think in the Australian male culture they are never quite sure that a woman can be in charge without being a matriarch.' So Eva proceeded cautiously. 'If you are pleasant, attractive and non-confrontational, I think you can win them over,' she admits.

It was an emotional return. How she wished her parents could have been there to see her. On her first visit to Adelaide, where the Salvation Army was founded in Australia, she knelt under the very gum tree where the first open-air meeting had been held more than a hundred years before to pray for God's direction.

This was one country where she didn't have to struggle to learn the culture. Even her Australian accent came back. An elderly man came up to her after she spoke at a men's hostel one Sunday and said, 'You know Commissioner, you speak real Ocker.' Eva smiled – Ocker was the talk of the common man on the street – and she knew she fitted in.

The staff soon learned that the new Commander was not to be trifled with just because she was a woman. One board member who habitually arrived late to meetings found himself locked out on Eva's instructions. Yet she also reacted compassionately and was not ashamed of her tears when her colleagues suffered personally.

Though she was the Territorial Commander of one of the Army's top commands, Eva never lost touch with the people God had called her to serve. Brigadier Jean Geddes describes seeing her talking with street kids, 'I saw her in conversation with a girl who obviously had a "chip on her shoulder." As Eva talked with her, I could sense the girl relaxing and responding. With her arm around her shoulder I saw Eva bend and gently kiss the girl on the cheek. I shall never forget the look, first of amazement and then of utter joy, on the girl's face.'[10]

One Saturday night Eva attended a youth fellowship meeting, and mixed with the young people, asking their names and what they did. She took the arm of one young man asking, 'What's your name and where do you come from?' He responded, 'Stephen Millar, Glenelg. What's your name and where do you come from?' 'Eva Burrows, Commissioner, Melbourne,' came the answer. Stephen's shocked response was, 'Oh God!' Her instant reply, 'No, just Eva Burrows.'[11]

Before Eva left Australia she received the *Order of Australia*, one of the highest honours conferred on those who have made a significant contribution to the community. Eva certainly had done that as she lobbied against laws legalizing prostitution and for lower taxes for the poor, provided homes for the elderly, and brought renewal to the stagnant 'corps' by bringing church growth training to officers throughout the Territory. Her four years in Australia were characterized by the same zeal and achievement she had demonstrated in her previous posts.

In April, 1986 Eva attended her third High Council to elect a general of the Army. In her heart she was aware that there was a strong possibility she would be nominated. Over the years people had made remarks that she would be general one day. She had had major assignments as well as vast experience in the Third World. At conferences she was always one to speak her mind forthrightly, and so she was well-known by the leadership throughout the Army.

She had three 'black marks' against her however. (1) A woman had not been general of the Army since Evangeline Booth more than 100 years before. (2) She was only fifty-six years of age. A general can serve for only five years and must retire by sixty-eight, so the High Council could easily have put her off for another term. (3) Her heart attack six years earlier caused some to question her physical strength.

Nevertheless when her name was suggested Eva went to her room to search her motivations for accepting the nomination. Did she want to accept this nomination because it would be the crowning pinnacle of her life? Did she want this position to prove that a woman could do it? After praying earnestly for God to reveal her true motives she came to the conclusion that it was his will, and right for her to accept the nomination. She knew there was a strong possibility she would not be elected, since there were six other good candidates and she felt at peace whatever the outcome.

Each candidate was required to make a speech to the High Council defining his or her understanding of what leadership of the Army meant. Eva struggled through a long night, crumpling up one piece of paper after another. Finally she decided to speak on how she would pattern her leadership style after Jesus. On the fourth ballot, and by the narrowest margin in the Army's history, Eva Burrows was elected as general of the Salvation Army and would have opportunity to put into practice that lofty ambition.

At the tumultuous welcome when she returned to Australia after the elections, Eva quipped, 'Well, there's only one thing left for me to do – and that's get married.'[12] It was obvious this general hadn't lost her sense of humour.

Suddenly General Eva Burrows became the darling of the world media. She used this public platform to announce with deep conviction that 'We are an evangelical movement with a social conscience.' Eva made it very clear that the Salvation Army will always preach Christ.

She moved easily and naturally into the hectic life of the International Headquarters (IHQ) in London. Her day started at 6 a.m. in her apartment in the Barbican, part of the old fortress wall of London, where she lived with a housekeeper. After time spent in prayer and Bible reading, she was picked up by her driver at 8 a.m. and taken to the IHQ on Queen Victoria Street across from St. Paul's Cathedral.

One of her first responsibilities as general was to appoint the Chief of Staff, her second-in-command. Within a few months she had set in motion a reorganization of the Advisory Council, encouraging them to come up with 'radical suggestions' for the Army. From the very first she acquainted herself with the financial matters of this global organization. One officer described her as 'shrewd and pragmatic' when it came to financial matters. Though Eva did not do the actual fund-raising, she was kept informed of the needs and progress. At one time a woman offered $100,000 a month for ten months to help the Army re-open its work in Russia. Eva followed up this relationship with personal notes and calls to encourage the donor and keep her informed of progress. 'As the general, I was often able to inspire people to contribute to a particular area of development,' Eva explains, 'but I had no authority to manipulate or apportion Salvation Army funds.'

Some considered her open-door policy a weakness, but Eva's love for people and desire to listen to her subordinates' opinions and suggestions was an integral part of her leadership style. Every night she took work home, prepared messages and communiques and dictated letters. One morning she stood dolefully at her secretary's desk saying, 'I have no dictation this morning,' as if she had failed her. In fact, Eva had spent the night in prayer about the disciplining of an officer.

About half her time was spent in travelling to visit the far-flung territories of the Army. In seven years Eva travelled one million miles to 61 countries. Fortunately one of the few perks of being a general was that she could travel first class, conserving her strength and allowing her to rest and prepare for her next meeting. Few people knew of the hundreds of postcards she wrote on each trip, or the handwritten notes and phone calls to family members after she returned from visiting one of their loved ones overseas.

Her exhausting schedule on her first visit to the United States tested the limits of her endurance. Everyone wanted to see and hear the new 'woman general,' and she spoke 64 times in five and a half weeks, with very little duplication. About a third of the way through the itinerary, even Eva had come to the end of her strength. She returned to her room and broke down in tears crying, 'Lord, I can't do it. I can't do it.' Tenderly God reassured her and restored her as she cast herself upon him, and after a good night's rest she was able to carry on. She learned more not only about total dependence upon God, but about the importance of controlling her own schedule.

The media didn't see these human sides of the General. One Canadian reporter described her as the 'Top Tambourine,' and wrote, 'She looks as though she could dress down the Almighty himself in the unlikely event that he stepped out of line . . . This is not a woman to be trifled with, and even the Mounties who escort her into Massey Hall to the strains of "The Maple Leaf Forever" look diminished in her presence. Her orations are down-to-earth and she stresses the good news of evangelism rather than the bad news of despair.'[13]

During the seven years of her generalship Eva met with 26 heads of state beginning with Prime Minister Bob Hawke of Australia and President Ronald Reagan in Washington D.C. in 1986, and ending with Fidel Castro in Cuba in 1992. When she asked Castro for permission to pray for him, he agreed. As she rose to leave after an almost two-hour visit Castro asked, 'Why are you leaving so early? You just came.'

In spite of her concern for individuals Eva could not help but realize that she held a very powerful position, with the right to make far-reaching decisions that would affect thousands of people. She was also aware of her spiritual power and authority from the Holy Spirit. Through the years God had become very real in her life and she felt that she was in tune with his will. 'I never had any fears in my whole life as a Salvation Army officer about taking spiritual authority.'

People loved her and responded to her leadership. However she admits that she had a short fuse and often pushed her subordinates too hard. When she was away the staff referred to having so many GFD's (general-free days) to catch their breath. Her driving desire was to do her best for God and she expected as much of those she worked with. As she looks back she admits it was 'reverting to the old syndrome of pleasing God by what we do, rather than what we are.'

One of the criticisms she faced from Army women was that she appointed so few women into top leadership positions. In fact, they complained that Eva was dismissive toward Army wives; she seemed to work more comfortably with men. Unfortunately, too often the Army appointed male officers to appointments designed for them, without significant leadership opportunities for their wives. Under Eva's tenure she appointed the wife of each International Secretary as Assistant Secretary for Women's Organizations for the part of the world for which her husband was responsible – an appointment that may or may not have been a happy situation.

In her own defence, Eva believes that women do not generally take as easily to administrative leadership as men, possibly because of lack of encouragement or experience. But she feels that the Army – and the world for that matter – will benefit greatly from more involvement of women in leadership, bringing in their sensitivity, intuition and concern for people. 'Women have a responsibility to use their feminine gifts, not their wiles,' says Eva. She also believe women must serve on boards and committees because of their gifts and abilities and not just as tokens.

Eva would have liked to appoint women into top positions, but contends that too few had been brought up through the ranks to be given a position in top leadership posts. She also struggled with the problem of appointing a woman above her husband. She did establish a committee to study all aspects relating to men and women in office. She included single as well as married women, ordained women and women from different nationalities. Their recommendations were placed before her successor. Eva felt confident that he would implement the findings for 'he happens also to have a wife who is very gifted and able, and he gives her total opportunity in ministry.'

The major organizational contribution General Burrows made was to restructure the International Headquarters, dividing it from a newly formed UK Territory. The need for this change had been discussed for years, but Eva made it happen. It took courage to divide financial resources so that the UK Territory operated totally independently from the International Headquarters. Because of the far-reaching consequences of this division, the High Council asked Eva to extend her tenure for another two years so that she could oversee the completion of the change.

It would be impossible to describe Eva Burrow's contributions to the Salvation Army during her seven-year tenure. Henry Gariepy, who wrote her authorized biography, *General of God's Army*, from which much of the information for this short biographical sketch is taken, describes her tenure as 'an era in itself.'[14]

In 1989 she visited an Afghan refugee camp in Pakistan. A cruel civil war in Afghanistan had produced the largest number of refugees in the world. Over three and a half million had fled into Pakistan where the Salvation Army was responsible for one camp of ninety-thousand people, its most ambitious project ever.

During her leadership Communism fell and General Burrows was able to lead the Army back into former Communist countries: East Germany in 1990, Russia and Czechoslovakia in 1991. That same year she spoke to an estimated thirty million people on the BBC World Service.

Eva Burrows herself described to her biographer how she would like to be remembered. 'I would like to feel that the Salvation Army is known more as a church and not just a social service agency. I would not mind so much if I'm forgotten, as long as the Army has grown. I hope I will be remembered as a General for the people, and especially a General for youth, because I believe in giving youth their place . . . There are many things I hope for, but if you ask my ambition, I would say very simply and humbly, my ambition is just to please God.'[15]

Her successor, General Paul Rader believes that Eva Burrows broadened the outreach of the Army in the larger evangelical community. 'In my judgment one of the most significant parts of the legacy of General Eva Burrows is her repositioning of the Army as an essential part of the Evangelical movement' Rader says. 'It was she who called us to join in prayer with other Evangelicals all over the world, praying for world evangelization on Pentecost Sunday. In so many ways she has contributed to a whole new perception of the Army in the Evangelical community.'[16]

Probably nothing is a more telling picture of Eva Burrows than seeing her kneel late at night in the snow next to a homeless person bundled against the bitter cold in London's 'Cardboard City.' Her officers tell of the time she recognized a man behind the wrinkled face and unkempt stubble. He had been a former night-watchman at the William Booth Memorial College. Now a widower in his seventies, he had fallen on hard times and was sleeping under the arches of the Royal Festival Hall. Eva put her arm around him to comfort him and pray with him. Then she kissed him on the cheek, and walked away with tears streaming down her face.

That gift of true concern is what made her the 'People's General.'

Notes

1. Edith Deen, *Great Women of the Christian Faith* (Uhrichsville, Ohio: Barbour, 1959), 220.

2. Henry Gariepy, *General of God's Army* (Wheaton: Victor Books, 1993), 39.

3. Ibid., 53.

4. Ibid., 77.

5. Ibid., 84.

6. Ibid., 101.

7. Ibid., 109.

8. Ibid., 120.

9. Ibid., 125.

10. Ibid., 144.

11. Ibid., 133.

12. Ibid., 144.

13. Ibid., 279.

14. Ibid., 11.

15. Ibid., 346.

16. Ibid., 347.

Twelve

No Room for Egos – Faith and Roger Forster, England

Now a certain Jew named Apollos, an Alexandrian by birth, an eloquent man, came to Ephesus; and he was mighty in the Scriptures. This man had been instructed in the way of the Lord; and being fervent in spirit, he was speaking and teaching accurately the things concerning Jesus, being acquainted only with the baptism of John; and he began to speak out boldly in the synagogue. But when Priscilla and Aquila heard him, they took him aside and explained to him the way of God more accurately.

Acts 18:24–26. (NASB)

When Faith Forster opened the letter of invitation to speak at 'Spring Harvest' her first reaction was one of surprise. This was the first time a woman had been invited to be the main speaker at the annual Easter conference which attracted up to sixty thousand Christians over four weeks on two sites in Britain.

Faith knew that in recent years some attendees had made comments about the fact that women were not represented on the speakers' roster. The organizers knew her, so she assumed they felt she was a reliable candidate for this first attempt to include a woman as a plenary speaker. She and Pat Cook had shared a seminar together on the role of women in ministry in 1984. That had been a breakthrough! Now two years later she'd been asked to speak on the Christian and social action, a subject dear to her heart.

Faith accepted the invitation as a challenging opportunity God had put in her life. Yet on the actual day of her debut, she had to admit to a certain nervousness. Not only would she be speaking to more than two thousand people, but she knew both critics of and advocates for women would be evaluating what she had to say. Her heart cried out to God for a favourable response both to her deeply felt message and to her as a woman messenger.

Just before the celebration service opened a group of Christian leaders, including several well-known speakers, gathered around her to pray. Suddenly she heard the voice of her seventeen-year-old son, Chris, praying fervently that

God would strengthen her and give her a word from God. She knew the whole family, including her husband Roger, were rooting for her. But the fact that Chris had left his youth meetings just to pray with her was particularly encouraging.

Standing before the crowd, she could still hear Chris saying, 'Go out there and sock it to them.' Even as she spoke she glanced down into the audience to see how her husband Roger was responding. She could pick out the curly grey hair wisping around his bearded face in the sea of faces. Dressed in a casual grey pullover he was sitting back with his arms crossed and his eyes almost closed, as if asleep. But she knew by the half-grin on his face that he was pleased and confident of God's answers to their prayers for wisdom as she spoke. Dear Roger – he was always there for her.

The only negative comments she heard about that night were from a few sceptics who asked, 'Why was this woman asked to speak when all those men were there?' But Roger just encouraged her to 'hang in there,' – that everything would be all right. And it was.

She and Roger had been encouraging each other in ministry for a long time. Could it be twenty years ago since they had begun Ichthus Christian Fellowship together? They had never dreamed it would become an evangelism ministry reaching into the heart of London, into many corners of Britain, and even the world. Or that the March for Jesus, which began as a testimony in a neighbourhood of prostitutes and pimps, would one day see more than ten million people around the world demonstrating for the King of Kings.

Ichthus had started out of an evangelism campaign sponsored by a group of churches in a poor part of London. From the beginning Roger had vowed that 'whatever God calls me to do, I need to be in a place where I can serve the poor and abandon privilege.' So they'd started in a working-class neighbourhood of southeast London where the once well-kept houses had endured the war, their stained glass windows dingy with age, or partly replaced with plain glass. The brick walkways were broken, the irregular fences rotting and paint peeling. Whole blocks were covered with drab council flats. And people with empty faces sheltered under their umbrellas in the seemingly constant rain as they scurried from the city commuter trains to their homes each night. It was here in Forest Hill that Roger and Faith began the first Ichthus Church and ministered to the poor, the vagrants, the addicted and the unloved.

Today Ichthus Christian Fellowship reaches more than three thousand men, women and children in thirty churches in greater London alone. But its ministry of evangelism is intertwined with social concern, biblical truth, the church as a community and the power of the Holy Spirit. Ichthus has established a school for poor children. (This also provided a place where Ichthus staff could enable their own children to receive an adequate education while living in a rundown community.) It has opened coffee bars, and job-training programmes, offered practical help of all kinds to the poor and needy, and provides special ministries to the elderly and teenagers.

And from the beginning Faith was right there beside Roger, doing everything that he did. She had grown up in a 'religious home' but her uncle took her to a Bible-teaching church where she committed her life to Christ when she was just four years old. Her capable mother served on the local education committee and became the mayor of the London borough of Southall. Faith was one of the youngest of nine children, and watched her mother raise the family without her father to help. Perhaps this combination of energy and leadership gave Faith the self-confidence and willingness to determine to serve God with all the abilities he had given her. In her teens, after devouring missionary biographies, she believed God wanted her to serve as a missionary. She gave up her university training to become a nurse, feeling that would better prepare her for the opportunities available to women missionaries at the time.

But she was also interested in linguistics and began working at Scripture Gift Mission, a British mission dating back to the Victorian period. One day as Faith worked alongside the translators a young man came into the office to visit one of his friends on the staff. She was introduced to Roger Forster.

Roger says, 'It was love at first sight,' though Faith won't quite admit to that. But she was impressed with this brilliant Cambridge graduate, who had something of her mother's fervour for justice and people in distress. Because Roger travelled a lot, speaking all over England, they began their courtship by correspondence.

As Faith got to know Roger, she was intrigued by his background. Ron Sider describes how he became a Christian

> . . .through the Christian Union (called IVCF in North America) while studying mathematics at Cambridge, one of England's oldest, most prestigious universities. In the liberal Methodist tradition of his childhood, he had never heard a clear message of sin, forgiveness and eternal life. But one night at the Christian Union, an Anglican bishop explained the gospel in a way that overwhelmed Roger with God's love. On the way home, he quietly gave his life to Christ.
>
> Soon he was going to every possible meeting of the Christian Union – prayer meetings, lectures, visits to hospitals and prisons. 'I was just hungry to know God.' He wandered around Cambridge with a Bible in one pocket and Thomas à Kempis in the other.[1]

After graduation Roger served as an officer in the Royal Air Force. But his main passion was evangelism and he preached and witnessed at every opportunity. Hundreds of men in the RAF accepted Christ and were nurtured into local churches through Roger's ministry.

Roger's commitment to Christ, and his avowed purpose to become a missionary, impressed Faith. As they shared their goals and dreams, Faith concurred with Roger's conviction that he should first demonstrate that the church can meet the needs of people at home before going overseas. The church in the mid-sixties did not make social action a common element of its ministry. But Roger felt it should be an integral part of evangelism. He had been impressed in reading about the Anabaptists, the radical evangelicals of the sixteenth century who believed in self-denial and brotherhood and practised community of goods and Christian charity. He grieved that there was little of that spirit in the local churches.

As Faith fell in love with this gentle, quietly-spoken man, she found herself agreeing with his dreams and visions. Ever practical, Faith could see how it could be done. They spent hours talking about having a house where they could bring in people off the streets. Roger was already living in Kent so he could be closer to a group of young people he was discipling. So Roger and Faith began looking at big old houses in a run-down neighbourhood where they would make their first home after their marriage. Their wedding gifts went towards the down payment on just such a house.

Faith admits to a sinking feeling as she walked into the empty rooms of the big Edwardian house with its peeling paint, broken windows, and stench of age and mildew pervading everything! She wasn't sure she'd intended to go quite this far in identifying with the poor! The physical appearance was daunting, but the hope of making an impact on the derelicts and needy on their doorstep, filled Faith's and Roger's hearts with excitement.

Young people from Roger's youth group came to help renovate the house; old furniture was resurrected from attics and basements. Faith did all she could to add touches of beauty. The long-neglected garden still provided colourful bouquets which somehow added a gracious touch to the dingy interior. Someone built triple-decker beds to stretch the accommodation. And as word got out local churches were more than happy to pass their problem people on to Faith and Roger.

Word spread quickly that the destitute and hungry were welcome here. The milkman became curious about increasing orders each day, and when he found out what was happening he spread the word out on the streets. Even the police would bring them homeless people in the middle of the night.

Faith cooked and washed, changed beds, comforted and counselled while Roger was often away continuing his evangelism ministry throughout the country. The gifts from these preaching trips helped to put milk and bread on the table for dozens of needy people. At weekends when they held mini-conferences in the house they crowded 40–50 people in the sitting-room, and packed nine triple-decker beds into the largest bedroom! Most days Faith cooked for at least twelve people.

When asked how often people stole from them, Roger and Faith ruefully agree, 'A fair bit.' But they hasten to add, 'We never had things like televisions or anything like that. We lived very simply so there wasn't a lot to steal. And because of that, most of them regarded us with a certain degree of affection... and didn't steal from us.' It would have been easy to become disillusioned because many of the people they helped ended back up on the street. But optimistically Roger notes, 'You get the occasional success,' which kept them going.

Emotionally the work was a strain, especially as babies, Chris and Juliet, joined the family within a year of each other. Now Faith was not only sorting out the deep personal needs of people who'd come into her home, but was caring for two babies in less than advantageous conditions. It was especially difficult in the damp British winter without central heating or hot water. But it was the lack of privacy that finally made the situation unbearable.

'We were all living in the same house, and we didn't have a flat of our own. For example, there was one very strange person who started to threaten our son. We couldn't risk leaving a child in the next room in the night.' With Roger away more and more, Faith became exhausted from overwork and emotional draining. After three and a half years they realized that unless they could get a larger house with a separate family unit for themselves, and help for Faith in the day-to-day responsibilities, they could not continue the ministry in Kent.

Moving back to London did not mean moving up in their lifestyle, for they settled in Forest Hill where they still live today, more than twenty years later. Roger explains, 'We have lived at a modest level financially and within the inner cities where the problems are bad . . . Obviously if my commitment had been to the university and business world, I wouldn't live where I'm living now. We've chosen this because we're on the doorstep of the council estate. We've tried not to live on a level that would be out of kilter with those around us. For years we've had very poor cars . . . in order to identify with the people.'

Perhaps their greatest struggle was over their children's education – Debbie came along when Juliet was nine and by that time inner-city schools had deteriorated even further than when they had first moved into the area. Where you attend school and your accent seem to carry a lot of weight in Great Britain. But the Forster children have all managed to overcome such handicaps. Chris graduated to become a leader in the Evangelical Alliance of Great Britain. Juliet, also a graduate, runs a theatre company outside London besides teaching. She loves Shakespeare and has directed and created stage designs for youth productions. Meanwhile Debbie followed in her father's footsteps, entering Cambridge in the autumn of 1995.

With Faith growing more and more involved in the ministry – teaching, counselling, planning – Roger realized he needed to commit more time to the family. 'A mother is particularly involved in the early years with the child because the child came from her body and is still attached as it were,' Roger observes. 'Then with the breaking down of that as a teenager, the father needs to be putting more time into the children.'

Roger also believes that a husband must make a conscious attempt to release his wife into ministry, if God so calls. And one way to do that is to lessen his own involvement, helping with the care of the children, so that his wife can participate. 'Men have to restrain and hold back in order to give room for their wives to develop their gifts. That is a godly thing,' he declares.

Faith confirms that Roger played his part as the children grew older. When they were small she purposely limited her involvement. 'I remember being asked to go on a trip and I wouldn't even consider it because my children were at an age where I didn't feel free to leave them.' But over the years as Faith began to travel, they always made sure that either she or Roger was at home. 'If I were going away I would write DEBBIE in capital letters in Roger's diary,' Faith recalls.

The family's closest brush with tragedy occurred when fifteen-year-old Chris was diagnosed as having inoperable lung cancer which had spread throughout his body. While the Ichthus congregations practise all the spiritual gifts, there is not a special emphasis on healing. Yet when Chris' test results came back indicating cancer through his lymphatic system and even in his spinal fluid, the congregation fasted and prayed that God would reverse his hopeless condition. Amid that holy tension a Canadian stranger walked into the hospital room to pray for Chris with extraordinary power and conviction. So fervent was his prayer that it could be heard up and down the halls of the hospital. The next morning Chris' pain and breathlessness was gone. A few days later his X-rays revealed no signs of the cancer. Even the doctors had to admit there was no other explanation except that God had miraculously healed Chris.

During the early years after their return to London, Roger continued his evangelistic ministry. As a result of a united evangelism campaign called Power Project, meant to stimulate the people into grassroots evangelism, many in the largely working-class Peckham District accepted Christ. Local churches found it hard to integrate these converts into their church bodies. Christians who had seen the benefits of the holistic evangelism approach didn't want to let go of the concept, but few churches were ready to make such a drastic change in their programme.

So Roger and Faith were asked to begin a church which was to integrate their evangelistic goals with the vision to meet the holistic needs of the community. Faith recalls, 'We really had to struggle with that for a while. We had not seen ourselves working in a local church but were more concerned for evangelism and facilitating churches in evangelism.' But their friends pleaded 'We just can't go back to the way things were before. We've got to do something and use our lives for God's sake. Would you lead us in evangelism?' Out of this vision Ichthus was born.

From the beginning Faith was responsible for organizing aid to the poor and needy called Jesus Action. The church posted notices throughout the community offering help for the unemployed, the sick, the elderly – even driving people to the hospital. Ron Sider tells the story of one of Faith's encounters:

> One day a woman who had just left a psychiatric hospital called the Jesus Action number. A single parent, she needed to shop for food and wash her clothes, and she didn't know how to get her six-year-old into school. Somewhere she had seen the Jesus Action number that Ichthus posts everywhere. 'Is this Jesus Action?' she asked Faith over the telephone. 'Yes,' Faith responded. 'Well,' the woman went on, 'I want the action, but don't want the Jesus. I don't want anyone coming around here ramming religion down my throat.' Faith assured her that would not happen. After Faith helped her with the washing and shopping, the woman invited her to sit down for a cup of tea. A mere ten minutes later, the woman blurted out. 'Okay, what's all this about Jesus?' Teasingly, Faith reminded her, 'We had an arrangement before I came that I'm not going to shove religion down your throat.' But the woman insisted. So Faith shared the Gospel and prayed with her.'[2]

Faith did more than care for the needy, however. She and Roger did everything in the ministry together. It was obvious to Roger that Faith's gifts of teaching and counselling, planning and organizing were every bit as valuable as his. More and more other leaders of Ichthus recognized her gifts. When Roger was away – as he often was – they came to her for advice and decisions. Faith found herself responsible for planning worship services, preaching, and organizing many programmes which grew out of the Ichthus movement.

Even as a little girl Faith had confidence and took it for granted that girls and boys should have the same opportunities. In grammar school she complained when girls were forced to choose sewing instead of woodwork – though when she was given the freedom to choose, she took the sewing class after all!

As Faith grew up in the church where she met the Lord, her pastor had recognized her special gifts and encouraged her to use them. As a teenager, she had sometimes been asked to lead the midweek service when the pastor was away. For Faith it was a matter not of feminist rights, but of using her God-given gifts wherever and whenever she had the opportunity.

Even though she was fully involved in all the activities at Ichthus, and often took Roger's place when he was away, the committee which led the work was originally made up of men. 'It was just not the habit among British churches,' Faith explains, 'at least not in the ones we were with, to have a woman in leadership. So it didn't really cross any of our minds. It wasn't a deliberate decision. I think it just happened. It was assumed that men would take the lead.'

But the issue came to a head when one of the committee was asked to draw up a chart of responsibilities and lines of authority. When Faith saw the chart she was taken aback. 'I didn't show up anywhere on the chart!' When she pointed this out to Roger he suggested that she go to see the person who had drawn it up and figure it out together. So Faith went to him and asked, 'Help me. Where do you fit me in this chart? If I'm going to function, I have to understand where I fit.'

The committee agreed that Faith was an integral part of the leadership, and at first put her name with Roger's. But Faith would not accept that. 'I am not totally interchangeable with Roger. There are things where Roger is particularly gifted, and there are thing that I am gifted in, so I don't think that is acceptable.'

Throughout the discussion Faith was concerned that it should not cause Roger embarrassment, and that Roger should not push it through for her. So she was relieved that one morning when the committee met as usual at their home, Roger was out of town. Faith was able to explain her feelings to the whole committee. 'I know you sometimes treat me as an extension of Roger, but you wouldn't say that about another brother's wife. She couldn't go into his office and take over his job, because she has a different role . . . But in areas where I do feel I am expected to take personal responsibility and authority in things . . . I like to know where I fit.'

In the end the committee decided to form an executive group which involved only the full-time staff, including Faith. The executive group met weekly during the day, making most of the major decisions, which were ratified by the 'elders' later. This led to a full discussion of the subject of women elders and the committee asked for Roger's teaching on it from the word of God. Today the central leadership team is made up of nine leaders, including Faith and Roger and one other woman. Each of the central leaders is responsible for leadership in one or more of the thirty congregations, and for one or two of the special departments in Ichthus' far-reaching programmes. And Ichthus appoints women elders in its churches as a biblically-sanctioned practice.

Over the years Faith's gifts and leadership skills have been recognized by others. She serves as the only woman on the executive of the Evangelical Alliance of Great Britain. As a result she became a 'member-at-large' on the World Evangelical Fellowship executive committee in 1992 along with Eva Sanderson of Zambia. Pressure from women on the WEF Women's Commission encouraged the leadership to give women representation. Since all other committee members are normally leaders of evangelical fellowships in their regions, it was realized it was unrealistic to expect that women would be appointed in the foreseeable future. But an unused by-law allowing for members-at-large to be appointed made room for the two women.

In analysing Faith's role on these decision-making boards, Roger believes that Faith has learned that she is going to be treated exactly the same way as men would be. Most men don't understand women's tears and they tend to withdraw and say, 'This woman can't work with us.' Faith agrees that sometimes she's likely to be too strong. 'I'm a very up-front person. I don't just function on the intuitive and emotional and therefore I don't find it difficult to tap into a man's world.'

Faith and Roger are also very up-front with each other. In committee meetings Faith is quite willing to disagree openly with him. 'We feel free to disagree with each other and everybody who knows us knows that,' explained Faith. 'I would say what I think but I'd say it to any member of the team.' However Faith reiterates that, in the end, the person in charge of the project must make the final decision, and she will abide by it, be it made by Roger or by some other team member.

Roger, as 'first among equals' in leadership, recognizes the wisdom of listening to others' opinions. 'If Faith disagrees on a point, there are probably two or three others that disagree as well. So it would be foolish for me to raise my head and say, "Well, I'm going to do it anyway." '

They are always aware of the danger of nepotism. Many secular businesses will not allow a husband and wife to work together for fear of collusion, or simply the temptation to stand up for each other which can cause personnel difficulties. When asked if people try to get something past her in order to get to Roger, Faith laughs and turns to him, 'Actually isn't it more likely to be the other way round? From very early on we realized that people try to manipulate a wife. But I don't think people work on me to get to you, do they?'

And Roger just grins. 'Sometimes they do.'

'But' he continues, 'we are very conscious that this is a possibility. It could be misunderstood if you want to insist on a point your wife is making or vice versa. I think it's a problem that comes with human beings interacting together. It can happen with friends too.' Obviously, it's an area in which Roger and Faith try very hard to be careful.

Faith and Roger realize that they have to work hard on keeping intimacy in their marriage and making time for each other. Their calendars are filled up a year in advance, often with trips that one or the other takes alone. Evidently some of their friends or colleagues saw the need for time set aside just for the two of them. A group of anonymous friends send them away for two or three days twice a year. The mystery donors check Faith and Roger's calendar through their office, and plan a getaway in a restful, beautiful place. It might be a bed-and-breakfast in the Lake district, or a cottage by the sea. But it's a place away from telephones and schedules, where they can pray and walk and talk, and renew their relationship with each other and with God.

While Roger has gained world renown as leader of Ichthus Fellowship and founder of the March For Jesus, Faith's gifts are being called upon more and more not only as a teacher and preacher, but as a woman of wisdom on national and international boards of various organizations. Many men would find it difficult to share the limelight with a wife, and sometimes to be overshadowed by her gifts. Ego keeps some men from allowing their wives to develop and express their gifts.

But Faith knows Roger's heart. 'He is not at all competitive or wanting me to get out of his way.'

When Roger was asked if he is ever resentful or jealous of Faith's growing public role he responds quickly, 'I just love it when Faith is given room to use what God has given her. It sounds a little patronizing, but I do think you have to make sure that you are giving each other room to use what God has given. And,' he adds, 'I have to be pleased even if it means that at times I can't be doing it.'

Notes

1. Ronald J. Sider, *Cup of Water, Bread of Life* (Grand Rapids: Zondervan, 1994), 31.
2. Ibid., 35.

Thirteen

A Woman's Place is in Government – Kay Coles James, United States

Queen Esther, daughter of Abihail, along with Mordecai the Jew, wrote with full authority to confirm this second letter concerning Purim. And Mordecai sent letters to all the Jews in the 127 provinces of the kingdom of Xerxes – words of goodwill and assurance – to establish these days of Purim at their designated times as Mordecai the Jew and Queen Esther had decreed for them, and as they had established for themselves and their descendants in regard to their times of fasting and lamentation. Esther's decree confirmed these regulations about Purim, and it was written down in the records.

Est. 9: 29–32.

The excitement of the crowd mounted as the Republican delegates to the 1996 convention prepared to nominate their candidate for president of the United States. Wearing red Kay Coles James was colour co-ordinated with the patriotic banners and slogans filling the auditorium as she stood to the side of the podium with other honoured guests. Her coffee-and-cream- coloured skin glowed under the brilliant lights and even without hearing her voice, observers could see this was a woman of vitality and energy. As secretary of the convention Kay would be calling the roll and number of votes to be cast by each of the fifty states.

While waiting to be called to the podium, Kay chatted with George Bush Jr., son of the former president, who was standing near her. She reminded him that it was all his fault that she was there. Eight years before she had dropped into the victorious Bush campaign headquarters to finalize some unfinished business before stepping back into private life. She'd got to know George Bush and his son during the campaign when as a representative of the National Right to Life Committee she helped endorse some of the Republican pro-life candidates.

She remembered how George Jr. had come out of his office to greet her. In the course of their conversation he'd asked, 'Kay, would you consider coming on board?' Seeing refusal in her eyes he'd added, 'Really Kay, you're a natural!'*

Shaking her head Kay had explained that her mother was dying of cancer and needed her full attention.

That afternoon when Kay visited her mother in the hospital, she'd laughingly told her of the offer, thinking it would cheer her up to know that her daughter had even been considered to work in the White House. Her mother was lying on a gurney, ready to go into the operating room. She could still hear Mama blessing her out, 'Girl, what's wrong with you? I raised you better than that! The son of the President of the United States asks you to serve your nation and you say no! How many people do you think get that kind of opportunity? How many black folks you think being asked? Girl, you bes' get back on that phone and tell them you was just kidding!'*

Her reverie was broken as the moment came for her to step up to the podium. The boisterous crowd finally quietened down enough for her to speak. It was time to call for the nominations. And she began, 'Alabama – fourteen votes.'

If only Mama could see her now!

Kay Coles had been born forty-seven years earlier in the tiny bedroom of her family's quarters, a converted army barracks, in Richmond, Virginia. Her father and four brothers were out in the swamps hunting bullfrogs while a neighbour helped to deliver their only sister, placing her squalling on the kitchen table for them to see when they got home.

The Coles family lived in poverty; their father seldom held a job for long and turned to alcohol in his frustration and hopelessness. A black man with the mind and desire to be somebody, he settled for the comforts of liquor as he drifted from one dead-end job to another.

Mama was the backbone of the family. Standing four foot eleven in her stockinged feet, she wielded a strong arm of discipline and held the family together, even after she could take her husband's abuse no longer and left him.

Kay remembers the day her mother and brothers moved to public housing in Creighton Court. Driving up to the rather pleasant-looking buildings surrounded by grass and playgrounds, her heart burst with pride to think they were leaving the tiny dilapidated army barracks behind. But once they stepped into their 'new' home her heart sank. The walls and floors were made of cement, chipped and gray, and regulations did not permit painting them.

But the most disturbing element were the cockroaches – roaches in the bathroom drains, on the cupboards, even in the beds. Kay would pull the sheets back at night, humming a little tune to keep her spirits up, to make sure that none of them were lurking beneath the covers. No matter how hard Mama tried to keep their apartment clean, there were always plenty of roachers in the building to move in with them.

Yet she felt secure, with five brothers (a fifth came along after her parents had separated) and lots of playmates around. There was a sense of community as neighbours kept an eye on each other's children, disciplining them when necessary. Even poverty was a shared commodity, and when there wasn't enough money to pay the rent because of loss of a job or other emergency, the family in need would throw a 'rent party'. They'd cook up some food, provide drinks, and neighbours would saunter over to buy the food and spend the evening sitting and talking. Kay describes these as 'benefit dinners without a planning committee.'

Though Kay's mother was on welfare she never allowed her children to feel sorry for themselves or believe that the world owed them a living. The most vivid example of this occurred when her oldest brother Ted came home with some stolen chickens. Meat was a scarce commodity in those days and the children's mouths watered as they imagined the delectable aroma of roast chicken.

But Mama took those chickens by the feet and began swinging them like a baseball bat, pumelling Tony who stood half a head taller than she did, shouting as she did so, 'Boy, I will starve before I let one of my children bring stolen food into this house.'*

Then opening the door she tossed the chickens into the backyard. Kay remembers that she and her brothers watched the neighbours pick up the chickens. They could smell the tantalizing aroma as they cooked, wafting back into their kitchen. In later years Kay would realize the value of the model of honesty and integrity her mother had set – and the sad example the other mothers were subtly setting for their children: it's OK to steal.

Mama had been born into an upper class family and was the only one of the six children in the family to have married 'beneath' her. The family had remained close and Kay enjoyed vacations spent with her Aunt Pearl and Uncle J.B., savouring the privacy of her own room, her very own bed, the new clothes.

But one day Mama took her on her lap and gathered her to her bosom, and Kay knew something was wrong. It was a common practice in black communities in those days for the extended family to help care for each other's children and grandchildren. Mama explained to Kay that Aunt Pearl and Uncle J.B. wanted her to go and live with them.

Kay remembers, 'I lay against her and cried in defiant silence. I didn't want new clothes and college. I just wanted to be at home in Creighton Court with my family.'*

Eventually the three youngest children went to live with relatives, and Kay's older brothers were able to get jobs so that Mama no longer had to face the insults and degradation of welfare.

Kay believes she is a typical child of an alcoholic parent: always working hard to prove herself. At Webster Davis elementary school, Kay had every opportunity to work hard. The teachers in this all-black school demanded the best of their students, preparing them for the world 'out there'. One of her teachers would point out of the window towards the white community and say, 'Those kids are going to be waiting for you when you get out of here. And you are going to be ready?'* Above all the students learned that they were survivors, not victims.

Kay remembers a teacher who stretched her to the very limit, requiring hours of homework and demanding her best. 'Her attention to detail, her insistence on excellence, nourished my soul. Her exacting standards waged a silent war with the message of a hostile society that I had internalized and believed, without realizing it; that I was worthless, inferior, lazy and dumb.'*

At home Kay faced another taskmaster as Aunt Pearl, also a teacher, supervised her homework. Unfortunately, Aunt Pearl began drinking beer as soon as she got home from school, and by the time Kay was down to her last assignment, she was berated for stupidity and laziness. She and her aunt got along well as long as her aunt was sober, but in her drunken stupor she would lash out at Kay, 'The Coles blood is going to ruin you! Bitch! You little Coles whore.' She was vicious when drunk.

By the time Kay was ready for junior high, the civil rights movement had flowered and school integration had become an issue. She was selected as one of twenty-six black students to attend a three-hundred-student white school. Suddenly she found herself in the midst of hostility and scorn. When she walked down the halls in the crush of students she felt pinpricks on her legs and back, so that sometimes she had to press her dress against her legs to keep the blood from running down.

At first her grades were poor – teachers seemed to demand more of her than of the white students, and would draw attention to her mistakes in front of the class. One teacher even remarked that they were having brownies for lunch, but she didn't know why since they seemed to have enough 'brownies' already.

Kay's greatest fear was finding herself alone in the halls with a group of taunting boys. One day her fear was realized as they surrounded her at the top of the stairs, gave her a push which sent her sprawling down the stairs and threw her books down after her. Everyone laughed and made crude jokes.

Then to her surprise one of the white girls came over to her and helped her gather up her books. She walked to the office with her, even as her friends called out 'nigger lover,' explaining that Kay shouldn't think that all white people were the same. Kay writes in her biography, 'That may have been the single most important incident in shaping my views on race.'*

As the years passed, Aunt Pearl's drinking became worse. On occasions she threw Kay's clothes out of the front door, or rang her mother to come and get her. She wrongfully accused Kay of drinking, smoking and running around with boyfriends. During high school, however, Kay's mother came to live with them for a time, and Kay enjoyed the creature comforts of Pearl's home, plus the security and loving care of Mama who polished and cooked and couldn't do enough for her only daughter.

Mama had always taken her children to church and Kay remembers the warmth and comfort of the black church with its joyous music and sense of family. She considered herself a Christian until one night, as they were sitting around the kitchen table having dinner, Billy Graham came on the TV. She found herself listening intensely as he talked about being confused, lonely, alienated, fearful. She felt as though he was speaking just to her as he explained, 'There is a place in our soul that only Jesus Christ can fill.'

After dinner she went to her room and 'gave her life to Christ.' She wasn't sure exactly what that meant, and didn't feel any different. But in the weeks and months ahead she noticed changes in her attitudes and reactions, found herself loving to read the Bible and pray, and knew for a certainty that she belonged to Christ.

Because of Aunt Pearl's and Uncle J.B.'s help, Kay could realistically think about attending college. She chose Hampton Institute, now called Hampton University, an all-black college not far from her home in Richmond. She'd had enough of integration for a while, and wanted to go where she was accepted, comfortable and where she could join any campus activity she wished.

Hampton is not a Christian school. It was founded to provide education for freed slaves and for native Americans. During the sixties the civil rights movement mushroomed on campus. Not only were rights demanded but the value of personhood was elevated. 'Black is beautiful' became the cry that lifted their spirits and gave them a sense of worth.

More importantly, Kay joined an InterVarsity group on campus, and saw that Christians were not fringe people or failures, but leaders and loving people who cared about others. Her growing knowledge of the Bible reinforced her sense of worth as she read passages like, 'For you created my inmost being; you knit me together in my mother's womb. I praise you because I am fearfully and wonderfully made' (Ps. 139:13,14).

Years later she would write, 'It was with a sense of childlike wonder that I grasped the fact that God loved even a fatherless, little nappy-haired (kinky-haired) girl like me. He had 'knit me together' in my mother's womb. He loved me even before I was born.'*

However, as Kay and other IVCF students shared their love for Christ, they found that students considered them sell-outs to the white man's religion. It was not popular to promote a Christian cause on black campuses.

When evangelist Tom Skinner visited the campus he encouraged Christian students. Kay remembers, 'We were trying to figure out what it meant to be black and Christian in the culture of that day, and we realized we were not going to find all the answers through groups like InterVarsity. What we found in Tom Skinner was a towering figure of a man straight off the streets of Harlem who had a real connection with our unique needs. He gave us hope and empowered us as Christ's ambassadors to those blacks on our campus who were sceptical toward Christianity.'[1]

Along with the cry that 'Black is beautiful' went the corrollary that black is natural. Kay went through a time when she wished she were ebony-skinned like a pure African, rather than the colour she was, which was the result of mixed blood in her past. She wore an Afro hairdo and would have worn African prints 'looking like a village queen' if they'd been available.

Kay completed her college courses a semester before the rest of her classmates. Since she couldn't find a teaching job in the middle of the year she decided to apply at the Richmond office of American Telephone and Telegraph for an interim position, possibly as an operator. To her surprise the personnel manager offered her a management position. Every company was seeking to meet its quotas of minorities and women to avoid lawsuits, and Kay was just what they wanted.

Many times over the years Kay has heard that she was hired because she was a woman, because she was black, because she was a conservative, because she was young. But she always reminds her detractors that in today's competitive job market, you also have to be competent.

Shortly after she began working at AT&T she was offered a promotion to Roanoke, Virginia. One woman passed by her cubicle and remarked loudly, 'I guess you have to be a Negro to go anywhere in this company today.' Kay shot back, 'No you just have to be good.'*

Roanoke proved to be a milestone in Kay's life. On her first lonely night there, a friend arranged a date with Charles James. The evening started out badly. Charles thought Kay stuck up. Kay saw a long-haired college dropout. But as they began talking over dinner the outer shells fell away and each began to see in the other a special person. After dating for a few weeks, they realized they were falling in love.

Kay faced one serious obstacle. Though he had been to church all his life, and knew more about the Bible than she did, Charles showed no evidence of a personal relationship with Jesus Christ. Religion was a formality to him. She knew she could not marry him and one night as they were ready to say good night, she explained that she couldn't see him any more. She began to cry as she got out of the car, and Charles asked, 'Do you need to talk?' Kay responded, 'No I have someone to talk to.'*

With that Charles began to cry too. Kay soon realized he was not crying because she was breaking up with him, but because he wanted to know Jesus Christ in such a personal way too. He had never realized that God was someone you could talk to and cry with. That night Charles gave his life to Jesus Christ.

Three months later, on January 6, 1973, Kay and Charles were married in Richmond. (On the 26th of that same month, the historic Roe vs. Wade bill was passed – which would later become a major focus of Kay's life.)

Because of the prevailing attitudes in the sixties, Kay didn't want a lavish wedding; people were getting married in parks and on beaches. She says, 'I had an arrogant disdain for tradition and ceremony. I have often regretted that I didn't make it more of me.' Rather, she simply told her mother and aunts the date and that they could plan the ceremony for her.

Kay continued to work for AT&T, and to this day credits the excellent training she was given for much of her management skills. She learned to respond to criticism with a sense of humour which has often stood her in good stead. For instance, while supervising the Directory Assistance department, one of the black operators had to deal with an obnoxious caller. Kay took over and asked how she could help. The customer shouted, 'Can you get me that number? That stupid nigger wouldn't give it to me.'

Kay responded, 'Well sir, this one can't either because the number isn't published.'*

Her career was taking off as she moved from one supervisory role to another, when Kay discovered she was pregnant. She and Charles seriously discussed which one of them should stay at home with the baby, but in the end realized that Kay was the nurturer and would do a better job at home. They were determined that their child would have the full attention of at least one parent.

Charles Everett James was born in June 1974 – a finicky, colicky baby. He never slept more than two hours, and Kay was exhausted and depressed listening helplessly to his screams. Meanwhile Charles' career was moving ahead and he would come home with exciting stories of events at the office, or packing up to go on a business trip. And then Kay discovered she was pregnant again – this time with their daughter Elizabeth. Three years later their son Robbie was born. Even though they were all unplanned pregnancies, Kay and Charles rejoiced in the gift of life God had given them.

Years later when Kay was involved in the National Right to Life campaign, reporters would stalk her, trying to get her to say why she was opposed to 'safe sex with condoms.' One day just as the family was getting into their car for an outing, a reporter appeared asking why she opposed condom distribution to teenagers. In her forthright, no-nonsense manner she said, 'Let me tell you something off-the-record. I have two condom kids. The result of condom failure for my husband and me has been two wonderful kids whom we adore and treasure. The result for someone else could be death.'

Charles and Kay had joined a white Presbyterian church in Roanoke, primarily for the solid biblical teaching they found there. During the difficult months of Chuck's infancy, Kay attended a morning Bible study for young mothers. She was able to leave Chuck in the church nursery and enjoy the teaching, fellowship and a good meal with other young mothers. One day a young woman told her about a crisis pregnancy centre where she was a volunteer and asked Kay if she might be interested in helping, since they often had young black women call for help.

As Kay discussed the issue with Charles, they both realized they knew little about abortion but felt instinctively that it was wrong. Charles encouraged her, and so once or twice a week Kay took Chuck to the *Birthright* Center as a volunteer. Kay writes, 'This was my first exposure to the issue. I was horrified at what I learned and saw. . . . When I began to read the literature and see the pictures and as I became more educated about the issue, I felt very deeply about it. Something akin to righteous indignation stirred within.'*

A few years later Charles was offered a promotion to Richmond and the family moved back home. Mama now came to live with them, and Kay had more free time to pursue a matter that was deep on her heart – to find her alcoholic father. He had remarried and cut off all communication with the family. However, after months of attempting to help him and encouraging him to go for treatment, she realized it was hopeless. Deep within her heart, however, Kay never lost the assurance that Daddy loved her.

In Richmond the Jameses once again chose a white Presbyterian church because of its strong teaching and emphasis on evangelism. Kay believes this was a providential move, for a young man fired up about the abortion issue felt Protestant churches should become more involved and provide institutionalized help for women in crisis.

He called a small group together to help set up a crisis pregnancy centre, and invited Kay to join them. While Kay realized that the black community had a rich history of caring for mothers in need (her own life is an example), it had not depended on organized institutions to do the job. Many black pastors who were called to get involved would respond, 'What do you mean? We are a crisis pregnancy centre. I dealt with five cases this week.'*

As the pro-choice/pro-life debate escalated, Kay realized that pro-choice really meant no choice. She heard young girls say, 'I'm choosing this abortion because I have no other choice.' Without guidance, loving support and options offered, a young woman whose boyfriend left her, or whose parents would throw her out, had no choice but abortion. Kay believed women would chose life if they were given viable alternatives. Because her children were small – Robbie was just a baby – she had limited time to volunteer, but Kay's heart had been captured by the defenceless unborn, and in the days ahead their tiny fingers would wrap themselves around her like Lilliputian ropes.

A few months after Robbie's birth, four-year-old Elizabeth, called Bizzie by the family, showed flu-like symptoms for several weeks. She complained of headaches, and often developed a fever towards nightfall. Routine treatments were not helping, and on December 3rd, 1979, Bizzie was admitted to the hospital. Within days Kay feared her daughter was slipping away from her. She was lethargic and incoherent, and the doctors could not diagnose her illness. Gradually her internal systems were shutting down.

One day a paediatric respiratory specialist was visiting the hospital and came to examine Bizzie. In two minutes he reported, 'She's got tuberculous meningitis.' He offered little hope. 'When the disease runs its course, it's usually fatal within three weeks.'

Kay still recalls how the church family, friends and the pastor came to their rescue – sitting with them in the hospital, taking care of household chores, looking after the boys and even putting up a Christmas tree and providing gifts.

One evening Charles noticed that Bizzie had slipped into a coma. As he touched her he was shocked to discover that her body was stiff as a board. She was having a fit! The emergency team rushed into the room, and the hospital chaplain took Kay and Charles out while the team worked to resuscitate their precious daughter. Though the team was able to stabilize her, the doctors felt she had to be moved to the Medical College of Virginia. Charles would not allow the rescue squad to move her until the Catholic chaplain came back to the room with a bottle of oil. Together they anointed Bizzie and prayed for her, each one laying a hand on her lifeless body. The doctors gave little hope that she would be normal even if she survived.

But a few days before Christmas Bizzie reached for her favourite blanket. Kay called her name, and Bizzie mumbled, 'Where's my mommy?' The crisis was over, but it would be many months before her atrophied muscles were strong enough for her to walk or even sit up.

Through the long ordeal and complete recovery, Kay and Charles learned lessons that have stayed with them. 'We are called only to have faith in our Lord Jesus Christ. To trust all that we have and all that we are into his care.

Throughout the spiritual and emotional ups and downs of Bizzie's illness, we hung onto his promise that "All things work together for good to those who love God, who have been called according to his purpose" ' (Rom. 8:28).*

While Charles and Kay were committed to giving their children adequate care and supervision, the cost of living in their region made it almost imperative that Kay go back to work. Once Robbie was in kindergarten, Kay took a management job with Circuit City.

When Charles' job called him to work in Washington D.C., the family decided to move to Annadale, Virginia, within reasonable driving distance. Aunt Pearl had died and left the family house to Kay and this became the down-payment for their home in Virginia. Kay knew that with the even higher cost of living in the D.C. area she would have to work. When she resigned her job at Circuit City, she was offered another job at their headquarters in Maryland. This was a 70-mile commute each day, but at last the family was living above the 'paycheque-to-paycheque just-scraping-by routine' they had known all their married life. In fact, Kay was able to hire a live-in nanny to relieve the burden of housework and make sure someone was there when the children came home from school.

Then one night she received the fateful phone call that would change the direction of her life forever. Someone from the National Right to Life Committee called to ask if she would participate in a black cable-vision talk show on the abortion issue. Kay's immediate response was 'Thanks, but no thanks.'

When she explained the call to her family still sitting around the dinner table, there was a shocked silence. Only a few weeks earlier Kay and ten-year old Chuck had had a lengthy discussion about abortion when he was helping her clear out some old literature. He'd never seen pictures of aborted foetuses and couldn't comprehend why anyone would want to kill a baby. His open-hearted question to her was, 'Why don't you and daddy do something about it?'

Kay had explained that the law permitted it, but that if she ever had an opportunity to help change the law, she would do so. Chuck now reminded her of her promise. Rebuked she called the committee member back the next day to say she would be willing to take part in the talk show, though her stomach churned at the very thought.

Kay debated a seasoned veteran of Planned Parenthood, armed with statistics and examples. Kay simply spoke from the conviction of her heart. The show went so well that a representative of the National Right to Life Committee asked to see the video. Kay invited him and his wife to dinner and at the close of the evening he asked if she would consider joining the staff. Kay politely demurred, thinking to herself *I finally have a well-paid job in the corporate world and I'm not ready to give up my well-earned security.*

But in her heart she did not have peace. Several months later as she was listening to a tape on her long journey to work, she heard an Episcopal priest make a compelling case for getting involved in the pro-life movement. Tears streamed down her face as she listened; as soon as she got to the office she phoned Charles to tell him she'd decided to accept the offer at the National Right to Life Committee. He was elated. She recalls the powerful pull God's Spirit had put on her life. 'Babies were dying because people like me didn't want to get involved. It occurred to me that while this battle for the lives of millions of unborn children was going on all around me, I could not hide myself behind a good job selling stereos and TV sets.'*

For the next three years Kay threw herself into the pro-life debate with all the energy and ability God had given her. She debated the issues in every setting possible – schools, businesses, government offices, radio, TV. Often her briefings were given to her scribbled on a half-sheet of paper as she took a cab over to CNN.

Part of her responsibility was to endorse pro-life candidates. On one trip she had just finished endorsing a candidate she did not know well, and was sitting in the lobby of a hotel with him watching his opponent give a speech on TV with several black people standing around him. Her candidate pointed at the TV screen, 'Just look at that! If I ran that stuff I'd lose half my supporters. Just look at him with those people.'* From that time on Kay carefully investigated her candidate's position on race and other values she felt were important before endorsing him or her.

Kay asserts that she would never support a pro-choice candidate over a pro-life candidate. She would rather just stay neutral. She states, 'There are principles that transcend politics. I could never do anything in the political arena that I believe would be the antithesis of what God called me as a person and a woman to do. That includes not only being pro-life, but against racism. God says more about being against poverty and caring for the poor [than almost anything else.]'

Kay found the media solidly biased against the pro-life position. Talk-show hosts like Donahue and Oprah favoured the pro-abortion leadership. Once she was asked to appear on the Donahue show with the leading spokesperson for Planned Parenthood, Faye Wattleton. But Faye refused to appear on the show with Kay, and so Kay was 'disinvited' and not even allowed to be part of the audience.

Preparing for a debate was always a harrowing experience. No matter how well she prepared, she knew that she had to have convincing answers on the spot. Kay made it a practice to spend two hours in her hotel room before a debate 'eating rug' – lying stretched out on her face before the Lord. She was totally dependent upon his wisdom and guidance as she entered these life-changing debates.

In her biography, *Never Forget*, Kay describes one such response to which her opponent had no answer:

> A woman in the audience angrily told me I was obviously so middle class that I didn't have a clue as to the conditions that poor black women face. 'if you realized what these women were going through, you would realize that abortion is their only choice.'
>
> I asked that woman to consider a poor black woman on welfare. She already has four kids and an alcoholic husband who has all but abandoned the family. Now she discovers that another child is on the way.
>
> 'How would you counsel that woman?' I asked.
>
> Without hesitation she answered, 'The most compassionate thing that woman could do for herself and the children she already has is to have an abortion. If brought into this world, that child would have a very poor quality of life.'
>
> 'I have a vested interest in your answer to that question,' I responded. 'That woman I described was my mother. I was the fifth of six children born into poverty. And in case you're interested, the quality of my life is just fine.'*

Even as the pace quickened and the opportunities broadened, Kay had a growing sense that her family was paying a price. One night when she phoned home from her hotel room after a debate Robbie asked plaintively, 'Mommy, why won't you come home?'

Kay and Charles had always sought God's will for their lives and for the welfare of their family. Not only had Charles been supportive, but encouraging as she accepted more and more responsibility with the Right to Life Committee. She believes 'The ultimate question is not whether I should work or not, but am I willing to go wherever God takes me? There comes a certain amount of confidence that if you are working in God's will, he will give you the grace for what he has called you to do. Someone else can't make the same choices that I made, because it may not be God's will for them. It is a very individual thing. I ask constantly, [if this is not your will] Lord remove the grace. And he's done that. The babysitter quits, the marriage is having a difficult time; there are behaviour problems. When that starts I know the grace is lifted and I know it's time [for a change].'

Now she sensed the grace had lifted and she needed to reconsider her all-consuming role in the pro-life movement. Shortly after Robbie's request, the family learned that Mama had cancer and would need care and support. Kay resigned from the National Right to Life Committee. As Mama's health deteriorated, Kay spent weekends with her in Richmond, enjoying the opportunity to care for her mother who had always served so many so willingly.

However, when Mama adamantly insisted that she should not reject the request of the son of the president of the United States, Kay reluctantly agreed to call George Bush Jr. back. She told him that since Mama didn't have much time, he should find the highest placed position he could so Mama could be really proud of her. As a result Kay was appointed Assistant Secretary for Public Affairs of the Department of Health and Human Services. As this was a subcabinet position her appointment required Senate confirmation. However, by the time Kay was confirmed, Mama was too weak to attend the swearing-in-ceremony, and she died four months later.

Whether it's the nature of public office, or Kay's own personality, most of her jobs have only lasted about two years before she has moved on to something else. After serving at HHS for a time she accepted an offer to reorganize a non-profit-making organization in Washington. Within a year she was asked to return to political office, this time as Associate Director for the Office of National Drug Control Strategy. Once again she faced Senate confirmation. Several questioned her qualifications for the job, but she reminded them that she'd grown up in a drug-infested inner city and had seen the effects of alcohol abuse within her own family.

Though Kay has nothing to hide, she finds the confirmations an invasion of privacy. 'Politics in America has become vicious. The civility has left the process,' she declares. 'I wasn't so much afraid of what was real in my life. I'm a redeemed human being and I serve a Lord who has paid the price. I've confessed my sin to him, but I really don't want to confess my sin before the nation.' Kay says that those who go through confirmations for major appointments must be ready to face accusations that are false and stories that are manufactured. She saw one of her dear friends crucified in that manner. 'Who would willingly, knowingly walk into that?' she asks.

After the Republican defeat in 1992, Kay felt she had done her political duty and was ready for a breather. She had no interest in going back into the political arena. But she had read many political biographies about people whom God had called into government service as reluctant servants. Friends reminded her that she was a patriot and loved her country too much not to serve if called upon.

Then one day the call came – from the office of George Allen, governor of Virginia, offering her a job as cabinet secretary of Health and Human Services. Kay refused as politely as she could, offering him several other names he might consider. But a second call put more pressure on her to reconsider.

She'd told several of her friends about the offer, and one called her saying, 'I don't feel right about this. Have you humbly and submissively taken this decision before the Lord?'

Kay knew her friend was concerned about her spiritual well-being; she had been her spiritual mentor for many years. Kay admitted she had not taken it humbly and submissively before the Lord because she was afraid of what he might say and she didn't want the job.

That weekend Charles and Kay and another couple went off to fast and pray. They came to the conclusion that if the governor called and offered the position again, Kay was to accept it. She knew he was actively looking for someone, and there were lots of people who would love to have the job. In her heart Kay was confident that the governor would not call a third time; that was unheard of! Some of her friends even encouraged her to call the governor herself and tell him she'd reconsidered. But she refused.

Charles and Kay returned home at six in the evening; at seven the governor called again. She had no choice.

Kay felt this confirmation would be the hardest of all. She knew she would be a lightning rod because of the positions she'd taken on abortion, contraception, and unmarried teenagers. 'I knew what would happen to me if I said yes. It's sort of like being willing to do what God has called you to do and being willing to pay a huge price.'

The head of Planned Parenthood said of her confirmation hearings, 'Never in the history of the Commonwealth of Virginia has a government's nominee been turned down, but this will be the first.'

She was wrong. Kay was confirmed as the head of an organization with a four billion dollar budget, nineteen thousand employees and seventeen state agencies under her. Her track record had proven that it wasn't just because of being black or being a woman, but because she had the capabilities to execute policy and manage that kind of bureaucracy.

Part of her skill is in being able to manage men. When asked if they treat her differently or patronize her she responded, 'Absolutely not. I won't tolerate it.' But then she smiles and adds, 'Being an aggressive, tough female in the political arena all day, and being a mommy at night, you have to change roles. But many times I find that what is needed in the work environment is a nurturing, caring perspective, but what's needed at home is a tough aggressive mom who's not taking any stuff off of kids. It's a complete package.'

While Charles and Kay have been strict disciplinarians, they have also given the children a sense of being totally loved and of prime importance to their parents. Kay has been fortunate enough to be high enough placed in her positions that she could make it clear to her employers, *My family comes first.*

'I have left cabinet meetings to go to birthday parties,' Kay explains. 'I committed to having dinner together at home with my family. Even when I was in the White House I did not do the Washington reception party scene. If you ask anyone in my office they will tell you that I don't care if the president of the university is in my office; I will always take a phone call from my children. My whole life has been about trying to create a better city, state, country, better world for them. This IS all about my children.'

How have the children fared now that they are almost grown up? Chuck is in law school and Elizabeth is studying at Hampton, her mother's alma mater, while Robbie is a senior in high school. Kay believes her children have benefited from her involvement in issues that matter. 'They tend to be far more confident, independent and self-assured [than most kids their age]. It could easily have gone in another direction. The only reason it didn't is because God's grace was there.'

Not long ago she asked them a question most mothers would like to ask. Were they drug-free, have they abstained from sex and from alcohol? All three said yes, which Kay believes is an evidence of God's grace. All three have made their public professions of faith and have made Christ Lord of their lives. But Kay adds wistfully, 'As their mother I'm looking for something more. When do they fall in love with Jesus?'

Kay has had a lot of help from Charles, who from the beginning has done his share of parenting. Kay believes they have developed an ideal division of responsibilities. 'It's funny to me when I as a conservative, female pro-family activist get 'criticized by the liberal feminists of this country,' she laughs. 'I think we have one of the most liberated marriages you will ever see with our ability to work out the roles of marriage and who does what. The lines are very blurred.'

Analysing her marriage, Kay realizes that Charles' personality and his bent are exactly right for her. He is very secure and not intimidated or threatened by who she is and what she does. Though their career tracks have taken different directions, he moved forward successfully with Bell Atlantic for many years. Recently he has become the director of personnel and training for the state of Virginia.

But Kay will be the first to admit how difficult marriage has been. 'For us it has been hard; being married is one of the hardest things I've ever had to do. Even though I'm confident that he's exactly the one God picked out for me, I don't want to diminish at all how difficult it is and continues to be.'

When asked why their marriage has stood the test for more than twenty years, Kay affirms that it is the commitment they made when they were married. 'Leaving is not an option; not working at it is not an option,' she says. Instead they have tried many ways to hone their relationship with counselling, marriage workshops, accountability relationships with godly people they admire and trust; reading. Kay confesses, 'I don't think it's fair that so many Christian couples we know make it look so easy.' They realize that they have an unusual amount of stress on their marriage, and cannot let up on working at it for one day. Charles surprised her and came out to the Republican convention in San Diego between the platform and committee meetings. Kay's eyes twinkled as she remarked, 'And the spark is still there, for the record!' Charles and Kay have made a conscious decision to be vulnerable about many aspects of their marriage. They have even taught an eight-week course on marriage and hope to do more of that in the future.

In March 1996 Kay moved back out of politics to become Dean of the School of Government at Regent University in Virginia Beach, Virginia. Chancellor Pat Robertson announced the appointment at a press conference. 'Because we wanted excellence in the school, we have spent a long time looking at many potential candidates,' Robertson said. 'And none quite filled the bill until today when we have had the acceptance of a wonderful person to become the dean of this very important school – Kay Coles James.'

The Robertson School of Government at Regent University prepares leaders for government, politics and policy-making. It believes that the source of enduring principles for government is the expression of God in Scripture and creation.

Kay believes God has her at Regent University right now to take the information, knowledge and experience God has given her to train up the next generation of leadership. She believes the combination of teaching with making practical use of the experience she's had in government gives her opportunity to influence the course of the nation.

If she moves back into the political arena, it will only be because God has made it unquestionably clear that it is his will. It will not be because of the status or power it offers. 'I have no interest in power. I have all the power that's available in this universe in Christ.'

Right Mama?

Notes

Much of the information and the quotes marked with an asterisks come from Kay James' autobiography *Never Forget*, written with Jacqualline Cobb Fuller (Zondervan 1992), and used with permission.

1. Edward Gilbreath, "A Prophet out of Harlem," *Christianity Today,* 16 September 1960, 40.

Fourteen

The Tug of War between Motherhood and Ministry – Ruth Heil, Germany

A wife of noble character, who can find? . . . Her husband is respected at the city gate where he takes his seat among the elders of the land. She makes linen garments and sells them, and supplies the merchants with sashes. She is clothed with strength and dignity; she can laugh at the days to come. She speaks with wisdom and faithful instruction is on her tongue. She watches over the affairs of her household and does not eat the bread of idleness. Her children arise and call her blessed; her husband also, and he praises her. Many women do noble things, but you surpass them all.: Charm is deceptive and beauty is fleeting; but a woman who fears the Lord is to be praised. Give her the reward she has earned, and let her works bring her praise at the city gate.

Pr. 31:10, 23–31.

Ruth Heil stood in front of the audience of women, their faces turning towards her expectantly. Perhaps some of them were surprised to see how young and relaxed this mother of ten looked. Her brown eyes sparkled with enthusiasm. She grinned frequently as she talked, the words spilling out rapidly in a voice that hardly needed amplification. In a day when few women wear hats, Ruth had crushed a broad-brimmed straw bowler over her unruly brown hair, giving her a little girl look.

'We were engaged less than two years,' she explained as she launched into her favourite topic. 'In that time we wrote countless letters, speaking about love. My previously unromantic man became creative – he even began to write poetry for me. I was overcome with joy – our marriage would never become boring. Our burning love for each other would continually renew itself.'

Then Ruth grew serious as she told how after their marriage the declarations of love were few and far between. The more she asked her husband Hans if he loved her, the more grudgingly he would answer, 'Of course!' Instead he criticized her cooking skills and lack of punctuality.

Ruth explained that while women need constant verbal reassurance of love from their husbands, men seem to feel that if they are caring and provide for their wives, that is enough – but not enough for a satisfying relationship, according to Ruth. 'We must learn to give to the other whatever he or she needs to feel satisfied . . . let each other know what you need to feel loved as a mate.'

These practical insights into love and marriage, and her ability to share the warmth and stress of raising a large family with candour and humour, have made Ruth Heil one of the most sought-after women speakers in German-speaking Europe. She and her husband Hans lead marriage seminars and train seminar leaders for the international *Family Life Mission* founded by Walter and Ingrid Trobisch.

Ruth's schedule is booked three years in advance. Besides leading marriage and family seminars with her husband, she speaks at the popular *Frauen Frühstück* (Women's Breakfast) meetings or to church women's groups. Her twenty-five published books include children's stories, books on marriage and beautiful gift books for weddings, anniversaries, and birth celebrations. She appears frequently on German television.

She could never have dreamed that her offer to help the Trobisches care for their children would have such a far-reaching effect on her life. At sixteen Ruth already knew she wanted to be a missionary. When she heard Walter Trobisch, a well-known German missionary, speak in their small Lutheran church, Ruth asked her parents to find out if there was any way she could help the Trobisch family.

Ruth's father telephoned Walter Trobisch, who had settled in a town near them, to find out if there was any way she could help. Walter responded enthusiastically, 'Yes, sure! My wife is coming soon. We have five little kids from two to nine, and coming from Africa, they are very wild.'

Indeed they were. 'I learned everything I needed during that year – how to cook and how to talk with kids. They were so wild. They wanted to put water on everything; sugar in the sheets. They'd ring the doorbell and when I opened the door there was no one there. Once they ran water into the bath, and it overflowed under the door, but they had locked the door so we couldn't open it.' Ruth laughs as she recounts these antics. 'That's when my desire to work with children grew!'

One day a young man came to offer his services as a translator to Pastor Trobisch, whose books on love and marriage were in demand in many parts of the world. Hans-Joakim Heil knew ten languages, including Greek and Hebrew, and was studying at the Lutheran seminary to be a pastor. Ruth eyed this tall slender man with interest, and made it a point to be nearby whenever he came to work with Pastor Trobisch. It was evident that a mutual interest was developing, but neither seemed to have the courage to speak up. One day when Hans was working on a translation, Ruth came into the room to talk with him. Kathryn, one of the children stood in the doorway observing them. Suddenly, as if making a discovery, she piped out in a loud voice, 'Er liebt Dich!' (He loves you). A warm glow still spreads over Ruth's face when she tells this story – 'It was so wonderful.'

But her parents weren't sure it was wonderful. She was only seventeen and still had a two-year nursing course ahead of her. And they insisted that Hans complete his examination for the pastorate before they marry. The day they announced their engagement Hans told his future mother-in-law, 'Mum, I would really like it if this were our wedding day.'

During the two-year engagement Hans and Ruth were separated much of the time, and pursued their courtship through correspondence. But when they were together they dreamed and planned as any couple does. That's when Ruth told him she wanted to have twelve children.

Hans still remembers those discussions. 'Ruth was crazy about children. Her suggestion of having twelve children seemed very unrealistic to me. I agreed to half a dozen. But in my heart I thought, 'It's no use arguing about this. If she has one or two children one day, she will see how much work it is [and change her mind.]'

Another concern to Ruth was her sense of call to the mission field – specifically to Africa. She hadn't told Hans about this. But one day when they were together Hans brought up an issue that had been troubling him. 'Ruth, there is one problem we should talk about. I think God called me to go to Africa. Could you imagine yourself going to Africa?' Ruth's heart leapt with joy. God was so wonderful. Not only had he called them together, but he had given them the same call to serve him.

The reality of God in her life goes back to Ruth's childhood. Born in 1947, just after the end of the Second World War, she knew extreme poverty as Germany reeled from its defeat. Living in a small town, the family faced many days without food. Her father had developed tuberculosis and could not work. Many a time her parents said to the children, 'Today there is nothing. Let's go on our knees and tell our heavenly Father.'

'Very early in life I experienced how God answers prayer,' Ruth recalls. 'I saw how God cared for us in time of need. On one occasion my brother was so impressed [at God's special provision] that he cried, 'Papi, that should go in the paper.' But my father sadly answered, "They wouldn't believe it." '

In spite of their poverty, her parents had a deep concern for people in need. 'My mother was a faithful pray-er, and set an example of hospitality,' Ruth remembers. 'They took in ex-prisoners who had recently been released. Often they were robbed. But in spite of that they helped again and again.'

Because of her father's severe tuberculosis, which was worsened by malnutrition, doctors warned that he would not survive past the age of thirty-five. But today at eighty he still visits prisoners to tell them about God's love. To Ruth, talking about the love of Jesus, and even the Second Coming (a taboo subject in the German church at that time) was natural as she followed her parents' example. Even as a child, she remembers setting up a 'church' in her back garden and preaching to the local children.

When Walter Trobisch visited their church the first time, her heart was smitten with the desire to go to Africa. She wanted to go to Bible school, but the only school available was charismatic and her Lutheran parents would not allow this. 'If you go,' her father warned, 'it would destroy the work that I'm doing.'

Ruth could not understand this block in her plans. Only in later years would she comprehend the deep divisions in the German church, and the inability of Christians from different backgrounds to understand and accept each other. She just remembers going into the little Lutheran church crying, 'No! No! No!'

But even at sixteen she knew how to listen to the voice of God. 'As I sat there, all that came to my mind was that if God wanted me to be somewhere, he could open the way. He had a plan; He was the master, and nobody could destroy his plan. I opened a songbook to an old song:

If I don't know the way, You know it.
If I don't know the plan, You know it.
You know the time, You know the way,
You know everything.

'And I said, "Lord, that's it. I give it all up into your hands. You know the time; you know everything. I know nothing. I'm just destroyed and angry and sad. But now it's in your hands." '

How beautifully God worked out his plan. Instead of going to Bible school, she spent a year at the Trobisches. As she cared for the lively children and watched their mother Ingrid show such love and patience towards them, she realized that children are a gift from God and motherhood a worthy role which he gives to many women.

At the Trobisches' she met Hans, so wise and well-educated, preparing for the ministry, and the mission field. Even though Walter Trobisch had warned them before their marriage that he'd never seen two people so different get married, Ruth and Hans joyfully entered marriage with high hopes for the future. Hans was appointed pastor of a small Lutheran church and they lived comfortably in the manse the church provided.

In the first year or two Hans and Ruth worked with a group of young people who had come out of the drug culture. God healed many and set them free – many who today are still 'uncle' and 'auntie' to the Heil children.

But the ministry in the church itself was less than satisfying. 'So much paperwork,' Ruth reiterates. 'Building a kindergarten, baptizing kids whose parents didn't believe, officiating at weddings and funerals . . . not really serving the people. We felt as though we were going backwards spiritually.'

And even as their spiritual vitality seemed to be drying up, Hans deteriorated physically. He suffered debilitating bouts of weakness and high blood pressure. He couldn't stand behind the pulpit for any length of time. He became so weak he couldn't even hold up a newspaper to read it. An underlying depression controlled his spirits, and there was little doctors seemed to be able to do to help him. In fact, doctors did not know the cause of his strange illness.

In the first two years of their marriage, Ruth waited expectantly to become pregnant. She was convinced that once Hans saw how wonderful it was to be a father, he would certainly want more than two or three children. When she did not become pregnant right away, Ruth even questioned in her heart, whether she married just to have children. Perhaps God was testing her.

With the arrival of Markus in 1969, the reality of caring for a child hit home. For a time she couldn't imagine taking care of a second. 'In spite of our precautions' she told an interviewer for *Lydia* magazine, 'I became pregnant at the first possible opportunity. In less than one year we had two children. Two children who were both still in diapers, who could not walk – and had a totally exhausted mother'.

'But still my deepest wish was to have more children,' Ruth admits. And two years later Demaris was born. And though by this time Hans was almost totally bedridden and unable to serve the church or to help her, Ruth never lost the joy of motherhood.

In *My Child Within* she recalls an evening after her three little ones were in bed.

> I've just completed my evening rounds – I go from bed to bed each night, making sure that my little ones are well covered and tucked in. When I looked at our sleepers in the light of the bedside lamp, I wanted to shout for joy: what a privilege, to be the mother of these sweet kids. Children's arms to hug you – what kind of a price tag could you hang on that? How wonderful to be a mother . . . What reason would I have to care about following generations, if I weren't connected to them through my children?
> 'Of course no one can guarantee me that our children will turn out well. Every single child is a hazardous undertaking. I can only continue to invest all my love in them. But they are calculated risks, for we often find both the possibilities and the joys of accomplishment in them. And I have faith in God's power; he will enable us to fulfil our assigned tasks.[1]

It became evident that Hans would have to give up the pastorate. After little more than five years his dreams had vanished; the prospect of Africa erased from his plans. Ruth not only had to care for the children alone, but also had to make the decisions about their move. Her parents suggested the family move into the town where they were living so that they could see each other more often. Ruth's mother warned her not to have any more children, since she could not physically help her care for more.

The church arranged a wonderful farewell. 'It was like a wedding,' Ruth remembers, 'with big cars and flowers. But Hans was so depressed he couldn't even talk.' As they drove out of the town and up the mountain in a procession of cars, Hans told her to look back at their lives. He fully believed there was nothing ahead.

With her natural buoyancy, Ruth tried to encourage Hans with descriptions of the quaint little town to which they were moving. Even though they had only two rooms (the church's disability stipend would cover only the rent), Ruth was confident it would be a new beginning for their family. When she asked Hans' opinion he replied, 'Just do what you think we should do. For me it's lost; it's over. Let's just move wherever you want to.'

Physically the move was difficult. Hans could not help move even a single piece of furniture. They were crowded and had little money for food or other essentials. There were days when Ruth didn't want to hear one more, 'Mummy I'm thirsty! Mummy, he hit me.'

Some mornings she woke up with not enough money in the house to buy bread. 'I didn't want to ask anybody because everybody said, "Stop having kids. You have no money; you have no future." ' So she asked God instead, and the experience of her parents' poverty and trust in God' taught her the lesson of faith all over again. 'Today I know that I needed that time to know that God provides everything!'

And God provided in unusual ways. Sometimes she asked for bread; and God provided bread. Once she asked for face cream, and a friend came over and apologetically said, 'I wanted to bring you flowers, but instead I brought you this.' Ruth reached for the paper bag, knowing that she'd find her face cream inside. Through these difficult times, the Trobisches remained faithful friends, encouraging and helping all they could, offering Hans small translation jobs whenever he could handle them.

God provided for the little things, but sometimes it seemed as though he didn't provide for the big ones. Hans was not getting better, and the doctors were suggesting he go to Heidelberg for extensive tests. To add to their problems, Ruth became ill with an infection. She wasn't prepared for the shock when the doctor told her she was pregnant again. Much as she had wanted more children, she wasn't ready for this one. On the way home she kept thinking of the way her neighbours would react. The curious and disapproving glances they would get. And what would her mother say? What would Hans say?

To this day she recalls her return home vividly, 'When I got home Hans was waiting. I walked in the door saying, "I have a kidney infection – and we're going to have another baby." "Hallelujah!" he cried, and threw his arms around me. Didn't he even see my discouragement? I didn't feel like being hugged – I felt like giving up. I kept thinking of all the women who conceive children without wanting them and simply have abortions. I knew exactly how they felt. I felt that I had a right to shake these troubles off. And I just felt too tired to cope with the added strain of a pregnancy, piled on top of the responsibilities of my little ones. It seemed impossible; I felt as if someone had tied lead weights to me and thrown me into the depths of the sea. Dozens of negative experiences, long buried in my consciousness, rose like giants to confront me. And memories of the last birth planted themselves in front of me like sinister shadows.'[2]

Yet Ruth not only survived but revelled in having children. Two years after Miriam was born, their second son, Ruben, joined their family bringing the total to five.

Hans' trip to Heidelberg provided some relief and gradually he began to grow stronger. By now he and Ruth were helping the Trobisches with marriage-counselling whenever they could. But God brought an unexpected challenge into their family – one only God could meet.

A neighbour worked with an organization that placed foster-children in homes. She was looking for a family to take in a ten-year-old boy whom no one wanted. He had already lived with six foster-parents, and was so difficult to handle that each one had rejected him. Ruth's neighbour explained the situation to her and then shocked her with her request. 'You already have five. You know how to handle kids. Couldn't you take this boy?'

Somehow God opened Ruth's heart and arms to this sick little boy, who soiled his pants, threw tantrums, and shouted insults at everyone around him. Often Ruth would lie in bed at the end of a day of turmoil and uncontrolled outbursts wondering how she could face another day. At one point she told Hans, 'I can't anymore; it's that child or me.'

But Hans, faithful and steady, would say, 'You have to go through with it.' And Ruth admits that through this experience God taught her that he loves everybody. After four years, the Heils adopted Freddie. He had settled down and surprised even the psychiatrists who had predicted that he would never finish school.

'As long as he lived in our family, God had a shelter around him,' Ruth reflects. Even though he left their home without committing his life to Jesus, Ruth is confident that God's arms are long enough to bring him back to himself and to the family.

By 1972 the family quarters were far too small for six children and the Heils moved to the village of Fishbach just eight kilometres from the French border. Today with eight of their ten children still at home, they have a roomy two storey house typical of southern Germany, with beamed ceilings and a peaked roof. The main room beyond the entrance hall is a large dining area with a long wooden table covered by a red checkered cloth. Hand-crocheted curtains hang at the windows, and paintings and craft work which Ruth has done over the years adorn the walls. The comfortable living room has a 'lived in' look with a sheepskin covering the ample sofa, books lining one whole wall, and a well-used upright piano with music spilling off the rack.

The garden at the back runs almost to the edge of a forest and is a virtual zoo. Besides four ponies, the children take care of chickens, rabbits, dogs and birds; more than fifty animals in all. Ruth has immortalized this aspect of their family life in several picture booklets and calendars.

On the lower level of the house, looking out over the lush green garden and field, Hans has a small office from which he directs the *Family Life Mission*. By the time Walter Trobisch died suddenly in 1979 Hans had regained much of his health and had been teaching marriage seminars with Ruth. The leaders of the Mission appointed him as the logical successor to Trobisch. He trains and supervises co-workers from Cameroon, Liberia, Ghana, Burkina Faso, Kenya, Burundi, Chad, Rwanda and Angola. His broad knowledge of languages is a tremendous asset. The Heils continue to hold marriage- and parenting-seminars throughout Germany as well, from which most of the funding for the mission comes.

Busy with caring for her family and home, Ruth never planned to have a public ministry. But one Sunday, after Hans had begun to preach in the local church again, he woke up with laryngitis. He could not utter a word. He handed Ruth a piece of paper on which he had written. 'I can't preach this morning. I have no voice. But there aren't many people going to be in this church. You go and preach.'

Ruth was shocked. Women didn't preach in German churches. Even as she protested, Hans wrote again, 'You've been listening to me all these years – you love the Lord and you can talk. Just go and give a witness. Just tell them about Jesus.'

So Ruth pored over the order of service and the liturgy, and took something black to wear out of her wardrobe. And she preached her first sermon. When she asked the congregation if anyone wanted to let Jesus into his or her heart, several people raised their hands. Even though two theological students in the audience expressed their disapproval, others invited her to come again. When they asked permission from the district supervisor, he agreed saying, 'We don't have enough "lectors" in this district. She can do it as long as we need her.'

It took a while for Ruth to feel comfortable about standing behind a pulpit preaching on a Sunday morning. 'Doesn't the Bible say that women have to be quiet in the church?' she queried. Han replied, 'It's not a church; it's a mission field. You would go to the mission field as a woman.' So for years Ruth spoke in local churches as God gave her the opportunity and the message.

Today she speaks in churches all over Germany; and the denominational barriers that were so divisive in her youth seem non-existent to her. 'I believe God's heart is suffering because his believers fight so much against each other,' she wrote recently. 'I see that denominations need a creed, a confession, a guideline . . . But one thing is far more important: to do the will of God expressed in Jesus' words – "A new commandment I give to you, that you love one another even as I have loved you . . . By this all men will know that you are my disciples" ' (John 13:34,35). (NASB).

God has endowed Ruth Heil with a gargantuan heart of love, which encompasses not only her own children, but children outside her home. Her first ministry role as a mother resulted from seeing so many children flock to her home. Children attract children. And soon she had started teaching them about Jesus – first at home and then in the local church.

She realized the importance of bonding with her own children. She cooked and cleaned with little ones on her hip or on her lap. 'All my kids grew up in the kitchen, not somewhere in the living room. They were always within the sound of my voice, feeling that I was very near,' Ruth says.

Staying at home to bring up children was easier in Germany in former years, for the German government paid a monthly stipend for the first year and a half after a child was born. This allowed mothers to stay at home, to breast-feed their babies and provide the warmth and nearness a child needs. Today, however, many mothers have to go to work, even in the early months of their child's life.

Closeness and warmth didn't cancel out consistent discipline, however. Hans and Ruth are asked to teach parenting all over Germany, and they can call on their own experiences with their large family.

'Discipline should not only be a reaction,' says Ruth, 'that is, only following misbehaviour. We not only punish, but teach and work on improving the character and behaviour of this child. This means speaking with the child about the situation, asking why he/she transgressed the rules, and explaining the consequences.' Ruth adds, 'There should be room for mercy too.'

For a toddler words are not enough. Ruth believes that teaching toddlers primarily requires doing things with them repeatedly, so that they can learn by doing. But by ten years of a age a child can understand verbal messages, and the consequences if he disobeys. Ruth adds, 'He must know for sure that my words are reliable, and that I will discipline him after he has not done what I told him to do.'

'There are three steps: One, say what must be done. Two, ask the child if he has understood clearly what I want; if not, I will explain until I am sure he knows. Three, the child has to act – and I will act, either praising him or disciplining him.'

She recalls an incident when she had told her ten-year-old son that he should clear up the mess in his room before dinner. During the afternoon she saw him playing and reminded him again that he only had an hour to complete his assignment. He indicated he would do so right away, but continued to play. Shortly before the deadline was reached he came to Ruth, head hanging. 'I haven't cleared up my room yet.'

Seeing that Ruth was angry he went on, 'Mom, it's okay that there is a punishment but please don't look so angry.'

Ruth sternly replied, 'You know that your pocket money will be reduced this week.'

Looking into her eyes pleadingly, he responded, 'That's very hard since I get so little pocket money. Can't we find another way? Maybe you could give me a short spank? Then I'll start doing what you wanted me to do, and it will be okay with the two of us.'

Would that all problems with children were so easy to handle! When one of their older daughters began showing signs of anorexia, the whole family agonized. Hans and Ruth encouraged their daughter to come back and live at home, and Hans spent many hours praying with and counselling her. The older children were distraught and wept a lot with their sister. Even the younger children began asking at the dinner table, 'Is this fattening?'

During this time Ruth wondered if she should give up her travelling and ministries outside the home. 'Should I give up everything for a few months?' she asked Hans. But he replied, 'Don't do that. For God, and for your sake it's important to leave once a week for an evening or morning [to do what God has called you to do].'

Much as Ruth advocates strong ties with and discipline of her children, she is also an advocate for her own self-development and personal growth. 'Each time I've had a child, I have done something [for myself],' she explains. She started playing the flute when Markus, her oldest son was born. Later she learned the accordion and typewriting. She took up painting, and the evidence of her innate talent can be seen throughout her home.

She recalls that those hours when she got away were happy times. The danger is that so often mothers feel like servants. 'And that feeling is not good for your child or for yourself. So if you can do something for the Lord and have goals – balanced goals – it is good.' In a recent issue of the *Family Life Mission* newsletter Ruth describes the feelings of a mother who considers herself a servant. 'I don't feel appreciated. Everything is taken for granted. I feel more like an object than a human being.'

Even more seriously, Ruth has seen that teenagers may reject their mothers because they see a lack of strength and ambition. Teenagers sometimes ask, 'Why didn't you do anything? Why didn't you build yourself up?' So she often tells young mothers, 'Find something you can do and do it with your heart. Then bring it back to your family.'

So Ruth continued to develop her gifts and interests. She played the guitar very well and began taking in guitar students. Many of these students accepted Christ through those classes, and she is still in contact with some of them today. She also taught Protestant religion in state schools for a year. 'Whatever God laid at my feet and what I could do in balance with my kids, I did,' she explains.

As her speaking schedule intensified, Ruth and Hans worked out home responsibilities so that each shared the burden. Hans does all the washing – twenty-five loads a week – and even hangs the clothes out to dry when the weather is nice. And he brings coffee to her in bed nearly every morning!

The children also share in the household duties, cleaning the table and helping in the kitchen. They are responsible for the care of the animals, including four ponies. But school timetables, music lessons (each child has an opportunity to learn a musical instrument) sports and roles in theatrical productions make this a busy family with a complex schedule.

Obviously Ruth is gifted with the ability to do several things at once, juggling housekeeping, disciplining children and writing without missing a beat. Hans observes, 'Ruth can sit down in the middle of the children's noise and bring her thoughts to paper. I need a longer period of peace to be able to work with concentration.' Indeed Ruth writes her quarterly column for *Lydia* magazine by jotting thoughts on scraps of paper as she rushes around her daily tasks.

When Ruth began travelling more and more it became clear she would need help, not only at home, but also occasionally when she travelled, especially when she took some of the children with her, which she likes to do when she can. Hans and Ruth prayed about this need earnestly. After a meeting where

Ruth had spoken, an older woman without family obligations came up and asked if she could help by serving as Ruth's driver when needed. What an answer to prayer Elizabeth became, travelling with her for years as well as helping at the home when necessary.

The spiritual development of her children is of prime concern for Ruth. Each one seems to go through his or her time of independence and even rebelliousness. One of the older daughters married a young American soldier who was not a Christian. It was with a heavy heart that Ruth said farewell to them as they returned to the USA to study. But some months later her son-in-law wrote to say he wanted to come back to Germany for a visit – and to be baptized. He told his in-laws, 'Miriam taught me what God's will is, and I want to live that way.'

Ruth speaks movingly of how the two youngest, Junias (5) and Salome (10), pray earnestly for their brothers and sisters. She admits, 'Some are lost and some are found again and some go through difficult times when I don't know where they stand. 'She remembers one rebellious teenage son who had gone away for the holidays. When he returned he told her, 'Mom, I know where I am again and where I stand.' She admits that the hardest part is waiting for God's timing. She often tells the Lord, 'I don't ask you when; I just want to be sure that all my kids will serve you.'

The Heils have always had family devotions at least twice a week. They gather around the piano, sing and read the word of God. They often read a book together, and there's nothing Ruth likes to hear more than 'Don't stop! Go on; go on.'

Hans still has difficulty travelling, but Ruth tries to take the children with her for holidays twice a year to Holland or Austria, somewhere 'that God gives us a house for free because we haven't much money.' These family outings help to make up for the many times the children ask her 'Why are you leaving again?' She confesses she loves to hear that. 'I feel I am needed and that they love to have me around.'

In spite of years of ministry Ruth still has a sense of hesitation over the 'authority' to speak. Recently she spoke to a group of eighteen men, trying to help them understand their wives. This is not her comfort zone, though she does not have any theological qualms about speaking to men. 'I feel comfortable talking to women. I don't want to be a teacher of men.'

Even when she speaks to women Ruth always wears a hat. She can't clearly define her reasons, except that it gives her a sense of shelter. She speaks with so many women who have serious problems with their husbands and children. After she has dealt with them and helped them to work through their problems, they generally leave with a sense of joy and freedom. 'They leave feeling wonderful . . . and I have problems with my husband and with my kids.'

By wearing a hat Ruth has a sense that she's going in the name of Jesus or of her husband. She confesses, 'I have a very loud voice, but inside I feel so little. I always wear long skirts so they can't see how [nervous I am.].' She reveals that before speaking she feels depressed and even like throwing up.

'But afterwards I am so happy that I feel I could sing all the way home through the woods and feel the Lord is using me.' With that upsurge of joy in serving God and helping others, Ruth returns to her busy, noisy brood with renewed vigour and strength to serve them too.

In his marriage seminars Hans-Joakim Heil reaffirms the role of his wife who has such a public image and yet overflows with love and compassion for him and their children. 'I have the impression that many husbands make a mistake [limiting their wives' freedom] for fear of the wives abusing their freedom,' he teaches. 'When I give my wife freedom to develop and she is free to make her own decisions, I have a contented wife. If I supervised her and led her by the nose, she would probably be dissatisfied.'

A sense of fulfilment and the joy of living pervades everything this mother of ten does. She knows who she is in Christ. She rejoices in her femininity. 'We seem to be soft, but we can carry a lot,' she says. 'God lets everything start through the women. He lets all the kids start at the breasts of the women, not of the men. And all men have to go through women. So God gave us strength even though we don't know we are strong. When women are strong they can help others and are free to work for the Lord.'

Notes

1. Ruth Heil, *My Child Within* (Westchester, Il.: Good News Publishers, n.d.), 64–65.
2. Ibid., 68.

Part Three

**Where Do We Go from Here?
A Word to Younger Women Still Uncertain
about What To Do with their Gifts**

So – What About You?

I love the story of Barnabas and Paul. I picture him as an older servant of Christ, generous to a fault, encouraging and correcting Paul – helping him get started in his ministry. Then Paul did the same thing for Timothy, loving and nurturing him, but urging him into difficult tasks, like setting that recalcitrant Ephesian church straight.

While those are only two specific examples of mentoring in the New Testament, the whole concept of 'preparing God's people for works of service' and 'bearing one another's burdens' tells us that God expects us to help each other grow into maturity.

That's the heart of this book – the desire to see you as a woman become all that God wants you to be. I want to encourage you to recognize how much God loves you and how special he made you, and to convince you that those gifts he's planted in your very soul are there to be unwrapped and used.

Perhaps by this time, you're feeling discouraged. You don't see yourself as an Eva Burrows, Kay Arthur, Judy Mbugua or any of the other strong, gifted women you have just encountered. God has very special ministries for these women and he endowed them with powerful gifts that you and I may never have. But we are not to be jealous – rather we can rejoice that God has distributed his gifts so freely to women. Whatever gifts we have, one or several; powerful or limited in impact, we can use them with joy. That's what God expects.

Let me remind you of a few practical suggestions that can help you unwrap, assemble and begin to use your gifts.

1. **Don't forget the batteries!** Using a gift without the power of the Holy Spirit is like trying to get a talking doll to say 'I love you' without a battery. No matter where you are in your journey, make your relationship with Christ,

your knowledge of the word of God, and your response to the Holy Spirit the number one priority.

2. **Know what you believe about the biblical role of women in ministry.** You don't have to go through twenty years of uncertainty as I did. Read and study, talk with women in ministry until you are at peace that you have discovered the truth for yourself. This is not necessarily the easy part, for leaders you respect and people you love may not agree with the conclusions you reach. Once you have settled this question in your mind, it will be a lot easier to fulfil whatever you are called to do.

3. **Seek God's will – not your own ambitions.** Start out by discovering what your spiritual gifts are – we discuss this briefly in chapter fifteen, but there are many excellent books on the subject. Once you know what your gifts are (and even that may unfold over the years) ask God to show you how to use them. Look for ways to develop your gifts by studying, experimenting, and volunteering. Above all, USE THEM. God has given us gifts in order to build up the body of Christ, whether it's reaching out to unsaved neighbours or to unreached people on the other side of the world.

4. **As you learn more about your gifts and God's leading becomes clearer, consider going back to school.** I was fifty when I earned my Master's degree, and am so glad I waited until then. I caught up with new trends and issues since I'd left college, and could apply my experience to what I was learning.

You needn't necessarily wait as long as I did – life is moving much faster now. But if God calls you into leadership you will need quality training, to be the best that you can be. It's still often true that a woman generally needs to be better educated and qualified than a man to gain the same respect and opportunities as he has.

If you're married and caring for small children, consider this to be part of your training. Running a home and organizing children takes administrative skills, creativity, and perseverance, all invaluable should God call you into a leadership role. At the same time, listen to your heart if God is already beginning to nudge you into using your gifts. Remember how Ruth Heil added a new skill or outreach with each new baby. It will keep you growing as a person, and inspire your children.

5. **Look for every opportunity available to minister in and through the church.** You will have noticed that most of the women in this book are leading ministries outside their denomination or local church. God may lead you in

that direction. You don't start an international magazine through a local church, or hold political office sponsored by a denomination.

However, more and more women are leading their own organizations because they could not find a leadership role within their own church. It may take some years yet before more doors for women are open, and you may find God leading you into a para-church ministry or to start up your own ministry. But I would encourage you to make every effort to be involved in your local church, to seek the church's blessing on your ministry, no matter what other call God puts on your life.

6. **Be willing to tough it out.** As we've read earlier, leadership for women is often harder than for men, not only because of our God-given natures, which Peter says are 'more fragile' (my paraphrase of 1 Peter 3:7) but also because it takes courage to step into an arena primarily inhabited by men. And it's especially difficult when we are also trying to be supportive wives and available mothers.

7. **If you're married depend on the support and encouragement of your husband.** The best of all worlds would be to work in partnership with your husband, sharing the joys and the burdens in the ministry and in the home. But if God has called you into a separate ministry, you need your husband's affirmation, encouragement and help. Even in an egalitarian relationship, husbands and wives submit to one another, and if your husband opposes you, I doubt it's from God.

8. **Be a mentor.** Robyn Claydon tells of how she has moved into this role. 'A major focus for me in the last couple of years has been the motivating, enabling and nurturing of younger women. We, as the current leaders of the church worldwide, are in the process of handing the baton to those coming up behind us . . . we need to run alongside those whom God is calling to lead the church in its ongoing response to the Great Commission.'

You may still be young – but there are already younger girls and women who need someone to get alongside them. Unfortunately in business today women who have reached executive positions are often unwilling to mentor younger women – perhaps fearing they will jeopardize their own careers. But in the body of Christ, it's a privilege to encourage those coming behind us – even if it's the teenage helper in our Sunday school class.

And don't forget your daughter. She's going to hear mixed messages at school and church about who she is and what she should do with her life. You are the best mentor she has, and you can tell her – and demonstrate by your example – how wonderful it is to be a woman created in the image of God and gifted by him.

Research shows that girls lose 23 percent of their self-esteem between elementary and middle school. A study by the American Association of University Women found only 29 percent of high school girls were happy with themselves, compared with 46 percent of boys.[1] Your affirmation and encouragement can make a difference in how your daughter sees herself and her gifts as she matures.

You can help your daughter appreciate the potential God has placed in her, rather than the limitations of her sex. And you can help your sons understand the same concept about themselves and about the women who will come into their lives.

9. **Work hard at maintaining a balance between your femininity and the strengths necessary to use your gifts effectively**. The radical feminist movement practised abrasiveness and expressed hostility towards men. Even the secular world wearied of their 'in-your-face' attitudes.

A mature Christian woman can demonstrate inner strength, confidence in God's leading in her life, and wisdom in decision-making while at the same time showing respect and appreciation for the men to whom she relates. We are not adversaries – we are meant to be partners. When it becomes necessary to correct misconceptions about women or patronizing attitudes, or when we have opportunities to explain our biblical understanding of women's role, we will make a far greater impact if we speak with love and grace.

10. **Be sensitive to your culture,** even when it goes against your freedom in Christ. Paul taught that we should be careful not to cause a weaker believer to stumble because of our freedom. Christian women in Muslim or Hindu societies may have to continue living under cultural restrictions in order not to offend non-believers they are trying to win. No doubt this was in Paul's mind when he urged certain restrictions on women in Jewish societies so that they would not offend outsiders.

On the other hand, because of the tremendous opportunities for women in the secular world today, the church's lack of opportunity for women can be offensive. A leader in Canada says that the largest unreached people-group in his country are professional women who find no place for their gifts in the church. Therefore, these women need to understand the radical relationships Christ demonstrated as he ministered to women. And we need to demonstrate the wholeness and freedom he has granted us, worshipping him and exercising patience with his church rather than giving up on her.

Enjoy serving Christ with the precious gifts he's given you.

Notes

1. Patricia Aburdine and John Naisbitt, *Megatrends for Women* (New York: Villard Books, 1992), 322.

Fifteen

What Have We Learned?

Therefore, since we are surrounded by such a great cloud of witnesses, let us throw off everything that hinders and the sin that so easily entangles, and let us run with perseverance the race marked out for us. Let us fix our eyes on Jesus, the author and perfecter of our faith, who for the joy set before him endured the cross, scorning its shame, and sat down at the right hand of the throne of God. Consider him who endured such opposition from sinful men, so that you will not grow weary and lose heart.

Heb. 12: 1–3.

The Bible is full of human examples – good and bad – to teach us how God deals with His children in victory and defeat. Paul urges the Corinthians 'Follow my example as I follow the example of Christ', (1 Cor. 11:1) yet he also admitted that he was the 'worst of sinners.' In the previous chapter he reminds his readers of the Israelites who had fallen into sexual immorality and pagan revelry and were 'killed by the destroying angel. These things happened to them as examples and were written down as warnings for us' (1 Cor. 10:10,11).

The stories of the twelve women we have just read about should serve as examples and models, not of perfection nor for their praise, but that their obedience, creativity and sacrifice will encourage women to consider how they might better follow God.

Women have had too few such models put before them, and therefore often fail to recognize that God may have gifted them for a ministry beyond their imagination. Women outside the church need to see models of capable and committed women finding fulfilment in obedient and giving service to their Lord.

That's what happened to author and professor at Eastern College, Dr. Mary Stewart Van Leeuwen when she went to Africa with the Canadian arm of the Peace Corps while she was working on her doctorate. In the seventies she associated with women activists who were basically Marxists, focusing on justice from a completely secular and materialistic perspective. Then she met some faithful believers in Africa. 'What made Christianity come alive for me was to meet so many intelligent and alive Christians from various traditions who were missionaries in Africa,' says Dr. Van Leeuwen.

Elizabeth Mittelstaedt echoes the need for models as one of the greatest needs for women in Europe. After a conference she held in Eastern Europe in the early days after the fall of Communism, when few churches permitted women to lead women's organizations in the church, a woman wrote to thank her. She explained that she had come to the conference fully determined to resign from leading the women's work in her church when she returned home. She couldn't face the opposition and criticism any longer. But after hearing one woman after another share how God had called her into ministry and was upholding her through many difficulties, the woman wrote to Elizabeth, 'I went home stronger than ever to obey the Lord in what He's called me to do.'

Lynn Smith, vice-president of student affairs at Ontario Bible College and Seminary, says, 'Modeling a Christian woman in ministry is an important result [of my ministry] for both male and female students, but particularly the females. Specifically the model of a woman who is not angry at men, nor unhappy about being a woman, nor unfulfilled as a woman is something badly needed in our culture.'

The women whose stories we have just read represent a great diversity of cultures, nationalities and ministries. But some common threads running through their stories can be helpful to any woman whom God is calling into a wider and perhaps unexpected avenue of service. What can we learn from their experiences?

The women recognized, developed and used their spiritual gifts

When my daughter was in college she called me one day to say, 'Mother I know what my gift is – working with little children.' I don't think she was really happy about that discovery for she probably had more grandiose aspirations at the time. But wisely she obeyed what God had shown her, went on to seminary to train as a Christian Education Director, and has proven to be one of the most creative and inspired children's workers I know.

It is important to study the three major passages dealing with spiritual gifts – Ephesians 4:11, Romans 12:4–8 and 1 Corinthians 12:7–11, 27–31 – and to realize that they are not gender-based. Every believer, man or woman, has one or more spiritual gifts which God intends to be used for the building up of the body of Christ.

Peter Wagner, in his classic book *Your Spiritual Gifts can Help Your Church Grow*, lists five steps to help you find your spiritual gifts:

1. Explore the possibilities by studying the Scriptures, reading extensively about spiritual gifts, and getting to know gifted people to find out how they discovered and use their gifts.

2. Experiment with as many gifts as you can by being available to help around the church and as a volunteer at Christian organizations. Try doing something in a small way to see if you 'fit.'

3. Examine your feelings. God matches our gifts with our temperaments in such a way that if we really have a gift we will feel good using it. Just watch Kay Arthur teach sometime, and you'll never doubt that she enjoys the gift God has given her.

4. Evaluate your effectiveness. If you have the gift you'll do well using it – you'll get results. That's why you start out small so if you don't have the gift others won't be hurt, and you won't be embarrassed.

5. Expect confirmation from the body of Christ. Since gifts are to be used to build up the body of Christ, they should be confirmed by other members. If no one else in your church thinks you have it – you probably don't.[1]

I believe that God expects women to use the gifts he has given them. No matter what position you hold on women's roles, there will be somewhere you can use your gift to build up the body of Christ either in the church, in your neighbourhood or in a para-church organization. With women making up more than half of the body of Christ around the world, they will remain the greatest untapped resource for evangelism until their gifts are fully utilized.

Jim Reapsome, director of Evangelical Missions Information Service says, 'I see in the apostolic example every encouragement to women to use their giftedness. The Spirit distributes gifts as he wills and there is giftedness all around . . . I think the church denies itself considerable spiritual value whenever it denies women in ministry.'

The women have overcome feelings of inferiority and low self-esteem

As a close corollary to recognizing their giftedness, these women have also overcome their feelings of inferiority because of their femininity, nationality or race. They realize that they are created in the image of God, equal in value and giftedness to men, and that they are daughters of the King of Kings. They are loved and cherished, precious in his sight.

This is the message women in ministry need to emphasize as they teach others. Women in every culture struggle with feelings of inferiority and self-worth – no wonder when an estimated 25 percent of women (as high as 80 percent in Pakistan) are battered in their marriages; when in many countries women work 16–18 hours of mind-deadening physical labour just to keep themselves and their children alive; when 57 percent of all women in the less-developed world are illiterate; when 75 percent of all refugees are women and children, without home or security. In many cultures women are told they are inferior to men. Wives are bartered for dowry; passed from the control of father or older brother to husband and finally to eldest son, with little to say about where or how they want to live.

A woman who is quiet because she is afraid to speak or because she has been told she has nothing to say, and whose submission is enforced rather than freely given, has been drained of inner strength to minister to others.

Yet Jesus gave dignity and worth to every woman he met. He touched the bleeding woman. He honoured the poor widow. He taught the women who followed him, breaking Jewish traditions. He discussed theology with an immoral woman. He appeared first to a woman and instructed her to inform his male disciples of his resurrection. Obviously no circumstance of birth or life lessened the concern and respect Jesus showed women when he walked on earth.

So too Paul commended women throughout his letters for their collegial ministry. Over and over again, we read the names of respected women serving in the early church. In his writings Paul did not imply that women were inferior. In a culture where women were often considered possessions, Paul instructs husbands to 'love their wives as their own bodies' (Eph. 5:28). He equates the value of the wife with the value of the husband when he says, 'he who loves his wife loves himself.'

Even a mother may sometimes feel she is serving others constantly without any time for herself as an individual. One pastor on Mother's Day told children to put their arms around their mothers and say, 'Hey, you're not just a wonderful mom, you're also a person.'

Women's self-image is bruised more severely in some cultures than others. Akiko Minato, a university professor in Japan says, 'Japanese women have experienced great difficulty in developing a strong sense of equality with men and of independence. A sense of "non-personality" or the subservience of individual personality to the broader group is still emphasized in contemporary Japan. Japanese Christian women must find their identity in their relationship to their Creator.'

As Juliet Thomas works with women in India, she encourages them to take a new look at themselves. 'We must place our identity in that which will not

Teresa Simbana - Quechua from Ecuador

Quechua Indian women are enjoying expanding opportunities unimaginable just decades ago, though women, particularly, still struggle in a society dominated by males, Mestizos and people of Spanish background. Teresa Simbana, mother of four children now aged fourteen to twenty-five, is president of the Association of Indigenous Evangelicals of Pichincha, one of Ecuador's twenty provinces and home to the national capital, Quito.

'The most important thing I am doing is finding equality in growth of the people. I want equality for the Indian people of Ecuador so that they have opportunities to grow and function in this country like other people,' she says.

The numbers of Indian believers in Pichincha are not as great as in other areas. But the local association, with 33 churches averaging 100–120 people, is growing. It has departments of community health, agriculture, bilingual education, theological education, a pastor's council and one for women and children.

'We have to get organized so there is a united effort,' Simbana says. 'We want to get to know people in authority. We want to claim our basic human rights. There are a lot of marginalized people who have very poor standards of living.'

The association teaches Quechuas to read and write, and provides health care, water and electricity services as part of its ministry. Simbana wants to set up training centers where women can learn to weave, knit, embroider and where men can be trained in trades.

'There are problems,' she said. 'It is hard for the women to find work. In the Indian culture, the men work the regular jobs, but not the women; they just work at home . . . I am just trusting the Lord for His strength to go on and fight.'

'There is a lot of response to evangelicals,' Simbana says. 'There are a lot of problems with alcoholism in these communities. Little by little there is change as they stop drinking and the family is stronger and relationships improve.'

(Adapted from article by Stan Guthrie
Pulse, July 1992) change – even Jesus Christ. Thus we establish our identity in Christ no matter what our feelings of inadequacies may be, no matter what voices are raised against us, through it all we stand secure in him, free, liberated to let God work his gracious purposes in and through us. Our "little" placed in God's hands, becomes much.'[2]

Pastor Robyn Peebles of Australia believes she is a better wife and mother since she recognized her gifts and began using them to serve God. 'I am a much better person. I am much nicer to live with because I am being fulfilled and I have a part to play in life . . . now I am serving out of my own personhood and the identity God has given me.'

Each one of the women we've come to know has overcome barriers of background, race, lack of education, social status or the challenge of being a woman in a man's world, to gain a godly sense of self-worth. They rejoice that they are made in the image of God, and accept that God declared all his creation 'good' including themselves. Only when a woman accepts who she is in Christ can she truly minister with his authority and power. These women have had a clear call from God to ministry.

A true call of God into ministry must come directly from the Holy Spirit himself, and you'll recall that these women turned to him for direction, listening to hear that voice behind them saying, 'This is the way; walk in it.'

There is no fast rule for recognizing God's call, but there is also no doubt when you have heard it, that it is from the Holy Spirit, if you are truly listening and your motives are right. 'Everyone's ways seem innocent to him or her, but motives are weighed by the Lord' (Pr. 16:2, revised). A truly godly leader is motivated first and foremost by a desire to be obedient to God, not to prove that a woman can do it, or to gain power and prestige. There is far too much of such motivation in the body of Christ.

On occasion a call is easy to detect, as Elizabeth experienced on the bridge as she contemplated suicide. Instead, God put the idea of a magazine in her heart. Of course she needed affirmation from her husband, and resources to put it into effect, but once the call was clearly discerned she moved forward with perseverance.

Sometimes the idea or plan comes to mind, but the assurance is slow in coming. That's when it's important to take time for a retreat alone, as Yolanda Eden did, or to gather prayer partners around you to fast and pray, as Kay James did before accepting the invitation from the Governor of Virginia.

God allows many women to go through early marriage and motherhood, collecting experiences like bargains at a sale. And then the day comes when we look into our basket of 'goodies' and realize that God has put together a whole

Dr. Roberta Hestenes - United States

'When I became a Christian during my college years, I received mixed messages in my new Christian sub-culture. Early in my Christian life I was asked to relinquish leadership of a small evangelistic Bible study which I had begun, through which several persons had come to faith. I did so willingly even though the group dissolved soon afterwards owing to the inexperience of the man assigned to replace me.

'I learned that men should be the visible, up-front leaders, while women quietly work behind the scenes making it all possible.

'I found myself eager to serve Christ, but gradually realized and accepted the assumptions of my Christian culture: that a woman can serve best by marrying a committed Christian man and supporting his ministry through homemaking and raising a family. So I married and tried to fulfil that understanding of my call.

'It didn't work out that way. My husband went into science and I went into full-time service in the church. God kept surprising me with new challenges and opportunities to get involved directly in ministry.

'It was an astonishing thing to discover, as the years went by, that my call to follow Christ went beyond traditional expectations. It was a clear call, straight to me, to serve Christ and the church in visible and recognized ways as a teacher, pastor and leader.

'This did not diminish my love and commitment to my husband and children, but instead my ministry opportunities helped to enrich our life together.'

Dr. Hestenes served as chairperson of World Vision International's board of directors for nine years. She also held the position of president of Eastern College in Pennsylvania. She has returned to the pastorate and shepherds a Presbyterian church in southern California.

Adapted from *Together*, a Journal of World Vision International
October–December 1992

array of experiences that could be used in a special ministry he's designed just for us.

When Luis Bush, the international director of the AD2000 and Beyond Movement, asked me to coordinate the AD2000 Women's Track, my first reaction was negative. I questioned, What did I know about women's ministries? What would it take to mobilize women for evangelism globally? But as I prayed and talked with people about the prospect, I realized God had been putting many experiences in my life that would be of help. I'd travelled widely internationally, served cross-culturally, had met Christian women in many countries, and perhaps most significantly was the mother of five children and of eighteen grandchildren, which gave me tremendous status in developing countries. In fact when the Koreans learned I was in my sixties, they smiled and nodded approval – even age was to my advantage!

Dr. Roberta Hestenes knows something of the personal sense of risk when one follows God's call in an unorthodox way. 'It can be frightening to move from invisibility to visibility. People don't scrutinize and criticize you when you stay in the shadows. I have needed courage and strength to respond to God's call when some people around thought it all wrong for me as a woman to answer yes. I have found that taking the risks is possible only because of the support of the Christian community and the comfort and power given by the Holy Spirit.'

The support of the Christian community, or at least a group of intimate friends and acquaintances whose spiritual maturity we respect, is invaluable. Proverbs says, 'Where there is no guidance, the people fall, but in abundance of counsellors there is victory' (Pr. 11:14, NASB). There are times when the Holy Spirit makes the call so clear that not even the advice of our closest associates can stop us. When Agabus prophesied that Paul would be handed over to the Gentiles in Jerusalem, the believers pleaded with Paul not to go. But Paul was 'compelled by the Spirit,' even though he knew prison and hardship awaited him. Sometimes we must follow the call of God to difficult and dangerous places – as Gladys and Elena did – because the Spirit overrides even our dearest counsellors

Women have the support of their husbands when they enter a ministry

A husband's support is critical for a woman to carry on a successful ministry, whether it's caring for babies in the church nursery or teaching seminars across the country. Mutual submission, as instructed in Ephesians 5:21, means husbands and wives encourage, nurture, support and help each other in

Eva Sanderson - Zambia, Africa

Eva Sanderson of Zambia describes herself as an 'ordinary person who has faith in an extraordinary God.'

This ordinary person is a wife, mother, former deputy mayor of Kitwe — a city in Zambia of over 500,000 people — chairperson for the board of the Pan-Africa Christian Women's Alliance and a member of the International Council of the World Evangelical Fellowship .

As a nurse she worked in a clinic when the AIDS epidemic surfaced in Zambia. Eva helped pastors and church workers understand how to help those affected by AIDS. 'Two-thirds of our church members are women. Many have unbelieving husbands. In some cases unbelievers come into the church, get converted and fall in love with young people in the church — and so AIDS spreads in the church.'

She urges 'Christians must stand against customs that force women to sleep with their late husband's relatives for spiritual "purification" . . . this only helps spread AIDS.'

Eva believes women can also make contributions in the political realm. 'The lack of Christian participation at policy-making levels has allowed lawmakers to enact laws that are totally contrary to biblical standards,' she declares.

In Zambia two-thirds of the church members are women. 'Being a woman should be no restriction to evangelizing the uttermost parts of the earth. A woman must hear God and move in obedience, as many have done before now.

'I have managed to do what I do because my husband is my number one supporter. He is willing to baby-sit for the benefit of other people. I do not think I would have been able to be involved to this level had God not given me such a husband.'

Now that her children are grown up, Eva continues to make her presence felt in the church, in the community and in her nation. She has recently formed a Christian entrepreneur trust to help women develop skills and start small businesses so they can be self-supporting.

Adapted from article by Diane Kesey in *A Great Company of Women*, published by the AD2000 Women's Track whatever God tells them to do. I have discovered that godly women who are seeing the Lord's blessing on their ministries invariably have husbands who back them. This seems to be true, even if the husbands are not born again. I know of one unsaved husband who is so eager to encourage his wife's ministry that he purchased a fax machine for her so she could more easily communicate with women in other countries.

A supportive husband is essential in helping to carry the burden of responsibilities at home, not only in the physical things like cooking or running errands, but also in the emotional support a woman needs. To be able to bounce off ideas, talk about sensitive situations that no one else should know about, cry over disappointment on your husband's shoulder is one of the greatest sources of comfort and strength a woman in ministry can experience.

Eva Sanderson of Zambia feels strongly that 'One of the reasons why fewer women are involved in God's work is lack of support from their husbands. There are many gifted women with a call of God upon their lives whose husbands do not share the vision or feel too insecure in their relationship to allow their wives to be involved in local and international affairs. I challenge husbands to see themselves as partners in their wives' calling, just as they [husbands] would like their wives to support them in their jobs and careers.'

Women who are involved in obeying God's call are particularly blessed when their husbands feel responsible for nurturing and developing their gifts. Dr. Chris Marantika is such an example. He saw in his wife Saria gifts of administration and teaching that are needed in the education field in Indonesia. He realized that as a Christian she could fill a top leadership position in education only if she had her doctorate. Dr. Marantika encouraged her to study in the United States which meant they had to be separated for a number of years, except for holiday visits.

Though not generally as common, at times God calls women into public ministries rather than their husbands. Unless the man is very secure in his own position in Christ, this can be very threatening. Perhaps this is the reason the Salvation Army refused for so long to put a woman in a leadership position above her husband. Yet when a man has strength of character and a longing to see the kingdom of God expand without a desire for personal credit or affirmation, he can affirm and encourage his wife in her call.

Kay Arthur describes how she and Jack worked through this dilemma. 'Jack is the president of Precept Ministries. However, he's not a teacher. Today the thinking is if you're a man, you're supposed to be on the platform, but that violates everything God says about spiritual gifts. I honour and respect what God has given Jack and he does the same with me. We don't try to make each other what we're not.

'Those early days, the most needed gift was helps, serving. This was Jack. He would take the load off me in every way, so I could study, teach and write the courses. He saw that things got done, not from an administrative platform, but as a doer. He was on the tractor, tearing down old buildings, building new ones, setting up the tape ministry, overseeing the finances. He was like Paul making tents. He made it happen.

'We've had adjustments in all this, but one of the things lacking today in many marriages where the wife is visible is recognizing what is of God. That's the thing I admire most in Jack. He's not threatened. He's never wanted to stand in the way of what God wanted, or where the ministry was to go.'[3]

Husbands like Jack Arthur, Roger Forster, Robert James and Ditmar Mittelstaedt are willing to take a back seat so that their wives, empowered by God's Spirit and strength, can run the race with confidence.

Women need to get as much training and experience as they can

Many years ago I attended a meeting of mission executives with my husband. In the crowd of more than a hundred mission leaders, the only woman, apart from the wives who had come along with their husbands, was one lone mission executive. I noticed that she carried a beautiful leather briefcase, and remarked on it. She responded, 'In this position a woman has to be the best in everything she does.' She didn't necessarily mean the briefcase. She had earned her PhD and had years of leadership experience on the mission field before she was appointed director of a small mission agency.

Unfortunately in the church or missions, as in business, there is often competition when it comes to leadership positions, and it seems that even though some women may be better gifted, they need to be better trained than men to qualify for these roles.

More importantly, in order to minister to the younger generation of women who are gaining opportunities in education and broad experience in the secular world, women need to be well-trained to meet the needs of the women who fill responsible positions in government, business and education.

Dr. Akiko Minato says, 'There is today a desperate need for training Christian women to assume greater leadership responsibilities. In order to reach the ninety-nine percent of Japanese who are not yet Christian, as well as the many others in Asia, the next generation of women Christian leaders must have an education that is not only solidly based upon biblical and theological studies, but is also genuinely international in preparation for ministering in a global context.'

Children are important but kept in balance with ministry

Which comes first? The Lord's work or the children God gave us? Any parent who has responded to God's call wrestles with this question time after time. In a sense the children must come first, for they are God-given responsibilities to us as individual parents, and without our training, discipline and love, they could easily be destroyed emotionally and spiritually. Children are a heritage from the Lord, and the hope of the future.

Yet, there is a very real sense that nothing and no one comes between us and the Lord who saved us, loves us, called us and enables us to live and serve. And sometimes that means our families take second place.

Dr. Robert Foster, a veteran missionary in Africa and past interdenominational director of the Africa Evangelical Fellowship, was left in a children's home in Canada at five years of age. His parents returned to what was then Northern Rhodesia, but could not take their children because of the serious health hazards and lack of educational facilities. Late in life Dr. Foster wrote, 'I can remember memorizing, "When my father and mother forsake me, then the Lord will take me up." I knew in a sense, they hadn't forsaken me. They loved me; but in a physical sense, they had . . . If I'd had my parents to depend upon I would never have learned to depend upon the Lord in the same way. This is one reason I can't be angry at my parents. I've realized that my folks made a sacrifice. I've always appreciated the fact that my folks put the Lord first, and that has been a tremendous example to me – to put the Lord first and to know that the Lord honours those who put him first. I know I have a responsibility to my family, but family responsibility is not first, not for me.'

But family responsibilities were very high on Dr. Foster's list, and family vacations and reunions even today remain very special. He and his wife raised seven children in Africa, sending the first three to a mission boarding school there, and home-schooling the four youngest when they lived in war-torn Angola. Five of the seven are back in Africa as missionaries – one of them is a medical doctor and another has his ThD. Their daughter Sheila remained in Angola with three children after she was widowed, to teach in one of the few Bible schools in the country.

What Dr. Foster said was not that he neglected his children – the results certainly prove that. But there are times when children cannot come before God's call on our lives. Though infants and toddlers need moment by moment care, as they grow older children can understand that God is first in our lives, and sometimes he asks us all to make sacrifices for him. A mother in ministry must be very sensitive to the personalities and needs of her children. But it may not hurt junior at all not to have mother at his ball game because she's

Akiko Minato - Japan

Akiko Minato is a delightful contemporary woman and a professor of Church History at Tokyo Christian University. When with Professor Minato you have a sense that she loves being Japanese, she loves being a woman, and she loves life! She is equally comfortable with academics and mothering . . . She regularly breaks the boundaries to be the first woman representative in the Christian community in what used to be a man's world.

Professor Minato speaks in women's language, but at the same time is a persuasive agent of change in the church, an advocate for the improvement of the woman's role in Japan.

During the war her grandmother educated all the grandchildren, teaching them English, which was forbidden at the time. Akiko was seriously injured when a bomb dropped on her school building, which left her with physical limitations.

Nevertheless her father who was a doctor urged her to continue her studies. In 1959 while working on her MA in New Testament at Wheaton Graduate School, she met and married Hiroshi Minato. Together they attended Harvard University under Fullbright Scholarships. Just as she completed her PhD course work she realized with delight she was to have their first child. Even as a busy mother of three she studied daily in fifteen-minute sessions taking advantage of the academic environment.

Back in Japan her husband died suddenly in 1977. With this unexpected change Akiko's ministry outside her home began to blossom. When the children became independent she began teaching full-time at Tokyo Christian University, teaching Church History and Women and Society. She serves as the chairperson of the Women's Commission of the Japan Evangelical Association and a member of the Women's Commission of the Evangelical Fellowship of Asia.

Adapted from an article by Sandi Wisley, *Japan Harvest*, 1994

counselling a teenager in trouble; or to ride his bike to his music lesson because his mother is preparing a Bible study for her neighbours.

When mother and father work together to make sure that children's needs are met, they can free each other for service. If the call is clearly from God, without ego-fulfilment or desire for position, children from very early in life can recognize the importance of what their parents are doing. They can be included in prayer-times for people in the ministry, and even participate whenever possible. Ruth Heil loves to take several of her children when she goes on a speaking engagement. Juliet's daughter became so convinced of her mother's burden for women, she wrote a theme song for them.

Throughout history children have paid the price, along with their parents, for a courageous stand for the gospel. There could have been nothing more traumatic for parents living behind the Iron Curtain than to see their children denied opportunities for education and position because they did not join the Young Communists and maintained a Christian stance. Russian parents sometimes lost their children to government foster-homes because they were caught teaching them the Scriptures. Pastors in Third World countries stay in the ministry even though it means denying their children material comforts and educational opportunities.

'Seek FIRST his kingdom and his righteousness' (Mt. 6:33) applies to all of us, including women who obey God's call to serve him.

Women were willing to move out of their comfort-zones

Some years ago I was in a conference in India where women delegates complained that though there were needs for women to teach in Sunday schools and serve in the women's groups, many women refused to accept the responsibility. One said, 'I think it's a cop out. I think women hide behind the fact that they are women.'

Ministry is demanding. Studying takes hours of time and energy. Counselling drains our emotions. Teaching children can be frustrating. Speaking makes our knees knock. Travelling wears us out and aeroplane seats are getting smaller. But above all, the enemy is after us when we're obeying God's call.

He discourages us; people talk about us; sin stalks us and results evade us. It would be a lot easier to sit in the pew on Sunday morning and enjoy the worship, spend quiet evenings at home with our husbands, plan long holidays, watch all the latest season-openers on TV, and spend hours going to Bible studies which we never share with anyone else. The enemy urges us to stay in the comfort-zone of our community rather than to find ways to befriend the poor and abused, the lonely women in ethnic neighbourhoods or even to go to some unreached people in another region or country.

Yet I believe the same words of comfort and challenge spoken to Jeremiah

Ingrid Kern - Germany

In 1957 Ingrid and Manfred Kern moved to the German Democratic Republic after completing their studies in West Berlin. Manfred had received permission from the authorities in the East to study in the West where he met Ingrid. But they both felt the churches in the Communist side were desperately in need of leadership and encouragement.

Ingrid will never forget the night of her husband's ordination. Many West Berliners had come over for the occasion, only to learn that the Communists had closed the borders and were building a wall separating the two sides. The visitors were able to return, but for twenty years Ingrid was unable to visit her parents.

'It was a time of confrontation between the government and the church, but,' says Ingrid, 'I was never afraid.' While Manfred pastored the church, she taught children, though it was forbidden, and was an active pastor's wife. She raised her four sons to stand for righteousness and truth — though they were not able to attend university because they didn't join the Young Communists.

In 1983 when Manfred was asked to lead the Evangelical Association of Germany, Ingrid felt lost. Now that she was no longer a pastor's wife she wondered where God would use her. Soon however, she was a pivotal person in the EAG office. The new pastor asked her to become a member of the church council, and soon the chairman of the board.

When Dave Howard, then head of the World Evangelical Fellowship, decided to form a Women's Commission he remembered the courageous godly woman in East Berlin who had persisted in her ministry in the face of great odds. He invited Ingrid to attend the first meeting of key women in Wheaton, Illinois. Though the wall had not yet come down, Ingrid was miraculously granted her visa within three weeks. She remembers how shocked she was that Americans equated freedom and materialism with God's blessing. She kept thinking, 'But we can be free behind the Wall!'

Ingrid served from 1992–1997 as chairperson of the WEF on Women's concerns Commission, a job which involved travel and public leadership. But of all the things she does, working closely with her local church, experiencing the sense of 'family' that gives, is dearest to her heart.

apply to any woman who hears God's call on her life and responds in obedience. This is how you might read Jeremiah 1:6–8

> *Ah, Sovereign Lord, . . . I do not know how to speak; I am only a woman. But the Lord said . . . 'Do not say I am only a woman. You must go to everyone I send you to and say whatever I command you. Do not be afraid of them, for I am with you and will rescue you,' declares the Lord.*

The women recognized they might face opposition

When women step into ministry-roles that have traditionally been held by men, they may face opposition. Yolanda Eden found pastors ignored her in the meetings she attended; Elena Bogdan faced criticism because she planted a church; Kay Arthur was questioned about her right to teach men; Judy was told to stay home with her children.

It is vital that before embarking on a public ministry that might draw criticism, a woman knows where she stands biblically, and that she is sure of her call. Unfortunately many people in the evangelical church have not yet arrived at a place where they can accept different interpretations of the role of women in ministry. Jim Reapsome says he sees increasing rigidity among younger men, especially as he visits Bible colleges and seminaries. Some students refuse to attend classes taught by women. When a well-known woman speaker was invited to speak in the chapel of a prestigious seminary, many of the male students walked out when she got up to speak.

Some opposition can't be helped but sometimes a little humour goes a long way to lessen the tension. When a pastor asked Jeni Rosian to speak in his church he knew there would be resistance. So when he introduced her he said, 'Sister Jeni will not preach. She will have a message.'

A board of deacons once wrestled with allowing Evelyn Christenson, well-known author and seminar teacher, to speak. They decided that as long as she stood on the lower-level platform rather than behind the pulpit it would be all right. A pastor told a missionary wife she could not speak in the morning service, but if she gave a 'report' in the evening there wouldn't be a problem.

Opposition may be as subtle and paradoxical as these illustrations. But a godly woman will do her best to avoid confrontation, to be gracious and sensitive to the situation – and courageously continue doing what God has told her to do. Women who are hostile and resentful towards their brothers in Christ will never heal the gulf of misunderstanding that still exists in so many quarters.

Women in non-Western cultures must be even more adaptable. As Akiko

Jeni Rosian - Romania

Early one morning on her way to work, Jeni threw her precious typewriter into the river. The Romanian secret police had questioned her the day before, and she knew that if it were discovered, she would lose her job.

Writing had been Jeni's passion, since the days she and her parents listened to Trans World Radio every evening. Jeni had copied most of Billy Graham's World Aflame by hand as it was read over the air.

Jeni grew up in abject poverty. Her stepfather lost his eyesight in a factory accident and could not work. In their two-room flat her mother worked long hours as a seamstress to care for him and the four children. Jeni remembers the dark green dresses she sewed for her — since the church they attended would not permit bright colors.

Jeni loved school, excelled in her work, and dreamed of being a teacher. The Communists allowed her to study engineering — but would not permit Christians to teach.

She found a way to reach children by starting a weekly paper. Since printing was forbidden, she put her 'magazine' on a large sheet of paper and hung it at the back of the church each week. Soon other churches did the same. Because of her knowledge of English, Jeni translated for Westerners who came to teach in Romania. Shortly after the revolution, one of these contacts gave her a copier machine, and her magazine, *Children's Friend*, was born. Her next dream was a library. Romanians love to read — a legacy from Communism — but there was little Christian literature available.

At thirty-one Jeni married Gusti after a very unorthodox courtship. On their wedding day a printing press was delivered to their front door — and took up half their apartment. They now have two little girls and the family lives in two rooms.

The colorful *Children's Friend* is now read by children all over Romania. Jeni has to draw the four colour separations by hand since she doesn't have computer skills to do that yet. 'Jeni's Library' serves several thousand readers. She also teaches Sunday School training seminars. With Gusti running the press, Jeni's dream has become a family affair.

Minato observes, 'It is impossible for women to develop and exercise their gifts in evangelism and ministry apart from the understanding and co-operation of men. This is especially urgent in Asia where societies are influenced by the model of the authoritarian patriarch.'

This does not mean women in Asia are giving up their call to serve. On the contrary, most house churches in China are led by women. In Korea the majority of house churches have women leaders. Women play a key role in the churches in the Philippines. Many have expressed frustration at their limitations in decision-making, but nevertheless follow the injunctions found in 1 Peter 3:8,9:

> All of you, live in harmony with one another; be sympathetic, love as brothers and sisters, be compassionate and humble. Do not repay evil with evil, or insult with insult, but with blessing, because to this you were called so that you may inherit a blessing.

Women in leadership are able to work comfortably with men

It helps to have been a girl growing up in a family of boys; to know the things they laugh and joke about, and to be able to hold your own in the give and take of family life. Women who work with men on an equal level need a certain amount of self-confidence that they have the qualifications and abilities to do what is being asked of them, and are not afraid to express opinions even though they may be in the minority.

Women who work well with men like men. One observation made about General Eva Burrows was that she preferred working with men rather than women, and that she tended to ignore the wives of officers and would discuss issues with their husbands instead.

Women who work comfortably with men aren't intimidated by their strengths, nor by their reactions. Roger Forster believes that women who work in leadership with men must accept the fact that in a mixed committee they are going to be treated exactly the same way as men would be when opinions are expressed and disagreements arise.

But while women may be treated the same as men – albeit often in Christian circles with a certain old-world gentlemanly charm (which can also be patronizing) – brain research reveals that men and women use their brains differently to process language. A bestseller in the United States, *Men are from Mars, Women are from Venus* contends that men and women respond differently in relationships and that this is the cause of much of the misunderstanding in marriage.

Robyn Peebles - Australia

Because Robyn grew up in a broken home, she always dreamed of having a perfect marriage. When she married Allen she lived, breathed and doted on him, making him the centre of her life. She was happy to let him make all the decisions, even about how she should spend her money. 'I was actually losing myself and didn't know it,' she says.

As her relationship with the Lord grew through Bible study it seemed as if God was saying, 'Hey I want to be your first love.' She gradually realized that her total dependence on her husband was unhealthy.

Robyn became very involved in youth work. This became disruptive to their home life. Allen admitted that he knew that God had placed a call on Robyn's life, but he didn't want to let her go. He liked to have her come to him for every decision, but in time he saw the value of her ministry and appreciated the new person she had become.

Robyn was involved in a revival at the local high school where three-quarters of the children accepted Christ. Many were not churchgoers, and began coming to the Peebles home for Bible study. Others joined and soon the house was too small on a Sunday morning to contain the group. The Lord told Robyn, 'You've got a church and I want you to treat it like a church.'

Robyn was sure the Lord would call her husband to pastor the new church. 'I was waiting for God to tap him on the shoulder.' Instead God spoke to her through the Scriptures: 'Do you love me? Feed my sheep.' Students at the Bible school she was attending also confirmed her call.

Robyn believes God has gifted her for the ministry — she is a visionary (some people would call this an apostolic gift) but she also has the gifts of teaching and evangelism. She is a motivator, and has delegated many responsibilities to the congregation which in seven years has grown to over three hundred adults and children. There is a healthy balance between men and women, both in leadership and in the congregation. She believes the secret of the church's growth is in the early morning prayer meetings which about a quarter of the adults attend.   (cont.)

> While she has been excluded from some of the minister's
> fraternals, she has been able to participate in co-operative church
> efforts in the community. She recently organized a national
> reconciliation event to confess the sins of Australian settlers against
> the first boatload of women who had been sent to settle in
> Australia, and who were raped by the crowds as they disembarked.
>   Of her marriage, Robyn says it's better than ever. With Allen in
> a secular leadership role, they have so much more in common than
> ever before. They enjoy going out on dinner dates just to talk about
> their mutual experiences. 'We have a good healthy respect for one
> another' she says.

Certainly women are generally more relational, sensitive and intuitive than men, although men also share these characteristics. Unfortunately women often suppress these natural gifts in the company of men, afraid that their response will be criticized as being too emotional. Men don't know how to handle women's tears, and women who work know that they dare not use tears as a weapon. However research indicates that crying appears to be the body's natural and healthy reaction to stress. As Eliane Lack looks back on her experience leading men she advises, 'I would say you can put a woman in leadership, but you need to let her be a woman. Let her cry if she wants to cry. I do not know why men cannot cry. I didn't do it, but I would now.'

Just because of the God-given differences between men and women, women leaders who work comfortably with men recognize that they can make a special contribution to discussions leading to decisions. The direction of the Holy Spirit seems to come through the intuitive, though that cannot be proven from Scripture. But Roger Forster points out that the last vestiges of female participation in leadership in the church were abandoned at the Council of Laodicea in 365 AD. 'From that point on,' he says, 'it is evident that the male rational approach dominated the church for centuries and has done great damage.'

Mary Stewart Van Leeuwen in her 1991 book *Gender and Grace* writes, 'The chief New Testament metaphors for being a Christian are not drawn from male-dominated activities such as warfare, politics, international trade, or even high art. They are mainly metaphors concerned with giving birth (witnessing so others can be born again,) nurturing (patiently discipling others,) caring for the body (of interdependent believers) and taking the lower status of a servant – all taken as the more natural domain of women.'[4]

Evelyn Quema - Philippines

In the Philippines, there has long been remarkable equality between the sexes. Women occupy important positions in government (Corizano Aquino served as prime minister), industry and business. In the home, except where there has been a strong Spanish influence, husband and wife have complementary, co-operative and fairly equal roles. So when such women come to Christ they naturally use their leadership skills in his service.

Consider twenty-four-year-old Evelyn Quema. Short, stout and single, she is hardly noticeable in a crowd of Filipinas her age. Yet she has planted four churches in three years; seen two hundred solid conversions to Christ plus several hundred more she has not been able to follow up; developed contacts with five hundred students, and taught thousands of children and young people.

At twenty-two, fresh out of Bible school, she and her mother arrived in the city of Baguio with six dollars, which was to last her a month, and an assignment: to plant churches. She had no contacts, nowhere to live, no church building. That was on Thursday. On Friday she rented a building. On Saturday she invited people in the market. On Sunday she conducted a service for thirty, and saw four conversions. Within a few months her congregation was self-supporting.

There are hundreds of Christian women like Evelyn in southeast Asia, giving leadership alongside men.

(Adapted from 'Women for Such a Time as This' by Miriam Adeney, *The Link & Visitor*, April, 1994, p. 10.)

The synergism of male and female working together represents the completed creation of God, when he looked at male and female and saw that all he had made was 'very good' (Gn. 1:31). Thus when men and women work together they combine their strengths and can more quickly and effectively work through solutions. Ingrid Kern, who serves as the chairperson of her church board in Berlin, sees a difference now that men and women are working together. 'Men discuss things at great length; everything must be very clear before they make a move. Women, who are more sensitive to the needs of women and children, say, "Let's not talk so long. Let's do something." '

But working together is not necessarily easy. Faith Forster serves on a number of international boards, often as the only woman. 'You have to be fairly thick-skinned. I'm not too thick-skinned, but I've learned that you simply have to get in there and do what you think it's right.'

Unfortunately sometimes women drop out of boards and committees just because they get fed up being in the minority, and realize that their opinions and contributions have limited effect. If the representation of women on boards and committees is to grow, women should realize that sticking it out faithfully is important, not only to the fulfilment of God's purpose for them, but to keep pushing the door open for other qualified women.

Not all women in leadership find it easy to work with men – and many of these choose to work in ministries with and for women. Eliane Lack has worked with men for many years but she confesses, 'Working with men is difficult. The biggest problem, at least with the ones I have worked with, is that they are very rational, objective men of God. I am a strong intuitive. I can use my brain and rationalize, but my relationship with the Lord is a lot of intuition. Sometimes I just sense things which I cannot always explain . . . I think the Spirit and intuition work together. I have learned to know, "this is the way; walk ye in it." But I need a word of confirmation. I need the leaders to agree by their guidance.

'I still believe that men are better equipped for leadership. They have wider inner shoulders than ours. In their inner being I don't think they receive the fiery darts of the enemy as we do. It doesn't affect them as much as women generally. I didn't want to become an iron woman.'

In the following chapter we will look at suggestions on how men can help women find and use their gifts. And one thing that will help greatly is to allow women like Eliane to use her considerable leadership and administrative gifts, without giving up her femininity in order to be accepted.

Prayer is the spiritual strength and support of women who are called to ministry

The great prayer movements of the twentieth century have been primarily spawned and nurtured by women. Perhaps because women have been limited in using their gifts in other ways, they have been forced to their knees. As a result they are a great powerhouse in the kingdom of God.

While men are joining this prayer force in greater and greater numbers, women have led the way in taking up the burden to pray for their families, their nation and the unreached peoples of the world who have never heard the Gospel.

Eliane Lack - Switzerland

From the balcony of the YWAM prayer retreat centre you can see the 'four sisters' including the Jungfrau towering in all its pristine beauty. Once the summer home of a wealthy family of Swiss bankers, the lovely retreat centre outside Innegen attracts intercessors and weary servants of the Lord to rest and be refreshed in him.

This is the dream of Eliane Lack who is responsible for the centre.

She grew up on the ski slopes of Switzerland, dreaming about becoming a ski champion. But at fifteen she had an encounter with Christ instead, and went on to study nursing. After attending Bible school she joined YWAM. One of her first assignments was to work in the office in preparation for the first Lausanne Congress in 1974. 'That Congress did something for unity in the city. The pastors got together and became friends. They realized they could love each other and work together even if they didn't always believe the same thing. And since then we've had unity, acceptance and tolerance and respect for one another.'

Well into her thirties Eliane married Rudy, a fellow YWAMer — but they soon both realized they had different gifts and ministries and had to work through that tension. While Rudy pursued his writing assignments, Eliane took a team of five young people in 1982, climbing into the mountains of Tibet to visit and pray for an unreached tribe. Another time she spent three months in seclusion and prayer.

Even before her marriage Eliane was the only woman appointed to the YWAM base council which was responsible for a staff of 70 people plus students in training. Later she was asked to serve as the chairperson of YWAM Switzerland — the first woman national leader in the global organization. The council has since dissolved, but if it is restored Eliane would like to serve on it again — not as leader however. She found it difficult. 'I would say to the men: listen to your heart more. I think there are lots of women out there that are very capable of taking on responsibility. I know there are lots of them that don't want to because there is a cost involved. . . . You can put a woman in leadership, but you need to let her be a woman.'

Women in ministry who are being effectively used by God to help build the kingdom recognize the absolute importance of their own prayer support team. Every time Evelyn Christenson travels overseas, her prayer partners pray around the clock while she is gone. Dr. Lee's ministry to the world through the Torch ministries began with a small group of women praying together in her living room. Roger and Faith Forster established a prayer centre which is open 24 hours a day. Ichthus staff have special days of prayer and fasting for the needs of the ministry, and for each other.

Without exception, these women have intimate and faithful prayer partners with whom they can share the joys and heartaches of their ministry. These groups often serve as accountability groups as well, ensuring that each leader keeps short accounts with God, and is made aware of any weakness which might be developing.

One of the greatest prayer warriors I knew was a young woman named Sandra who was completely incapacitated by multiple sclerosis. Every day her mother would dial a phone number so she could call a blind man and share a Scripture verse she'd memorized. Her room was lined with pictures of missionaries and maps of where they worked, and she would pray around the world each day. I believe the angels of God carried those prayers to the throne, and many of us who were working in distant places gained new grace and patience, wisdom and strength for the day as Sandra prayed. Women called by God to serve him, MUST have such power behind them.

It's Never Too Late

When I was a young missionary speaking in a church, a woman came up to me with tears in her eyes to tell me God had called her to the mission field, but she had turned him down. Instead she had married and now had four children. She wanted to know if there was still an opportunity for her to take God up on his offer.

I have no idea what I said to her, but I remember thinking, 'Lady, it's too late. You chose marriage and family instead and you're stuck!'

But I was wrong. It may be too late to become a missionary doctor, or a Bible teacher in a seminary because we don't have the education. It may be too late to do prayer journeys in the mountains, or teach primary health care in the jungle, because our bodies have weakened and our bones are getting brittle. We may not be able to respond to the call that God whispered so faintly back in our college days because we were madly in love – and thought we really had better plans!

But we can start listening now to God's call for this time in our life.

Juliet spent twenty years in the 'wilderness' of domesticity and frustration before God called her to her nation-wide prayer ministry. Elizabeth was already forty, feeling that she'd wasted her life, when God gave her a magazine. Yolanda was in her fifties when she was given a church. I was sixty-two years old when God called me to lead the Women's Track – about the time most people retire.

Eliza Davis George, Afro-American daughter of slaves, spent almost sixty-five years in Liberia, rescuing baby girls from aged husbands, starting schools and planting churches. When she was seventy-one years of age, however, her mission station had burned down, the children had scattered, and her supporters in the United States said she must retire.

Instead Mother George and Otto, one of her trusted 'boys', trekked into the interior of Liberia to a piece of land that had been condemned by the chief because it had been cursed. No one would work the land or build on it. When they neared the crest of a small knoll with virgin jungle spread out before them and a murky creek pulsing over submerged logs at the bottom of the hill, Otto asked, 'Mother are you sure you want to build a mission on this land?'

And Mother's confident reply was, 'Son, there is no place where God has told us not to stay. This is going to be my life's work. We're not going to move anywhere else.'

Over the next twenty years the Elizabeth Native Interior Mission, trained hundreds of Liberian young people through five primary schools and a technical training school. When she died at a hundred she left a legacy of more than one hundred churches started by her spiritual children. Today Liberia has been utterly devastated by years of tribal fighting, with buildings destroyed and over half the population killed. Yet heaven is populated with some of Liberia's best – the spiritual children of an elderly woman who kept hearing God's call and responding to it.

Notes

1. Adapted from Peter Wagner, *Your Spiritual Gifts Can Help Your Church Grow* (Ventura, Calif.: Regal Books, 1944), 109–26.

2. Juliet Thomas, *After God's Own Heart* (Bromley, U.K.: Pilot Books, n.d.), 17.

3. Nanci Carmichael, "Any Bush Will Do," *Virtue,* January–February 1994, 30–31.

Sixteen

Helping Men to Help Women Use Their Gifts

Why is it that he gives us these special abilities to do certain things best? It is that God's people will be equipped to do better work for him, building up the Church, the Body of Christ, to a position of strength and maturity.

Eph. 4:12 (LB.)

Indeed, true comrade, I ask you also to help these women who have shared my struggle in the cause of the gospel.

Phil. 4:3 (NASB.)

Men and women enjoy working together. There's a certain intensity of interaction – like 'steel sharpening steel' – when men and women tackle a problem together or work out goals and new directions. What a blessing our brothers in Christ who have seen women as partners rather than as subordinates have been to us. How thankful we are for those who have opened the doors of opportunity, encouraged our gifts, and affirmed our ministry. They are a growing band – and it is these men who are going to help women make the transition into full partnership in the body of Christ.

I have been impressed with the openness of many Christian leaders who want to help women get involved in Christian leadership, but sometimes don't know what to do.

At a meeting of key Christian leaders, one of the few women in attendance spoke about the desire of women around the world to use their gifts more fully. She told of a Filipino woman leader who said, 'Our women are tired of crocheting doilies for the church. We want to use our gifts in a more meaningful way.'

The Holy Spirit brought an attitude of repentance to the men. One asked very solemnly, 'But what can we do to change the situation?'

Quickly the speaker replied, 'Start by treating women as Jesus did.'

Books have been written about Jesus' relationship with women, but let us briefly remind ourselves of some of the ways in which he radically departed from Jewish tradition while on earth. He allowed women to travel with him and his disciples – even married women who possibly had children (Luke 8:1–3); spoke to them in public (John 4:7–27) discussed theological issues with them (John 11:17–27), taught them (Luke 10:38,39), used women as models and in parables (Luke 8:43–49); gave a woman the responsibility to deliver the report of his resurrection to men (John 20:11–17) – and never gender-differentiated his teaching. Though he didn't call women into the intimacy of the Twelve, neither did he include Gentiles – who were certainly to be involved in the leadership of the Church after his resurrection.

Treating women as Jesus did starts by treating them with respect as equals and as mature, gifted partners in the work he has instructed us to carry out.

Put yourself in their shoes

Sometimes men are simply unaware of their attitudes. Several years ago a new video was shown at a conference to depict the growth of evangelism around the world. Ten to fifteen 'talking heads' – leaders of mission and evangelism ministries – reported on the exciting growth of the global church and the powerful impact of global prayer ministries. It was well done and very effective.

But at the close women from all over the audience crowded around the facilitator of the meeting; some were in tears, others obviously angry. Somewhat bewildered, the leader listened to the complaints of the women. They were asking questions like – Why wasn't there a single woman in the video? What about all the women involved in the evangelism prayer movements? What about women missionaries? Why weren't women involved in the organization sponsoring the video included?

Now you may feel these women were overreacting or looking for attention. The truth is THEY were bewildered and hurt. Put yourself in their shoes. What if all the testimonies had come from women, totally ignoring the contribution that men were making? Wouldn't you be concerned about the kind of message going out to the body of Christ as a whole?

Fortunately, the story ends well, for the organizers admitted the omission, and redid parts of the video to include some of the women involved in the programme. They had not intended to hurt or ignore women; they were simply so used to featuring and quoting men that it never dawned on them to do differently.

Jim Reapsome tells the story of being on a panel of mission executives. After several hours of questions and discussions, a person in the audience stood up and asked, 'Why aren't there any women on the panel, since there are more women than men on the mission field?'

Jim later wrote in his editorial in *Pulse*, 'Ignoring women is just as easy as slipping into your car and pulling the lever into drive. Sure, neutral and reverse are important – we couldn't live without them – but they just get in the way of drive. That's exactly how we slight women habitually and unconsciously, all the way from long-range planning to our preaching and writing about world missions.'[1]

Men can help women by trying to identify with their desires and hurts. Often women don't talk about this because it makes them appear aggressive, resentful, or even unbiblical. Husbands can encourage their wives by openly asking how they feel about restrictions or lack of opportunity for certain kinds of ministry in their church. Pastors and church leaders could bring women together in an informal gathering where frankness is encouraged to ask where they would like to use their gifts.

Though we don't sing many hymns in our worship services any more, think about the male-oriented words that exclude women. A hymn I found hard to sing was 'Rise up, oh men of God'. Or consider the insensitivity of that powerful hymn, 'In Christ There is no East or West'. In the third verse it calls us to:

> 'Join hands then, brothers of the faith. Whate'er your race may be; Who serves my Father as a son is surely kin to me.'

Written in 1913 at a time when *racial* discrimination was rampant, John Oxenham beautifully expressed the oneness of the body of Christ – 'All Christly souls are one in Him/Throughout the whole wide earth.' He didn't intend to leave out half of those souls – he probably never realized he did. And very likely at the beginning of the twentieth century, most women did not consider this neglect. They were used to a male-oriented world, and in their hearts they automatically transcribed 'men' to read 'women,' and 'son' to read 'daughter.' But please realize that times have changed; language is important; and most women don't transcribe those words any more.

Unfortunately, when women say they feel left out or like second-class citizens, they are often labelled radical feminists, aggressive or just plain unspiritual. You can help women understand their feelings and how they can use their gifts if you listen sympathetically. This is not a minor issue that affects a radical fringe in the church. This is an issue that concerns more than half the body of Christ.

And it is not simply a western issue. As I have travelled around the world for the AD2000 Women's Track I have listened to women on every continent express their heartache and concern. Women are saying what Florence Nightingale once wrote, 'I would have given the church my head, my heart, my hands. She would not have them. She did not know what to do with them. She told me to go back and crochet in my mother's drawing room, or marry and look well at the head of my husband's table.' They long to get into harness, using the full strength of their gifts to move the church forward. But often they feel they are made to ride in the back of the wagon, handing out sweets to keep the children quiet.

Many women, it is true, feel strongly that the Bible limits the use of their gifts and the role of women in leadership positions in the church. But as more and more women study the issue and read new hermeneutical expositions, especially of Paul's position on women, they are unwilling to accept the restrictions placed upon them without discussion and prayer. Younger, educated women are rising to top leadership in business and government. More than 40 percent of small businesses are operated by women in the United States, and I suspect the percentage is far higher in the developing world. These women need the sympathetic understanding of men of God who are leading the church, or they may take their gifts elsewhere.

One of the best ways to put yourself into the shoes of women is to read what is being written about the whole issue of women in the church. Excellent biblically-sound studies on the role of women in the church are available, though unfortunately not often in your local Christian bookstore. Even though you may end up disagreeing with the new paradigm, at least you will understand that these are serious, honest students of the word of God, seeking truth, and rejoicing that they have found ways to free women into ministry. It may not be your interpretation, but it is a respected interpretation, as one writer describes the biblical interpretations that are not at the core of our salvation faith. Instead of deriding and criticizing their findings, be open-minded and accepting.

Reading and listening will help you to understand the gifted women around you and enable you to open the doors of opportunity as far as you can. Men can help women use their gifts by taking the initiative.

Teaching people how to find their spiritual gifts is a popular subject in our churches. Countless books have been written; lengthy self-tests designed. This is certainly a first step in helping women use their gifts.

Though many women know what their gifts are and respond to God's call to use them, others need the encouragement of older, more mature Christians to step out boldly into ministry. Some churches today teach 'networking' classes, where they help students not only to discover their gifts, but also to put them to use in the local church.

Older Christians can mentor younger Christians, finding ways to develop latent gifts into strengths. Younger women nurturing small children may need to be encouraged that they are doing the most important job they can right now, and that God may open doors for other gifts in his time. For some finding their spiritual gifts means they will have a desire to teach children about Christ long after their own parenting responsibilities have ended. Though the secular world says that women who take time out to be a mother never seem to catch up, there is always a place for servants in the kingdom of God, and maturity and experience in the walk of God make their offerings all the richer.

While women will benefit from personal mentoring, church leaders need to look at every aspect of church life to see if women are equitably represented, not by numbers but because of their gifts. Organizational staffs should remind each other to seek out qualified women to be involved in task forces, prayer programmes, budget-planning, building committees, mission boards, and any other leadership role in which the church or organization is ready to include women.

Rita Adhikary, a World Vision project manager in Bangladesh, confirms the need for men's support. 'Men can help remove barriers hindering the advancement of girls and women by changing their attitudes. They can begin by showing respect to women and girls in all sectors of society, starting with their own family members.'

But some Christian leaders complain, 'I have offered women leadership positions, and they refuse.' As Eva Burrows discovered when she took office, women had not come up through the ranks and thus were not ready to take top leadership. We must be sure that the women we are inviting into leadership truly have the gifts; understand and accept their own capabilities; are at a stage in life where they can relinquish some of their home responsibilities; and have a sense of God's call to that particular ministry.

Many women do not want leadership. They are far more comfortable in a supportive role, and if this is God's call for them, they should not be pushed into a public ministry or heavy responsibilities.

An Indian woman writer offers another reason why women hesitate to step out into leadership. She writes, 'The culture itself still tends to perpetuate the old values. And so do many of the women themselves, because they have internalized the culture's values. A woman will forego many opportunities because she thinks that these opportunities are not appropriate to her primary function as defined by her culture.'[2]

Christian leaders need to keep their eyes open for those women whose gifts are not being utilized, but who hesitate to reveal their desire for responsible service because they feel it is inappropriate or they are unqualified.

If you are on a board in the local church, para-church organization, or mission, you can help sensitize your colleagues to the need to invite qualified women on the board.

While this is becoming more common, unfortunately a 'token woman' is far too often asked, and that's as far as it goes. Tokenism is a beginning, but is very unfair. A lone woman on an all-male board is pushed into a very vulnerable position. The reason you've invited a woman is not to satisfy the critics or as a public relations move. It's to gain the benefits of godly women's perspective, experience and intuition as you solve problems. Since a woman will often suggest different solutions, and ideas that haven't been previously considered, it is very difficult when she is outnumbered. Support and input from other women can strengthen her position.

Evelyn Christenson tells the story of a time she served on an all-male board. Evelyn is not a shy, introverted person, but surrounded by top male church leadership, she found it difficult to make a point. It seemed every time she tentatively raised her hand, the chairman called on someone else. Finally, one of the other men boldly interrupted and said, 'I think Evelyn has something she wants to say.'

Ignoring a woman's contribution is probably not intentional, but may be a hangover from the 'old boys' club' attitude that the 'guys understand what's going on.' A South African committee met to plan a major event in the country. The committee members were all male except for one woman, who was highly educated, articulate and experienced. But every time she made a comment it was ignored and someone else was called upon for other input. She needed an ally – and a sensitive man would have understood not only her need for backing but the value of what she had to say. Better yet, two or three women would have reinforced her comment.

This is not to say that men and women are necessarily adversaries, but the synergism of men and women together works much better when there is more of a balance between the sexes.

In order to help women develop and use their gifts, we should consciously recruit women to participate in leadership conferences and training opportunities. We should be able to do better in global congresses than a 75:25 ratio between men and women.

Another way to encourage women is to provide models of other women who have responded to God's call. In his parables Jesus told almost as many stories about women as he did about men. He demonstrated the value of women by going to great lengths to heal them – the women with an issue of blood and Jairus' daughter are two cases in point.

Men could provide more women-models by inviting them to speak at conferences and as workshop leaders. By doing this, women will gain affirmation and encouragement, and men will actually see and hear how God has gifted his daughters. It may mean that some male leaders will not have as many opportunities to speak and teach as they would like. Roger Forster commented on this possibility: 'We've had a head start as young men to get involved in our ministries while our wives have had some years bringing up the children. Then they come on to the scene and they can't do it so well yet. The men have to restrain and hold back in order to give room for them to develop their gifts. That is a godly thing.'

Men can help women by understanding their style of leadership

Men say that they don't like 'masculine women' but somehow they expect women to be masculine in their discussions and decision-making. Probably the most commonly heard criticism of women in leadership is that they are too emotional. Yet it may be the emotional and intuitive side of women's personalities that are needed to bring balance and wholeness to our ministries.

A couple with serious marriage problems asked the church leaders to arbitrate their dispute over their children. Several elders and pastoral staff were called in. Can you imagine how the wife must have felt without even one woman to empathize with what she was feeling?

In an article, 'What Men can Learn from Women (and Jesus) about Leadership', authors Edna Valdez and Kim Wright list three major areas where 'the women's approach' may be important for men to understand – and even adopt. They write, 'Men typically are characterized by independence, while women tend to be more interdependent.'[3] Women tend to emphasize community and co-operation, and will work through a problem until there is a mutual solution. They tend to be more collaborative than competitive, listening to all sides and working towards a solution that embraces all participants.

Dr. Deborah Tannen in her book *You Just Don't Understand: Women and Men in Conversation* writes, 'For men, conversation is a language of report.' But for most women 'conversation is primarily a language of rapport; a way of establishing connections and negotiating relationships. Emphasis is placed on displaying similarities and matching experiences to increase unity.'[4] The difference in style will result in decisions reached by consensus rather than hierarchy.

Women need to be encouraged in meetings to express openly their gut feelings about the matter being discussed, and not to be afraid to make suggestions for fear of ridicule. Men need to take what women say seriously. Bringing the strengths of both sexes together can downplay the inherent weaknesses in both, and result in resolutions that are best for the whole body of Christ. If a woman occasionally sheds tears, men need to understand this is not meant to be manipulative, but reflects the caring concern in her heart.

General Burrows reinforces this thought, 'I agree . . . that man and woman are of two different psyches, and each has its own gifts to bring. I see a difference in the style of leadership. Men are more ambitious and plan ahead. Women are more involved and concerned with people. It isn't just culture-conditioning; it is their nature. I wouldn't think of myself as leading in a masculine way, which is normally aggressive and competitive. Women have more sensitivity to people and a greater tolerance than men.'[5]

Men should go as far as they can to open doors for women

A Baptist pastor who did not believe women should take leadership roles in the church learned that his daughter had decided to study for the ministry. When asked how he felt about her decision his response was, 'I would not dare to stand in the way of what she sees as God's call on her life. She is responsible for her obedience to him.'

This pastor had to accept that his daughter's decision was between herself and God, based on her understanding of what the Scripture says. While he may not permit women to hold such a role in his church, he can love and support his daughter in her ministry. Knowing his daughter as he did, he knew she was not a radical feminist looking for power.

As changes come into the church, you may fear that you are compromising your biblical position by encouraging women in leadership. But you have only to look at the Old Testament to see that God used strong women such as Miriam, Deborah and Huldah in leadership roles over men. Priscilla taught a man; Phoebe was very likely a leader in her church; and Romans 16 lists ten women 'fellow-workers' with Paul – all must have been significant leaders to have their names preserved in the word of God. There are those who feel these were exceptions because there were no men to fill their place, but there is no evidence of this in Scripture. In fact, Miriam was called to lead along with two strong male leaders (Micah 6:4).

Even if these were exceptions, can you not make exceptions too? If there are gifted and called women in your church or organization who could fill a position better than a man, why not use them? You have ample support from Scripture.

Men can help women by risking change

Today there are a growing number of pastors and Christian leaders who bemoan the fact that we are losing a huge potential for significant leadership by limiting the role of women. But it means being willing to risk the cost to bring about change. Other issues seem more important. Pastors are over-worked as churches are understaffed, and programme-orientated. Issues such as family breakdowns, ethnic violence, racial hatred, political unrest and persecution of Christians in many parts of the world weigh heavily upon God's servants. A virulent AIDS epidemic is decimating the church in parts of the world. Illegitimacy and immorality plague our youth. And millions of people live and die without ever hearing a clear presentation of the gospel. How can a pastor add one more potentially divisive issue to his goals as he faces these desperate needs?

There is, however, another side to this question. How can Christian leaders not release the greatest force for evangelism into the work of the body of Christ? How can we limit the very segment of the Church that is most sensitive to the relational problems among believers, and most ready to get involved in the healing process that must take place? How can we afford to develop programmes to help the poor and needy without the planning and decision-making assistance from the very part of the body that would best understand their problems?

Some years ago World Vision leaders realized they must study the role of women in ministry and take a position on how to use women throughout their global organization. They set up a task force to study the question, gleaned opinions from others in the organization and authorized a paper to be written by Katherine Haubert which became a basis for discussing the issue in the light of Scripture in the worldwide body. The introduction states, 'The purpose of this paper is to enable the saints to overcome any obstacles in relation to women in leadership that might hinder the full potential of God within his body.'[6] Out of these deliberations has come a World Vision policy on women in development and leadership which celebrates the diversity and dignity of women and men as expressed in Scripture.

Unfortunately, in some churches and organizations the 'women's issue' is considered too divisive and confrontational to be dealt with. Sadly, some church boards who do discuss the issue do not allow women to participate in the discussion. Instead of being willing openly to debate the subject, we fear reprisal and rejection if we reveal our position.

Rather than avoiding the issue, let us make use of the many illustrations and stories about women in leadership who demonstrate the grace of God. How often do we hear sermons based on their lives which would encourage both men and women in the audience? How many Sunday School classes are being taught on the role of women in ministry? Could we risk teaching the interpretations of both traditional and partnership models and allow students to make their own decisions? (A bibliography at the end of this book lists just a few titles presenting each position.)

What difference will it make?

Enabling women to use their gifts frees up countless resources to the body of Christ and helps to destroy the gender gap that has plagued the human race since the Fall.

Bryant Myers, vice-president of mission and evangelism for World Vision International believes women are a critical force for reaching those who have never heard the gospel:

> The first key will be to recognize the possibly critical importance of women as a responsive entry point to resistant people-groups.
>
> The second key will be to recognize the importance of women as the ones most likely to have opportunities to speak to unreached women and to present the gospel in ways they understand.
>
> Women in mission may have the only opportunities to develop relationships with women who may be the key to reaching an unreached people-group. As the work of Juster and Gilligan suggests, women speak 'in a different voice,' which may mean that they will more effectively communicate the gospel in terms other women can understand.
>
> 'What's the bottom line? We need to give preference to recruiting, training, and supporting far more women if we are to reach the unreached. The twin tragedies of the disappearance of the women's mission movement in the US and the marginalization and under-utilization of women within evangelical missions [around the world] may be among the major reasons we have not been able to make gospel breakthroughs in the 10/40 window during the last half of this century.[7]

If for no other reason than to enable women to help fulfil the Great Commission, it is worth every effort to encourage, develop and affirm their gifts to serve God where he calls. And men can help make it happen!

Notes

1. *Pulse,* 9 October 1992.

2. Dr. Radha Paul, "Are Men Capable of Seeing the Need?" *Together,* October–December 1992, 22.

3. Edna Valdez and Kim Wright, "What Men Can Learn from Women (and Jesus) about Leadership," *Together,* October–December, 1991, 14.

4. Ibid., 15.

5. Henry Gariepy, *General of God's Army* (Wheaton: Victor Books, 1993), 205.

6. Katherine Haubert, *Women in the Bible and the Implications for Leadership*, 1991), 2.

7. Bryant Myers, "Recognizing the Connection: Women and Missions," *Marc Newsletter,* September 1993.

Seventeen

What Does the Future Hold for Women in Ministry?

You also, like living stones, are being built into a spiritual house to be a holy priesthood, offering spiritual sacrifices acceptable to God through Jesus Christ . . . you are a chosen people, a royal priesthood, a holy nation, a people belonging to God, that you may declare the praises of him who called you out of darkness into his wonderful light.

1 Pet.2:5,9.

You have made them to be a kingdom and priests to serve our God, and they will reign on the earth.

Rev. 5:10.

A news item from Pakistan in our local paper read: 'Hundreds of women, chanting and carrying signs, demonstrated Sunday against a court decision requiring them to get permission to marry from male guardians.' Pakistani authorities have passed the Muslim shariah laws which require a father's consent for a daughter of any age to marry. But Muslim women are joining forces to protest against the injustice of the law.

Even though their individual rights are restricted, these women are learning there is strength in unity, and are voicing resistance in peaceful but powerful ways.

In another part of the world women have banded together to stand up against violence and injustice. After the withdrawal of peace-keeping troops in Somalia, the warlords renewed fighting and killing. The women of Somalia had had enough. They formed peace committees made up of the elderly, respected women of each of the clans. They confronted the warlords reminding them that it was their children who were suffering, and their farmlands which could not be planted or harvested. They challenged the warring factions to take responsibility for the welfare of the community.

A social worker familiar with the situation said, 'These women are literally engaged in negotiations with the leaders of these different factions one outburst at a time. Without a government structure, without an official head of state and with many of the international governments pulling away because there's an absence of a state structure to relate to, these peace committees become the negotiators for peace, the providers of food, the distribution network for what little supplies get into the country.'

These women learned that they could make an impact without guns or positions of power in the areas of life and death affecting their homes and children. Development workers have come to the same conclusion. They find women tend to be more reliable, more effective in implementing changes in their communities that will help their children and raise the standard of living. Thus around the world women are being given more responsibility in development programmes and entrusted with funds and other resources to improve the quality of life in their communities.

In their book, *Megatrends for Women*, Aburdine and Naisbitt state, 'When it comes to "saving the world" or a part of it, street by street, neighbourhood by neighbourhood, women are the catalysts through whom the critical mass of social change will be achieved.'[1] Politically, women have wielded power either behind the throne or on it, since ancient times. But while US citizens have not even had the opportunity to vote for a woman president in the twentieth century, other countries like Great Britain, Ireland, Norway, Bangladesh, Pakistan, Israel, the Philippines, Nicaragua, Turkey, and India have had women heads of state.

During the closing decade of the twentieth century only thirteen countries in the world had at least 20 percent women parliament members, five of them being the Scandinavian countries. Finnish women won 40 percent of seats in Parliament in 1991.[2] Today as educational opportunities expand and democracy flourishes, more and more woman are running for public office, and winning. For what it's worth, *Megatrends'* authors predict that in the United States 'The first woman president will come on the national scene early in the twenty-first century.'

Whether in business, politics, education or social services, opportunities are increasing for women to use their leadership, administrative and relational gifts to make a contribution to society. What about the church of Jesus Christ? How are women going to be able to use their gifts in advancing the work of the kingdom of God in the next century?

A group of key leaders of denominations and global mission organizations were asked 'What role do you think women will play in the evangelical church in the 21st century?' Their response could be summed up in the words of British-born Stuart Briscoe, pastor of a large interdenominational church in Wisconsin, and internationally-known speaker and author:

Unfortunately, the church has not always recognized the spiritual giftedness of women and, accordingly, has felt perfectly justified in limiting their activity to changing diapers and pouring cold drinks. This is not only an insult to the Spirit but is also a great hindrance to the work of the church as many vital members of the body are not functioning optimally.

I believe that an effort must be made on the part of the leadership of all the churches to come to some agreement as to the optimum way in which women's ministry is acceptable and should be encouraged. Even if, for theological or other reasons, it is felt that limits should be put on what women are allowed to do, this should not mean that there should not be careful thought and encouragement given to women to do all that they possibly can do.

Under Briscoe's leadership a number of women have served in pastoral and leadership roles and the male elder board has honestly and earnestly wrestled with the theological issues, and continues to do so.

Most leaders responded that the theological issue is the most difficult hang-up. Chuck Bennett, president of Partners International, believes another major problem is that many evangelicals hold the mistaken assumption that the 'descriptions of Jewish patriarchal society in the Bible – which are descriptions, nothing more – are God's mandate for all societies in all ages.' He says, 'People who have that mindset are not likely to change.'

Patrick Johnstone, author of *Operation World*, is concerned that we take a careful look at the 'entrenched theological presuppositions of those who most need to welcome the ministry of women as equal and complementary to that of men.'

Some leaders like Gerry Seale, head of the Evangelical Association of the Caribbean, feel that for changes to occur 'men need to mature to greater levels of self-confidence and "faith-confidence", so that they can release women to be all God intended them to be without feeling threatened.' Seale says women have played a vital role in the church and as general 'gophers', but he believes they will be 'increasingly released by the Holy Spirit into administrative and leadership roles within the body of Christ.'

South African Johann Combrinck points to the fact that women in Africa have done much of the leadership and work of keeping the church alive. 'Throughout Africa,' he says, 'we are noticing an increasing change in the role of women in ministry and also in leadership, especially among evangelicals. There is a much greater freedom for women to share equal platforms with male leaders.'

While mission writer Jim Reapsome believes that there is an increasing rigidity about women's roles in ministry among younger men and students in American Bible colleges and seminaries, other leaders are encouraged that there is a change with younger leaders worldwide.

Chuck Bennett says, 'Evangelicals face a daunting task to effect change but it will probably happen as the present generation of leaders passes from the scene. I'm sure the changes will be uneven, but I think the overall trend is irreversible.' Author Jim Engel adds, 'The existing group is probably hopeless.'

A young Chinese woman who leads an interdenominational mission in Singapore reveals her pain when she says, 'When will more women make it into evangelical leadership? About the same time men really understand the idea of "dying to self." All their world-view on women and culture must die, and when they really understand that at the feet of Jesus there is neither male nor female – we'll be in leadership. Today it is the rare exception, the near martyr, the exceptionally gifted woman that makes it to international leadership.'

Paul Cedar, who leads the Lausanne Committee in the USA under the banner 'Mission America', strongly affirms the role of women. 'Women are not "second-class citizens" in the kingdom of our Lord Jesus Christ. God has used women greatly in the history of the church at Pentecost, in crucial ministry roles in the early church and in strategic and significant ministries down through the pages of church history.'

But even some who are very affirming of women in leadership see limitations to the roles they will play. John Kyle, former director of United World Missions of the Presbyterian Church in America, admits, 'We will not see a tendency to change the position of not ordaining women as elders and deacons in the church, but women will continue to have very active ministries in that denomination.'

Male leaders of the church are not the only ones who limit the full use of women's gifts. Stuart Briscoe observes, 'There are women who are very comfortable in the "traditional role" because it is singularly undemanding as far as sacrificial ministry in the fellowship of believers is concerned.'

Greg Fritz, director of Caleb Project, voices even deeper concern, 'If women really want to lead they will need to pursue a legitimate preparation process. This implies giving up other freedoms and opportunities that women have traditionally enjoyed . . . I do not see nearly as many women as men who are willing to take the risks and responsibilities associated with leadership.'

It is not necessary that women feel they must seek leadership positions to the same extent as men do. But utilization of their gifts to the degree that God calls them is a different matter. Denying or refusing to use our gifts when God calls us, is an insult to the Holy Spirit. So is denying to those who feel God's call freedom and opportunity to use those gifts.

It is my observation that there is a general consensus about the role of women in the evangelical church in the 21st century.

1. An increasing number of Christian leaders want to help women develop and use their gifts in ministry. However, the tension between those who believe women should use their gifts in decision and policy-making, and those who do not, remains high.

2. The theological position on the biblical role of women will continue to be the major determinant as to what roles woman are allowed to play in the church. Hopefully there will be more open discussion and willingness to consider new paradigms by Christian leaders.

3. Changes in the roles of women in the church are irreversible. No matter what theological position a church takes, it must cater in some way to the educated, qualified, gifted and experienced 21st century woman who has gained so much in the marketplace.

Jane Hansen, international director of *Women's Aglow* which ministers to half a million women around the world, sees an encouraging picture. She believes that 'God will bring us back to what he purposed' when he created Adam and Eve and instructed them to take dominion over the earth together. 'Men will become more accepting of our service (they've always done that) and ministry. God will bring the two halves together as he intended when he said it was not good for man to be alone.' She believes men and women will come together in a complementary not a competitive relationship, working together without fear and intimidation to deal with issues in a non-threatening way. 'Where there are blind spots,' says Hansen, 'only God can reveal truth.'

How will the major evangelical organizations which focus on evangelism deal with the question of the role of women in the 21st century? We will consider the direction being taken by the parent bodies of three organizations which are sponsoring the publication of this book: the AD2000 and Beyond Movement, the Lausanne Committee for World Evangelization Women's Network, and the World Evangelical Fellowship Commission on Women's Concerns.

The World Evangelical Fellowship represents over one hundred and fifty million evangelical Christians in 116 national and regional fellowships. WEF traces its roots back to the formation of the Evangelical Alliance in England in 1846 and was officially organized in 1951. In 1986 David Howard, then international director, wrote a history of WEF. He said, 'Throughout most of the years of WEF's ministry one must recognize with some shame that women were largely ignored. References to women in WEF documents, either in any roles of significance or in terms of the special needs of women, are few and far between.'[3]

In 1980 a steering committee of international evangelical women met in London to discuss the purposes, structure and programmes a women's movement would take within the WEF. However the dream was almost derailed when WEF leaders recommended the group be called the Commission on the Christian Family. Many women expressed deep dissatisfaction that the leadership was ignoring 'women in leadership, in participation, and in influence'. In 1984 a new executive committee met to draw up the purposes and goals for the newly formed Commission on Women's Concerns. At the WEF Assembly in Manila in 1992 the Commission on Women's Concerns was asked to study the role of women in the home, church and society and bring its findings to the international body. It was out of this consultation that this book grew.

The opening paragraph of the foundation statement of the Commission on Women's Concerns, drawn up in 1992, reads, 'We believe that men and women were created to live in relationship with God and with one another; chosen to be a holy nation, a royal priesthood; redeemed to be the body of Christ, the Bride of Christ; expected to live in community, in harmony and unity, with Christ as the head; and commanded to submit to one another in love in order to reveal the true nature of God to the world around us.'

In 1993 the WEF Theological Commission began to touch on the issue of women in a consultation on Evangelizing the Poor. The Commission considered the injustices which women face such as violence, violation, rape, abortion and prostitution. It stated, 'The church adds to the problem with its unequal treatment of women and in not more openly condemning mental, physical and sexual abuse in the home and their lack of control over their lives.'[4] It concluded:

1. *We need to affirm the theological basis of the equality of women and men.*

2. *We must work for justice for women in society and the church.*

3. *The church must recognize and use fully the gifts of women.*

4. *We must model in our structures the love and responsibility God gives to women and men.*

5. *We urge processes that will enable men to recognize their responsibilities to be faithful to and care for their wives and children.*[5]

In its final recommendations to the WEF the Commission recommended 'that the Theological Commission take the issues raised in this Consultation further by appointing a Task Force on Community, Family and Women's Issues.' One major issue raised was 'to look into ways to promote the biblical interrelationships between women and men in church, home and society.' As of this writing the findings of the Task Force have not been circulated.

Meanwhile Lynn Smith, Vice-President of Student Affairs at Ontario Bible College and Seminary, developed a study guide on the role of women for the Commission on Women's Concerns titled *Gender or Giftedness, The Basis for Service.* Smith serves on the Commission and has been part of its ongoing study process since 1992.

The introduction to her seminar takes a further step in helping leaders of the church understand and utilize the giftedness of women and I believe it is a very strong option for the direction the church will take in the 21st century.

Smith begins by seeking a biblical framework and then introduces a new paradigm:

> Most Christians have been taught the hierarchical model for relationships between men and women, and thus also for the role of women within the church – sincerely believing it to be the biblical teaching on this subject.
>
> In this model, the function of women is restricted by their gender, whereas men function according to their abilities, gifts and call. Since patriarchy is the social order into which Christ came, it is therefore perceived to be the determinant form for Christianity for all time.
>
> . . . Since power is understood as residing in a man who is in authority, women are perceived as usurping the rightful power of men if they are given power. Any effort on the part of women to gain equality is seen, then, as a move against the will of God and is to be resisted.
>
> This results in a power struggle which can be illustrated by a continuum with male dominance at one end, female dominance at the other. Since very few today would espouse either extreme, the ideal is perceived to be more or less toward the middle. Equality is seen as a midpoint between two extremes.

	X	
Male dominance	equality	female dominance

> . . . This power-based model has a major flaw. No matter where you agree to place the balance point on this continuum, the position can only be maintained by tension between the two opposing ends. If one gives a little, the other gains a little. If one gains a little, the other loses a little. Thus men and women are set in an adversarial position, and no matter where you decide the ideal point should be, it can only be maintained by resisting the encroachment of the other's power. Men then fear encouraging the 'power' of women and women resist the 'power' of men.
>
> As long as the church uses this model and attempts to find the balance between the dominance of men and the dominance of women, tension persists. Tension is created by fear; fear of the power of others; fear of one's own power; fear of being controlled; fear of losing control. Dominance always begets fear. But the message of Scripture has nothing to do with dominance. Rather, the message of Scripture is that life in the community of believers is characterized by a servant attitude. The goal is to build one another up in love within the body of Christ. A paradigm that fosters dominance rather than servanthood cannot be our model.
>
> What then, does a model look like that is created by love: that rejects dominance as unbiblical?

. . . Scripture portrays a new model which moves the questions about the theology of women from the continuum of dominance into the sphere of development. In this framework, questions are asked out of a different worldview and the continuum of authority, command, power, mastery, reign and rule gives way to the sphere of encouragement, nurturing and community. Instead of a power-based model, we have a gift-based model in which authority is not 'over' but 'on behalf of'. Equality is not maintained by one giving up power to another, but is an inherent value of the community.

The words used in reference to this sphere are: gifts, service, encouragement, nurturing, community. Authority is placed in the word of God and positions of authority are given for the good of others, not in order to have power over others. Submission is seen as mutual submission to the body and to Christ. Function flows out of giftedness rather than gender.

It was the redemptive act of Jesus, rather than the consequences of sin, that established this new paradigm, and He expects us to see all of Scripture through the 'window' of that redemption rather than through the 'window' of the Fall.

When the paradigm through which we see and interpret Scripture is that of the Fall, the reign of sin becomes prescriptive rather than descriptive. The natural outcome is to see the effects of sin as established by God. If, however, the paradigm is that of redemption, the results of sin are seen as unwelcome and the need to redeem all from the effects of sin becomes our goal. That includes the dominance of the male – not to be replaced by the dominance of the female, nor even to be held in balance by tension between the two – but by entirely moving away from a dominance model and embracing the new model – the new order – which Christ came to establish.

This is the place to begin to look at the issue of women in the church.[6]

While the movement has been slow in encouraging leadership gifts of women in the evangelical churches, the WEF is working towards defining women's roles and this is encouraging.

Robyn Claydon, Senior Associate for Women for the Lausanne Committee for World Evangelization (LCWE) agrees that giftedness is the key to understanding women's roles. 'The call to take the Good News of Jesus to the world is a call to all believers and the gifts given by the Spirit for the building up of the body are not gender-related.'

Though LCWE has given women leadership opportunities and included the importance of their role in the Lausanne Statement of Faith, its current leadership recognizes there's still a long way to go. Fergus Macdonald of Scotland, the Executive Chairman of the Lausanne International Committee, writes,

The book of Genesis provides us with two accounts of creation . . . each narrative underlines both the equality and the diversity of the sexes. I think it is true to say that churches and mission agencies find it difficult to honour this biblical balance. Traditionalists so stress diversity (in particular men's headship) that women lose their spiritual equality. Radicals so emphasize equality that women in Christian leadership are often under pressure to act as men rather than as women. Most of us have a long way to go in our corporate ministries to harness all the riches of the male-female chemistry which God has made an integral part of our humanity.[7]

Tom Houston, minister-at-large for LCWE, has spent much time studying life in the former Soviet Union. He was impressed with the warm respectful relationship between wives and husbands. Yet, he observes,

> It was also true that the family Christians fought to preserve was the patriarchal family that dated from pre-revolutionary Russia. There seemed little role for women in the church that was not essentially domestic.
>
> As I reflected on the secular and Christian realities of the USSR it dawned on me that it was going to be a major problem with the 'liberated' Soviet women who got converted and tried to join a church that was still defending a patriarchal type family. I spoke to some women who were trying to make that transition. They said it was agony and that many women just gave up and left. They could not stand it.

Houston went on to say that this is still a major problem in the countries of the old Soviet Union, and is even worse in countries where emerging Islamic authorities are in control. He also warns, 'This problem is not unique to the countries of the old Eastern bloc. It must be faced and ways discovered to solve it if the role of women in evangelism is to be significantly developed.'[7]

Argentinian Luis Bush serves as international director of the AD2000 and Beyond Movement which focuses on the goal, 'A church for every people and the gospel for every person by the year 2000.' Bush recognized the importance of the role of women in evangelism right from the beginning of the movement in 1989. The AD2000 Women's Track was one of the first networks to be established and a woman was appointed to the international board.

Bush observes a growing role for women in all aspects of society. He says,

> From a secular perspective there is an increasing openness to and desire for involvement of women in decision- and policy-making roles, and an understanding of the contributions they can make.
>
> In India, where I have visited a number of times, I've seen women playing a key role, especially in community development. African women seem to have a cultural edge in implementation, planning and reliability.
>
> I believe women will have a very significant, and more directly influential role in evangelical circles in the 21st century. However, in the church men are still a bit chauvinistic about women in leadership. But that resistance is rapidly decreasing, and there is a spirit of repentance about past attitudes.

While there is openness and empathy for women's aspirations, women remain as token representatives on boards, in planning sessions and in being given meaningful leadership appointments in the national initiatives of the AD2000 Movement. Progress is very irregular, and unless women continue to remind leaders of their presence, their capabilities and their willingness to be involved, I fear that the status of women could slip backwards.

Megatrend's authors define critical mass as 'that point when a trend becomes a megatrend; it is the point when one accepted social paradigm no longer makes sense and is replaced by another.'[9] Critical mass regarding women's ability freely to use their gifts in the church has not yet been reached. But, as we've seen, more and more men of God are recognizing the importance of women's gifts, and are promoting their use.

At a Leadership Summit in 1996 at the world-famous Willow Creek Church in Illinois, pastor Bill Hybels asked a key woman on his staff, Nancy Beach, to speak to the three thousand five hundred delegates concerning the role of women in the church. Nancy pleaded with the male leaders to 'wrestle with the sticky passages' and not to 'snuff out those gifts and make women run away into the market place.' Then in an emotional appeal she spoke to the women in the audience, 'Tell your daughters "God did not make a mistake when he gave you that gift. It was no cosmic screw-up and the gift was supposed to go to a boy." '

A short time later Bill Hybels replayed her appeal for his fifteen thousand-plus congregation and promised, 'We're going to take another look at this; we're going to look beyond gender. We're going to invite women into the game. We want to lift up the leadership skills of everyone in this church.'

If this truly takes place in Willow Creek Church, and churches around the world, the gifts of women will be unleashed in the 21st century in a way never seen in the history of Christianity.

When the 'middle wall of partition' is broken between men and women, the synergism of male-female partnership may well be the greatest redemptive force this world has seen since Pentecost.

Notes

1. Patricia Aburdine and John Naisbitt, *Megatrends for Women* (New York: Villard Books, 1992), 265.
2. *The World's Women* (Washington, D.C.: Population Reference Bureau, 1995).
3. David Howard, *The Dream That Would Not Die* (Carlisle, U.K.: Paternoster Press, 1986), 197.
4. Bong Rin Ro, ed., *Sharing the Good News with the Poor* (Seoul, Korea: WEF Theological Commission, 1993), 30.
5. Ibid., 30.
6. Lynn Smith, *Gender or Giftedness: The Basis for Service* (unpublished manuscript).

7. Arne H. Fjeldstad, ed., *World Evangelization* (Norway: LCWE, 1995), 2.
8. Ibid., 23.
9. Aburdine and Naisbitt, *Megatrends,* xvii.

Appendix: Mission Statements

The AD2000 and Beyond Women's Track

Mission Statement

To be a catalytic force for God to unleash the under-utilized resource of women around the world through the power of prayer, encouragement and training for world evangelization.

Purpose

1. *To develop and maintain communications between a growing network of global women leaders in many denominations and para-church organizations who share the vision.*

2. *To gather and disseminate stories, activities, accomplishments and needs of women involved in reaching the unreached peoples of the world and providing available resources as needed to do so.*

3. *To gain greater acceptance and affirmation for women from male leadership of the church, praying for more open doors of opportunity for women to work alongside them in ministry.*

4. *To work cooperatively with other organizations which share the same vision and goals, avoiding competition and overlap, but using the synergism of historical experiences and cross-cultural insights to mobilize a mighty force of women around the world into the harvest fields.*

For further information contact: AD2000 and Beyond Movement, 2860 S. Circle Drive, Suite 2112, Colorado Springs, CO 80906. Tel: 719–576–2000, Fax: 719–576–2685

Lausanne Committee for World Evangelization

Mission Statement

To affirm the contribution of women in the task of world evangelization.

Goals

1. *To implement the Manila Manifesto (Lausanne II conference, 1989) which affirms that 'The gifts of the Spirit are distributed to all God's people, women and men, and their partnership in evangelization must be welcomed for the common good', particularly since 'God is calling the whole church to take the whole Gospel to the whole world.'*

2. *To equip, encourage and enable Christian women to use their gifts and opportunities to share the Good News of Jesus Christ faithfully, urgently and sacrificially until He comes.*

3. *Through emerging leaders' networks and mentor groups, to motivate and train young Christian women to recognize their potential in Christ and to be prepared to exercise their ministry in the church and in the world.*

4. *To organize conferences, establish networks, set up mentor groups and produce a newsletter so that ideas and models of evangelism which women are exercising throughout the world can be shared.*

The basis of belief is the Lausanne Covenant and the Manila Manifesto. Copies of both are available from: Lausanne International Communications Center, St. Olavsgate 23, 0166 Oslo, Norway. Tel/Fax: 47-22-20-03-58.

World Evangelical Fellowship Commission on Women's Concerns

Mission Statement

1. *The Commission on Women's Concerns exists to meet the unique needs of women around the world through evangelism, encouragement, fellowship, education and networking.*

2. *The Commission on Women's Concerns will work through the World Evangelical Fellowship's regional and national alliances and commissions where they exist.*

Action Plan

The Commission on Women's Concerns will:

1. *Help Christian men and women understand and appropriate the truth that they are equally created in the image of God, called and gifted for ministry.*

2. *Encourage the body of Christ to identify, train and maximize the use of God-given gifts of men and women.*

3. *Mobilize women to meet more effectively the needs of people in the church, home and society.*

4. *Provide systems and opportunities for women to network for resources, edification and encouragement.*

For further information contact: World Evangelical Fellowship, P.O. Box WEF, Wheaton, IL 60189. Tel: 630-668-0440, Fax: 630-668-0498.

If You Want to Study Further . . .

The introductory reading list below will lead you into a deeper study of the biblical role of women in ministry. Titles marked * reflect a more traditional interpretation.

Bilezikian, Gilbert. *Beyond Sex Roles.* Grand Rapids: Baker, 1990.

Booth, Catherine. *Female Ministry, or Women's Right to Preach the Gospel.* London: Morgan and Chase, 1859.

Bushnell, Katherine C. *God's Word to Women.* Oakland, Calif.: Katherine C. Bushnell, 1923.

*Elliot, Elisabeth. *Let Me Be a Woman.* Wheaton: Tyndale House, 1976.

Grenz, Stanley J., with Denise Muir Kjesbo. *Women in the Church: A Biblical Theology of Women in Ministry.* Downers Grove, Il.: InterVarsity Press, 1995.

Hasscy, Janette. *No Time for Silence.* Grand Rapids: Zondervan/Academie Books, 1986.

Hull, Gretchen Gaebelein. *Equal to Serve.* Old Tappan, N.J.: Revell, 1987.

*Hurley, James B. *Man and Woman in Biblical Perspective.* Grand Rapids: Zondervan, 1981.

Keener, Craig S. *Paul, Women and Wives.* Peabody, Mass.: Hendrickson, 1992.

Kroeger, Richard, and Catherine Clark. *I Suffer Not a Woman: Rethinking 1 Timothy 2:11–15 in the Light of Ancient Evidence.* Grand Rapids: Baker, 1992.

Malcolm, Kari Torjesen. *Women at the Crossroads: A Path beyond Feminism and Traditionalism.* Downers Grove, Il.: InterVarsity Press, 1982.

Mickelsen, Alvera. *Women, Authority and the Bible.* Downers Grove, Il.: InterVarsity Press, 1986.

Penn-Lewis, Jesse. *The Magna Carta of Women According to the Scriptures.* Minneapolis: Bethany Fellowship, 1975.

*Piper, John, and Wayne Grudem, eds. *Recovering Biblical Manhood and Womanhood: A Response to Evangelical Feminism.* Wheaton, Il.: Crossway, 1991.

Spencer, Aída Besançon. *Beyond the Curse.* Nashville: Thomas Nelson, 1985.

Swarthley, Willard M. *Slavery, Sabbath, War, and Women.* Scottsdale, Pa.: Herald Press, 1983.

Van Leeuwen, Mary Stuart. *Gender and Grace.* Downers Grove, Il.: InterVarsity Press, 1990.

If you can't find these books in your Christian bookstore, many are available from Christians for Biblical Equality, P.O. Box 7155, St. Paul, MN 55107-0155.

Lorry Lutz (M.A., Wheaton College) is currently the International Coordinator of the AD2000 and Beyond Women's Track. She has a rich lifelong background in international ministry having served with her husband for more than twenty years as a missionary in South Africa with the Africa Evangelical Fellowship and later working with Partners International. In her role with the latter mission she traveled worldwide visiting missionaries and reporting on the work of national churches. Her interest in the need for training and encouragement of women grew out of these experiences. She is the (co)author of several books including *Mission: A World Family Affair* and *Partnering in Ministry.*